HEALTH CARE

ISSUES IN

BLACK AMERICA

HEALTH CARE

ISSUES IN

BLACK AMERICA

Policies, Problems, and Prospects

Edited by
WOODROW JONES, JR.,
and
MITCHELL F. RICE

CONTRIBUTIONS IN AFRO-AMERICAN AND AFRICAN STUDIES, NUMBER 100

 GREENWOOD PRESS
NEW YORK • WESTPORT, CONNECTICUT • LONDON

Library of Congress Cataloging-in-Publication Data

Health care issues in Black America.

(Contributions in Afro-American and African studies,
ISSN 0069-9624 ; no. 100)
   Bibliography: p.
   Includes index.
   1. Afro-Americans—health and hygiene.
2. Afro-Americans—Medical care. 3. Medical policy—
United States. I. Jones, Woodrow. II. Rice,
Mitchell F. III. Series.
RA448.5.N4H39 1987   362.1′08996073   86-14233
ISBN 0-313-24886-9 (lib. bdg. : alk. paper)

Library of Congress Catalog Card Number: 86-14233
ISBN: 0-313-24886-9
ISSN: 0069-9624

First published in 1987

Greenwood Press, Inc.
88 Post Road West, Westport, Connecticut 06881

Printed in the United States of America

∞

The paper used in this book complies with the
Permanent Paper Standard issued by the National
Information Standards Organization (Z39.48-1984).

10 9 8 7 6 5 4 3 2

This book is dedicated to our parents,
Mr. and Mrs. Woodrow Jones, Sr.
Dr. and Mrs. Joseph M. Rice

Contents

Tables

Preface

Health beliefs and behaviors are determined by a number of factors, including the availability, accessibility, and quality of the health care delivery system. In addition to these factors, race has been shown to be particularly relevant to these components. Although it has admittedly been difficult to separate the influence of related variables, such as socio-economic class acculturation, the fact remains that blacks face barriers to the attainment of adequate health services.

This book focuses on the context and nature of barriers to health care in America, especially for those situated at the bottom of the economic ladder. Barriers such as cost, availability, and access influence the demand and utilization of medical services. Furthermore, in the treatment situation the treatment provider may be unable to respond to the patient's personal needs because of race and cultural differences. In addition to cultural differences, we find a disjunction in policy design and implementation of programs which directly affect the promotion of health in the black community.

For health professionals and students, our book narrows this disjunction by examining the problems and experiences of blacks in the health care system. First, we explore the general health status of blacks using epidemiological data; second, we examine specific health problems and concerns of specific subpopulations in the black community; and finally, we assess the adequacy of governmental response given legal initiatives. Thus, the health professional will be sensitized to the barriers of the present health care system and will be directed toward possible changes within that system.

The editors gratefully acknowledge the contributions of all the authors who shared in the labor and joy of preparing this volume. A special note of thanks goes to Jane Hansen whose kind words of advice and editorial comments were deeply appreciated. Finally, the editors express appreciation to their colleagues for encouragement and support during the many trials of this project.

PART I

Black Health Care
and Health Status

1. Black Health Care: An Overview

Woodrow Jones, Jr., and Mitchell F. Rice

Over the past twenty years the health care industry in the United States has become an important sector of the economy. It is no longer merely the provider of medical services but a multibillion dollar industry. The number of practitioners and health care workers has increased dramatically with the size and complexity of modern institutions. Correspondingly, the demands for governmental support and assistance have also grown. The result has been an increase in federal responsibilty for medical research, hospital construction, and the training of physicians, nurses, and allied health professionals. The effects on the health care sector have been contradictory: some subsidize the supply of health care services, whereas others enhance competition.

Despite the advances in the reduction of mortality and morbidity, there are still disparities between blacks and whites on every measure of illness and death. These disparities have become a consistent reality for each new cohort and do not seem to be diminished by governmental policies. Furthermore, many federal programs are so poorly implemented that their desired impacts are at best sporadic. In addition, programs are not targeted at blacks as a special group but at more general categorizations (e.g., the poor, maternal and child health). As with other federal programs, health programs suffer from vague statu-

tory guidance, inept administration, poor coordination, and unanticipated results.[1]

The difficulty of assessing the health conditions of blacks in America
stems from a general inability to conceptualize good health adequately.
Professional disagreement on what constitutes good health is pervasive
in policymaking arenas, planning boards, and the medical profession. In
fact, the concept of good health is constantly changing with the social
and political matrix of the society. The World Health Organization's
definition covers many aspects of a healthy life: "[Health is] a state of
complete physical, mental, and social well-being and not merely the
absence of disease or infirmity.[2] Obviously, it is difficult to consider such
a definition valid given the conditions of most blacks and most poor
individuals in the United States. A more reasonable view is to conceptualize health as a lifestyle in which an individual attempts to maintain
balance and to remain free from physical incapacity while maximizing
social capacity.[3] The critical ingredients of this definition of health are
the implicit emphasis on personal choice and the individual's responsibility to do the best he or she can to maintain and maximize personal
capacities.

The condition of an individual's health is the result of three forces:
heredity, environment, and behavior.[4] Heredity, unlike environment and
behavior, is beyond the control of individuals. A black person with a
family history of sickle cell disease or hypertension has a high risk of contracting these genetic disorders. In such cases, all an individual can do is
take preventive measures to reduce the risk of the onset of the disease.
Although genetic conditions are not amenable to direct manipulation or
change, their impact can be reduced by health screening and promotion.

Figure 1.1
Determinants of Health

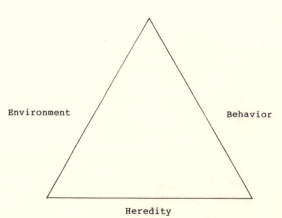

Environmental determinants, including such diverse elements as clean or polluted air, affluence or poverty, war or peace, directly impact the health conditions of populations. These determinants are directly influenced by public and private decisions about the production of resources, as well as by governmental policies to reduce the effect of the environment on health. Policies on air and water pollution, housing, poverty, welfare, and families all contribute to an environment that is either supportive or repressive of healthful activities and can influence the individual's feeling of well-being.

Individual health practices are important in reducing the risk of many illnesses. Yet, environmental and social constraints work to limit the ability of blacks to develop beneficial health practices. Because of poor housing, single-parent families, poverty, and unemployment, health practices are not of the highest priority for blacks generally. Their inability to gain a sense of control results in gross inequities in health status between blacks and whites. A fundamental health practice such as nutrition cannot be of primary concern to a welfare family. Furthermore, lacking control over their environment prevents many blacks from attaining adequate physician care. Even if physician intervention is possible, that role is limited by the nonsupportive environment in which blacks live.

This book critically examines the environmental and behavioral factors that shape the health status of blacks, and in so doing helps ascertain the impact of detrimental health practices. This book also examines the critical issues in delivering health service to the black community. Service delivery decisions by Congress and implementing authorities affect both the environment and health practices. Moreover, no study of black health care would be complete without an examination of specific subpopulations and behaviors within the community. Age, sex, and environmental location all create differential health practices and experiences.

The thesis presented here is that specific problems faced by the black community prevent them from developing the health practices necessary for a healthy lifestyle. The resulting inequities in health status and condition have social, political, and human costs. Therefore, we need an explanation as to why these conditions are allowed to exist in an abundant society.

INEQUITIES IN BLACK HEALTH CARE

Health care reflects the general conditions of people within the population. It reflects the matrix of social, economic, and political factors that segment American society. Race and ethnicity influence socializaton to the health care system and personal habits that allow the maintenance of a healthy lifestyle. Cultural diversification can serve only to exacerbate these differences when patients interact with medical practitioners whose orientation toward the health care system is totally different. However, these factors are only symbolic of the larger variables.

There are three major explanations of the health conditions of black America: institutional racism, economic inequality, and access barriers. Institutional racism as an explanation focuses on the exclusion of blacks from the medical care system. In contrast, economic inequality has a direct effect in determining how much medical care one can purchase. The final explanation focuses on the barriers to access to medical institutions experienced by blacks. Each of these approaches has a common thread: each views race as the primary factor in the distribution of health care services.

Institutional Racism

Institutional racism has been an important part of the explanation of why blacks underutilize medical services.[5] Discrimination in the vision of medical services stems from the historical relationship between blacks and dominant medical institutions in the South. During the post-Reconstruction era blacks were excluded from receiving medical services in most Southern states. During slavery, they were given better primary care because of their property value.[6] In the North, blacks received poor health care as a result of biases in public facilities and the lack of black medical personnel.

The covert racism that exists in many institutions today is manifested in a number of ways, most often in the adoption, administration, and implementation of policies toward the poor. Many rules and regulations governing the present health care system discriminate in the quality of care provided to the poor. The poor are most likely to experience long waits, to be unable to shop for services, and inevitably to receive poor care. Thus, institutional views toward the treatment of the poor overlap their attitudes toward blacks.

Overt racism is evident in the observable practices of institutions in the delivery of health care. The admission practices of hospitals, bed assignments, and the assignment of physicians have historically provoked blacks to seek help from noninstitutional sources. When these sources are not readily available, long periods of travel become necessary for the acquisition of services, especially for indigent blacks in rural areas. In contrast, the delivery of primary care in the inner city usually takes place in emergency rooms.

Despite federal and state civil rights laws, present mortality statistics support the argument suggested by this view. Invariably, institutional racism results in little or selective rewards to blacks and helps maintain present levels of inequality. As one member of the Kerner Commission summarized, "We've got to see [racism] as a system and attack it as a system."[7] Instead, present policies have tended to deny the impact of racism in any systematic way.

Economic Inequality

The economic condition in which most blacks find themselves directly affects their health care. The ability to purchase adequate health care is presently linked directly to employment. Households without adequate funding tend to be composed of members who are in a poor state of health. Poverty in these households is an important prerequisite for attaining public assistance. However, in those households made up of the working poor there is a greater probability of noninsurance or underinsurance of health care.

The uneven distribution of resources is reflected by a number of indicators from census reports. With the black unemployment rate double that of whites and with nearly 41 percent of black families with no employed member, there is little hope for adequate health care. In 1984, 22 percent of the black population made less than $15,000; in 1978, a little under 16 percent was at that level. In 1984, 35.7 percent of black families were below the poverty line, in comparison with 12 percent of white families. Alarmingly, 36 percent of the black female heads of household fell below the poverty line in 1984.

Despite this shocking condition, some segments of the black population have experienced significant changes, most notably black families where both spouses work. Such families earned a median income of $20,648 in 1984, which was 78 percent of the median income of white families with both spouses working. In the case of black females not working, the median income decreased to $7,742, or 55 percent of the median income of similar white families.

Lacking the resources necessary to obtain adequate health insurance, black families have a much lower utilization rate than whites. Blacks are more likely to seek care from nonprofit clinics or public free clinics. The present deluge of homeless persons needing assistance can only be seen as a sign of the ever-increasing demand for health services at these clinics. Many of these clinics are staffed by interns and other paramedical aides, which is not a condition for adequate primary care. Clearly, the present socioeconomic conditions of blacks promote inequality in the access to health services. This problem is further compounded by crowding in urban environments and by poverty in rural environments. In both contexts, blacks are the victims of an economic system that dictates both their ability to receive health services and the quality of their health.

Access Barriers

Use of health services can be viewed as an individual choice. Much attention has been focused on the determinants of health care utilization and how these determinants act as potential access barriers. The resulting governmental studies have tended to focus on these barriers and to lead to policies that might augment the delivery of services. Yet, effective health service access and utilization require additional forms of assistance that are informational, psychological, and organizational.[8] Accordingly, the models used to explain health care barriers for blacks can best be described as a set of attitudinal and situational factors. Attitudinal factors include attitudes that might serve as determinants of health behaviors. For example, perceived health status, perceived racism, and perceived social stress might limit the patients' seeking of services when illness occurs. As a consequence, blacks usually delay seeking medical care until all folk remedies are exhausted.

Among attitudinal barriers are beliefs about health and health behaviors, including fears about medical care, physicians, and diseases. These beliefs stem from the socialization and religious experiences of blacks. Studies indicate that their feelings of apathy are generated by the loss of control they experience in hospitals and in physicians' offices.[9] Having little sense of competency about the events that take place in these environments, many black patients develop a sense of fear of the environment and do not seek medical health services.

Situational barriers include cultural and financial conditions that might prevent health service access. Each situational factor partially elucidates underutilization behaviors, and together they link with social inequality explanations to provide an environmentally determined interpretation of underutilization. Functioning in an environment of inequality, it is difficult for blacks to adjust to the attitudinal dimensions of modern health services.

Situational factors also include geographic accessiblity that is, the "fiction of space" which is a function of the time and physical distance that must be traversed to acquire care. Rural settings are the extreme in the divisions of physical distance and time. For example, black rural patients tend to view a physician visit in terms of hours of travel, whereas inner-city patients tend to regard the physician's visit in terms of "freeway minutes."

A final set of situational factors is composed of the socio-organizational dimensions of the service provider. These attributes include the organizational perceptions and treatment of the patients.[10] The doctor-patient relationship as viewed through the eyes of the patient is critical for followup treatment. All aspects of this relationship can be influenced by such factors as sex, age, fee structure, specialization, and organization of the practice. When the patient perceives these factors as obstacles, then utilization behaviors decrease.

In sum, these three sources of inequality—institutional racism, economic inequality, and access barriers—prevent the reduction of present black health care inequities. Unfortunately, many of these inequities are a direct result of the failure of governmental policies to plan for and deliver health services adequately. This failure is due to the interface between a pluralistic government and an inadequately organized health care system.

PROBLEMS WITH GOVERNMENTAL INTERVENTION

Federal programs have widened the access to health services and have therefore increased consumer demand. The federal government provides more than $70 billion for the delivery of health services, most of which is directed toward Medicare and Medicaid programs. Although each state must make a contribution to these programs, the federal government ensures that a large amount of funds will be available to those citizens who are entitled. Agencies such as the Veterans Administration, Department of Defense Armed Services health system, and Public Health Service make a direct provision of services. In addition, tax incentives to stimulate the purchase of health insurance amounts to another $10 billion.[11]

In contrast to these stimuli to demand, the federal government has also been actively engaged in restraining the cost of health services. Such programs as Peer Standards Review Organization (PSRO), health maintenance organizations (HMOs), and health planning are intended to lower the actual cost of these services to the federal government. These restraints are countered by the heavy subsidization of biomedical research, which stimulates more utilization rather than less. Consequently, federal policy is mired in contradictions of goals and purposes, which necessarily undermine legitimate authority and attempts at regulation and control.

In examining the federal government's intervention record in the area of urban health, we find a lack of centralization around black health concerns. Instead, federal intervention has resulted in segmentation of urban health and adoption of new legislation in the areas of air, noise, marine, and other environmental concerns.[12] Although these areas of urban health are important for black residents, they only superficially deal with primary inner-city health concerns.

Three areas of concern have shaped the failure of federal efforts in the delivery of health services to blacks. First, federalism dictates the distribution of authority for the delivery of services. Second, the distribution of health professionals affects the probability of access to health services. Finally, the government's ability to plan dictates the ability of the system to change to meet new demands. Each of these areas will be examined within the framework of federalism and within the limits of its operationalization in the black community.

Federalism

The separation of powers between state and federal authorities in the delivery of health services to the poor has had mixed results. The federal government's expectations are that the state health authority should be recognized as the instrument of planning and implementation, whereas the state health authorities' expectations are for more federally financed interventions to promote health. Ultimately, many federally financed programs directed at local health problems actually undermine state authority. Robert Alford has noted that local neighborhood health councils which were encouraged by federal authorities were expected to assume responsibilities for policy determination despite the fact that state authorities could not relinquish control in certain areas.[13] The decentralization of power in a federal health care system has created problems in policy design. Wildavsky observes that within local communities there is a greater lack of medical knowledge and a more rigid viewpoint.[14] In addition, Woodrow Jones and Mitchell Rice have argued that "local client-based associations tend to narrow health policy to a single issue preventing the exercise of authority."[15] These local associations exert tremendous influence and may partially be responsible for the creation of an ineffective health care delivery system for blacks. Area-wide health plans produced at the local or community level tend to avoid specific programs for black residents. The plans seldom specify the physical distribution of resources to specific users.[16] In most instances decisions concerning physical distribution, location of equipment, and other resources are reserved for political authorities and not health planning units. In the end, however, because health planning authority is fragmented among policy bodies, political decision-making units are unable to set significant health care goals that can appease the pluralistic bases of urban health care.[17] Thus, state health policy decision-makers have found it difficult to develop intervention strategies that would make directed change possible through health planning.[18]

Health Professionals

Further compounding the problems of federalism is the lack of adequate representation of blacks and other minorities in both allied health fields and the major science fields. Black representation is sorely lacking in specialties that are important providers of adequate health services in urban areas. Lack of black representation in the major medical science fields can be traced to segregation in medical schools and schools of allied health fields.

Acceptance of blacks in medical schools has been slow in the United States. According to Seham, a black first received an American medical degree in 1847.[19] Since that time, the majority of practicing black physicians have graduated from two black medical schools, Howard University College of Medicine and Meharry Medical School. Prior to the creation of Howard, the first black medical school, black physicians received their formal training either in white U.S. schools or abroad. By 1860 nine Northern medical schools admitted blacks.[20] After the Civil War, Howard University School opened in 1868 and Meharry Medical College in 1876. Several other black medical schools were opened, but they closed after a short period. By 1938-39 only 22 of 77 medical schools in the United States admitted black students. In 1955-56 the numbers had changed to 50 of 82 schools, and in 1961-62 a total of 57 of 85 schools admitted black students. In 1970-71, 21 medical schools still had no black students.[21]

A similar pattern existed for black medical interns and nursing students. In the 1930s only three large white hospitals accepted black interns, and among the black hospitals only 68 internships were authorized, leaving a large disparity as nearly 100 blacks graduated yearly. Later, the total number of internships rose significantly, and by 1974-75 this figure had risen to 421.[22] However, it was not until 1964 that the American Medical Association accepted blacks as members.[23] In 1941 only 14 white nursing schools accepted black students, and in 1962 165 of the 1,128 nursing schools still refused to admit blacks.[24]

The term "health personnel" includes not only the usual category of physicians, dentists, and nurses, but all the occupations that are important in the delivery of health services. Health workers range from the more technical scientific positions to basic orderlies. Table 1.1 shows the distribution of black health personnel in 1972 and 1982 in selected health occupations. Although the percentage of black physicians remains relatively stable at 2.5 percent, the number of black health administrators has declined since 1972. In contrast, allied health occupations have an overrepresentation of blacks. The evidence clearly indicates a pyramidal labor force, with blacks underrepresented at the top and overrepresented at the bottom.

The small number of black physicians creates maldistribution and shortages. Thompson argues that black physicians tend to populate urban areas where there are high concentrations of blacks.[25] Furthermore, Reitzes notes that there is a regional imbalance between the black population and the distribution of black physicians.[26] Gray observes that

Table 1.1
Persons Employed in Selected Health Occupations,
1972 and 1982

	1972	1982
Dentists	2.2	2.5
Pharmacists	2.4	3.6
Physician, Medical and Osteopathic	2.4	2.3
Health Administrator	6.8	3.5
Registered Nurses	6.4	8.2
Therapists	3.5	7.9
Health Technologists and Technicians	9.2	9.7
Health Service Workers	23.8	22.4
Aides	21.6	15.3
Nursing Aides	26.1	29.0
LN's	24.5	16.3

Source: U.S. Bureau of Labor Statistics,
          Employment and Earnings, monthly
          (1984), and unpublished data

only 32 percent of active black physicians practice in the South,[27] whereas Rocheleau finds that only 25 percent of all black physicians live in nonmetropolitan areas, creating a shortage of black physicians in these areas.[28]

Closely related to the number of active black physicians is the number of blacks enrolled in and graduating from schools of medicine in the United States. Table 1.2 shows black enrollment in U.S. medical schools between 1969 and 1980. An examination of the overall pattern of black enrollment indicates a slight increase in the number of blacks graduating from medical schools. However, the total black enrollment from 1978 to 1980 shows a slight decrease. A similar decrease is also noted among first-year enrollment of blacks. These figures may indicate future man-

Table 1.2
Minority Percentage of Total Enrollments in Medical
Schools in the U.S., 1969–80

Academic Year	Black	Total U.S. Minority
69	2.2	3.6
70	2.8	4.3
71	3.8	5.7
72	4.7	7.0
73	5.5	8.3
74	6.0	9.5
75	6.3	11.2
76	6.2	11.4
77	6.1	11.7
78	6.0	12.1
79	5.7	12.2
80	5.7	12.7

Source: Health of the Disadvantaged, DHHS
          (HRA) 80-633.

power shortages for black physicians. Obviously, as the black population increases, the present level of black physicians in practice and training will not be adequate. By 1982 there were about 10,212 (2.3%) black physicians out of approximately 444,000 physicians. Using this figure, we find the ratio of black physicians to the black population is 1 to 2,700 (based on the 1982 population figure of 27,589,000). Sullivan observes that, even if the black population figure remains constant, "the optimal physician ratio will not be reached for another twenty years."[29]

Health Planning

The present conceptualization of health planning embodies a very traditional view of community. With a complex array of skills, technical knowledge, and information, the health planner has the responsibility of defining the community which is the subject of the plan. In the case of city planning, this problem is easily solved by the political boundaries established by political authorities. Because of their area-wide nature, health units are not easily defined by the realities of political boundaries.[30] Even if planners use their skills effectively, they still have to face the problems of motivating and coordinating divergent interests within the health and black communities.

Clark argues that the lack of identification with a defined community can prevent planners from acquiring legitimate authority.[31] In comparison, the natural communities of the urban environment are desirable. Jones and Rice comment that "these idealized communities are an impossibility when the temporal nature of health care delivery is noted.[32] Consequently, Panzetta observes that the main focus of the planner's identification tends to be the catchment area community rather than the natural community in health planning.[33] The catchment area approach to the study of community stresses the demography of an area. Such a community can easily be isolated on a map or graphically displayed as a service area. With this approach, Kelty argues that the great temptation is to assume that the people within the service areas actually represent common health problems, interests, and values in the area of planned change.[34]

The catchment area approach has failed because its focus is on objects and goals rather than on people. The role of people in the planning process is not an implicit bond that relates person to person. Instead, as Panzetta notes, people in the planning process are guided too much by formal rules and regulations.[35] As a consequence of this approach, only highly visible black problems are targets for planning. Drugs, sickle cell anemia, and hypertension are examples of highly visible black problems which give planners the illusion that they are changing the health conditions of the black population. The reality is that when time is applied to these problems, we note that planning and programs have had a relatively small impact. The phenomenon under study has usually been an artifact of the time of observation, and consequent response to the phenomenon is inappropriate for the duration of the study. Too often, the end result has been a short-range solution that has been inappropriate for the long-range problem.

Another problem with the conception of the community as a catchment area is that the black community has not, for the most part, participated in the formulation of alternatives. The black consumer's role has been limited to the consumption of services as defined by the health service agency. Although black consumers do have significant roles in blocking actions by authorities, they do not have the knowledge to formulate alternative conceptions of health care. Given the reality of the catchment area approach, lower income blacks are dependent on what could be an arbitrary program designed by professionals with no mandate from the black community.

RETRENCHMENT POLITICS AND BLACK HEALTH

The Reagan administration has developed a firmly articulated set of administrative, constitutional, and political defenses for restructuring the state-federal relationship as part of its program for economic recovery. In rethinking federalism, the administration questions the distinction between federal priorities and local responsibilities. According to Donald W. Moran, Associate Director of the Office of Management and Budget for Human Resources, the Reagan administration has clarified this distinction in the following manner: "National government is mainly responsible for defense and those matters which have any direct impact on interstate commerce. . . . A national issue [is where] . . . clearly and unambiguously everybody benefits."[36] In other words, the Reagan administration has "sort[ed] out public function by level of government in order to restore the 'traditional' separation of responsibilities. Federal, state, and local governments would become fully responsible for financing their own services."[37] Thus, the increasing federal involvement that has manifested itself in previous administrations has been assessed as an unacceptable intrusion into state authority. Claude Barfield observes, "The administration has set out to reverse the trend of decline in influence and authority of the state governments."[38] Moreover, it is argued that devolution of programmatic authority would allow a better division of labor and a redelegation of decision-making to the lower levels of government. Flexibility, efficiency, and decentralization would be accomplished by forcing lower level decision-makers to set priorities and to handle the political struggles that accompany them.[39]

In order to achieve retrenchment, for fiscal year 1982 the administration proposed to consolidate all or part of over 90 program categories into a system of four block grants (two in health) to the states with a 25-percent reduction in funds. This included a proposed consolidation of 25 health grants categories into two block grants. These block grants were to provide a lump sum of money to state governments according to functional area. Each state was to be responsible for the allocation of funds to local committees. Like the special general revenue-sharing bills in the early 1970s, there were to be few requirements for how the states would implement these grants. For instance, there were to be no provisions for matching funds by the states, no earmarking of particular categories, and no requirement that the state maintain any minimum level of effort for funding a particular program. Each grant was designed to cover a particular service area previously covered by various categories of grant programs. Programs proposed to be included in the block grants are listed in Table 1.3.

A secondary consideration was to develop a formula for the equitable distribution of resources to states and localities. No such formula has yet been developed to provide for the equity of services delivered. However, discrimination on the basis of race, age, or sex is prohibited in any grant program area. Under the block grant plan, fiscal year 1982 state entitlements were to be based on what their total grant funding was for fiscal

Table 1.3
Major Health Block Grants, 1984, 1985
(in $ millions)

	1984 Amounts	1984 Request
Primary Care	523	534
Maternal and Child	400	408
Alcohol, Drug Abuse and Mental Health	462	473
Preventive Health Services	88	90
Social Service Block Grant	2,675	2,200

Source: U.S. Detailed Budget, Executive
          Office of Presidency, 1985.

year 1981 less 25 percent. Furthermore, states were to be required to publicize their plans for spending and to provide some opportunity for public comments, thus mitigating some of the discretion of the states.

A third consideration was the overall reduction of spending for budgetary reasons. As part of the general effort to balance the budget, each block grant was to reduce the amount of governmental spending on program categories either by elimination or by underfunding. It is much easier for the administration to justify programmatic cuts in specific block grant areas. Congress acceded to the Reagan block grant plan and consolidated 77 program categories into 9 block grants—4 in health, 1 in education, and 4 in social services.

Thus, all three considerations are important for understanding the relationship between the New Federalism and black health care. Despite the rationale for congressional action, President Reagan's New Federalism gives the states more authority with far less fiscal support. Many programs that target minority groups will be consolidated into block grants and subsequently reduced to accomplish budgetary goals. The implications for black health care can be assessed on the basis of the program categories slated to be terminated.

The two major areas of black health care that were discussed previously (health planning and health personnel) are designated to be cut or consolidated into block grants. Four of the nine block grants created for fiscal year 1982 were 13 percent below the level of the individual program categories for fiscal year 1981.[40] Considering the present disparities in black/white mortality rates, these reduced budgetary requests can only lead to an increase in mortality differentials.

In the areas of mental health and health promotion, funds for staff development, drug abuse, alcohol treatment, and community mental health centers were reformulated into a block grant and cut by 25 percent over fiscal 1981.[41] These budget cuts have severe consequences for black mental health and mental health promotion. One other health block grant, the Preventive Health Services Block Grant, suffered a similar overall reduction for fiscal 1982. The Primary Care Health Block Grants received the same level of funding for both fiscal 1981 and fiscal 1982.[42] Concerning health, Judith Feder and her associates note that "the Reagan administration believes that decisions of the adequacy of service should be left to state and local governments."[43]

The response of the states to the block grant system has been mixed. Almost all states accept the ideals of increased discretion, administrative freedom, and program flexibility. But the typical response has been to retain existing program categories and to spread reduced funding across programs. Programs and projects funded directly from federal monies are continually at risk of state termination. Findings from a survey by the Urban Institute, reviewing the budgetary data of 25 states, reveal that states are reluctant to replace federal funds lost through block grants.[44] State action to replace lost federal funds hinges on the state's fiscal condition. A state with a surplus budget balance is more likely to replace lost funds. However, most states are under severe budgetary pressure and are making budgeting adjustments as a result.

The probability that state funds for black health care needs will be reallocated is slight. Many programs for blacks are considered federal initiatives and are a low-priority item for state governments. Programs that offer broad entitlements are likely to be protected by the political appeal of beneficiaries. For example, child care programs that entitle larger segments of the population will be viewed more favorably than substance abuse programs, which have large numbers of black beneficiaries. The difficulty of generalizing about the total impact of retrenchment politics on black health care is compounded by the inability to predict where state service reductions will occur and their direct consequences for the black community. Nevertheless, the themes "reallocation" and "efficiency in management" do signal a curtailment of health services to blacks and other underserved groups.

The pressing need for a more adequate health care system is nowhere better illustrated than by examining how the present system treats minorities. The authors represented in this volume are concerned with the status of black health and discuss contemporary issues surrounding the delivery of health services to the black community. Part I provides basic comparative data on the health status of blacks and whites. Included in this section is a special focus on black women and their problems in the health care system. Part II focuses on U.S. national health policy and the public health policy process. Little research has been done on the response of political institutions to the policy needs of black Americans. In this part specific attention is devoted to congressional politics, health policy implementaton, and health policy compliance/enforcement. Of special interest is a discussion of the politics of policy design and implementation. Part III provides policy analyses of important health problems that affect the delivery of health services to blacks, including substance abuse, mental health, long-term care, and inner-city health care. The final chapter on competitive health care serves as a general conclusion to the volume. Consequently, it emphasizes the need to formulate a more comprehensive strategy to handle unmet health demands.

This volume is unique in that it explores nontraditional policy concerns. Each chapter adds to our understanding of the complexity of health care delivery and provides basic information on the failure of the present system to adapt to the urban environment in which most blacks live. Our purpose is to elucidate these problems and to suggest means by which policy changes can eradicate the problems of this segment of American society.

NOTES

1. See Henrik L. Blum, *Planning for Health* (New York: Human Sciences Press, 1974), p. 92.

2. See John Romano, "Basic Orientation and Education of the Medical Student," *Journal of the American Medical Association* 143 (June 3, 1950): 411.

3. Ibid.

4. Walton Purdom, *Environmental Health* (Orlando, Fla.: Academic Press, 1980), chap. 1.

5. See Joseph N. Gayles, "Health Brutality and the Black Life Cycle," *Black Scholar* 5 (May 1972): 2-9.

6. On this point, see Mitchell F. Rice, "On Assessing Black Health Status," *Urban League Review* 9 (Winter 1985-86): 6-12.

7. *Report of the National Advisory Commission on Civil Disorders* (New York: Bantam Books, 1968).

8. L. A. Crandall and P. R. Duncan, "Attitudinal and Situational Factors in the Use of Physician Services by Low Income Persons," *Journal of Health and Social Behaviors* 22 (1981): 22-64.

9. C. Windle, "Correlates of Community Mental Health Centers' Underservice to Non-Whites," *Journal of Community Psychology* 8 (1980): 140-146.

10. Richard F. Gillum et al., "Determinants of Dropout Rates Among Hypertensive Patients in an Urban Clinic," *Journal of Community Health* 5 (Winter 1979): 94-100.

11. See Aron B. Wildavsky, *Speaking Truth to Power: The Art and Craft of Policy Analysis* (Boston: Little, Brown, 1979).

12. See Woodrow Jones and Mitchell Rice, "Liberalism, Politics, and Health Planning," *Journal of Health and Human Resources* 3 (1980): 56-66.

13. See Robert R. Alford, *Health Care Politics: Ideological and Interest Group Barriers to Reform* (Chicago: University of Chicago Press, 1975).

14. Wildavsky, *Speaking Truth to Power*.

15. Jones and Rice, "Liberalism, Politics, and Health Planning."

16. See S. Levey and P. Loomba, *Health Care Administration: A Managerial Perspective* (Philadelphia: Lippincott, 1973).

17. See William Schonick, *Elements of Planning for Area-wide Personal Health Services* (St. Louis: C. V. Mosby, 1976).

18. See Leland Kaiser, "The Effective Health Planner," *American Journal of Health Planning* (1976): 38-48.

19. M. Seham, *Blacks and American Medical Care* (Minneapolis: University of Minnesota Press, 1973).

20. Ibid., p. 20.

21. Ibid.

22. Ibid., p. 21.

23. Ibid.

24. Ibid.

25. See Theodis Thompson, "Selected Characteristics of Black Physicians in the United States," *Journal of the American Medical Association* 229 (1974): 1758-1761.

26. D. C. Reitzes, *Negroes and Medicine* (Cambridge, Mass.: Harvard University Press, 1958).

27. L. Gary, "A Mental Health Research Agenda for the Black Community," *Journal of Afro-American Issues* 4 (1976): 50-60.

28. B. Rocheleau, "Black Physicians and Ambulatory Care," *Public Health Reports* 93 (1978): 278-282.

29. L. Sullivan, "The Education of Black Health Professionals," *Phylon* 38 (1978): 225-235.

30. Alan Panzetta, "The Concept of Community: The Short-Circuit of the Mental Health Movement," in R. M. Kramer and H. Specht, eds., *Readings in Community Organization Practice* (Englewood Cliffs, N.J.: Prentice-Hall, 1975).

31. See N. M. Clark, "Spanning the Boundaries Between Agency and Community: A Study of Health Planning Staff Board Interaction," *American Journal of Health Planning* 3 (1978): 40-46.

32. Jones and Rice, "Liberalism, Politics, and Health Planning."

33. Panzetta, "The Concept of Community."

34. See E. J. Kelty, "Mental Health and Health Planning: Fitting Square Problems into Round Holes," *American Journal of Health Planning* 3 (1978): 65-70.

35. Panzetta, "The Concept of Community."

36. Donald W. Moran, quoted in Claude E. Barfield, *Rethinking Federalism: Block Grants and Federal, State and Local Responsibilities* (Washington, D.C.: American Enterprise Institute, 1981), pp. 23-24.

37. John L. Palmer and Isabel V. Sawhill, eds., *The Reagan Experiment: An Examination of Economic and Social Policies Under the Reagan Administration* (Washington, D.C.: Urban Institute Press, 1982), p. 12.

38. Barfield, *Rethinking Federalism*, p. 24.

39. Ibid.

40. Ibid., p. 32.

41. Ibid., p. 31.

42. Ibid., p. 33.

43. Judith Feder et al., "Health," in Palmer and Sawhill, eds., *The Reagan Experiment*, p. 291.

44. George Petterson, "The State and Local Sector," in Palmer and Sawhill, *The Reagan Experiment*, pp. 180-181.

2. Racial Differences in Mortality: Blacks and Whites

Antonio A. René

The health problems that affect different populations are related to a number of factors, but it is usually difficult to ascertain the specific contribution of these factors. In recent years there has been increased interest in the role of the U.S. health care delivery system in accounting for health status differences. This chapter presents an overview of vital statistics and other health-related statistical data, with particular emphasis on the difference in health status between blacks and whites with respect to morbidity and mortality. This information should provide the background for further discussion of health care utilization patterns, quality and types of health care in the black community, and other factors influencing differences among populations.

The major indices used in this chapter to describe the health status of the black population are births, deaths, and life expectancy. Birth rates can give us an idea of how fast a population is growing; death rates can indicate the extreme state of ill-health in the population for certain diseases. Life expectancy can be used as a basic measure for indicating general health conditions in the population.

FERTILITY AND BIRTHS

The fertility of American women has declined substantially during the past three decades. From 1950 to 1980, the crude birth rate decreased by 33 percent (from 24.1 to 15.9 births per 1,000 population), and the fertility rate decreased by 32 percent (from 106.2 to 68.4 births) per 1,000 women 15 to 44 years of age. Whereas both white and black women have experienced declining fertility, a sizable differential still exists between the two groups. Birth rates for black women have been substantially greater than those for white women. These differences are particularly large for third and higher order births (see Table 2.1). An interesting exception occurs for the 25 to 29 year age group as the result of delayed childbearing among white women. Since 1970, black women 25 to 29 years of age have been experiencing lower fertility than white women of the same age, and the rates for each race in the 30 to 34 year age group have become more similar.

Large differentials in teenage childbearing exist between the races. In 1980 the birth rate for black teenagers 15 to 17 years of age was approximately three times that of white teenagers in the same age group. For those 18 to 19 years of age, the rate for black women was nearly double that for white women. The largest differential occurred for teenagers under fifteen years of age, with the birth rate for black teenagers seven times that of white teenagers. Teenage women are at higher risk of various complications of pregnancy such as toxemia and prolonged labor than women in their twenties.[1] These problems are related to several factors, including poor nutrition, physical immaturity, and inadequate prenatal care.[2] The incidence of delay or the absence of prenatal care is greater for teenagers than for older mothers. This pattern is inversely proportional to the age of the mother.[3] Whether these factors are considered individually or in combination, there is little doubt that they present a serious health risk, not only to the young mother but also to her infant.

There may be several reasons for higher birth rates in the black population. One explanation offered is that for one reason or another black women prefer to have children. This explanation is probably the most ludicrous. Second, black women may not obtain abortions, undergo sterilization, or practice contraception with the same frequency as their white counterparts. These practices, in turn, may result from greater financial barriers, less awareness of the availability of these services, lack of affordable services, less acceptance of these services, or less availability of these services in the black community.[4]

INFANT MORTALITY

Because another chapter in this book (Chapter 7) discusses the importance of the problem of infant mortality in the United States, only a brief discussion of the problem will be presented here. Four indices can be

Table 2.1
Live Births, Crude Birth Rates, and Birth Rates by Age of Mother
According to Race: United States, 1950-80
(Data are based on the National Vital Statistics System)

Race	Year	Live[1] Births	Crude birth rate	AGE								
				10-14 years	15-17 years	18-19 years	20-24 years	25-29 years	30-34 years	35-39 years	40-44 years	45-49 years
White												
	1960	3,600,744	22.7	0.4	35.5	154.6	252.8	194.9	109.6	54.0	14.7	0.8
	1970	3,091,264	17.4	0.5	29.2	101.5	163.4	145.9	71.9	30.0	7.5	0.4
	1980	2,898,732	14.9	0.6	25.2	72.1	109.5	112.4	60.4	18.5	3.4	0.2
Black												
	1960	602,264	31.9	4.3	—	—	295.4	218.6	137.1	73.9	21.9	1.1
	1970	572,362	25.3	5.2	101.4	204.9	202.7	136.3	79.6	41.9	12.5	1.0
	1980	589,616	22.1	4.3	72.1	138.8	146.3	109.1	62.9	24.5	5.8	0.3

[1] Live births per 1,000 population.

Source: National Center for Health Statistics: Vital Statistics of the United States, 1980, Vol. I. Public Health Service, DHHS, Hyattsville, MD.

used in describing infant mortality: (1) infant deaths, (2) maternal deaths, (3) fetal deaths, and (4) neonatal deaths. For the purposes of this discussion, infant deaths are defined as mortality for infants under one year of age exclusive of fetal deaths. As can be seen in Table 2.2, the infant death rate for whites and blacks has declined by more than two-thirds since 1940. Despite this dramatic reduction, the 1980 rates for the black population (21.4 per 1,000 live births) remained nearly double that of the white population (11.0 per 1,000). This pattern persists with respect to fetal deaths.

Beginning in 1970, fetal deaths included only those deaths with a stated or presumed period of gestation of twenty weeks or more; for prior years, this category included deaths in which the gestational age was not stated. Table 2.2 indicates that fetal deaths for blacks and other minorities was 68.3 percent higher for blacks and others compared to the white population. Data for blacks alone were not available; however, if one assumes that it follows the same mortality pattern for other causes of death, there should be a greater than 70 percent differential between blacks as compared to whites.

Mortality for infants under 28 days of age, excluding fetal deaths, are termed neonatal deaths; this category of infant mortality accounts for the majority of infant deaths. As can be seen in Table 2.2, the rates for blacks in 1980 (14.1 per 1,000 live births) were one-third the rates 40 years prior (39.9 per 1,000 live births). However, in 1940 the neonatal mortality rate differential was approximately 1.5 times higher for blacks compared to whites. Data from 1980 indicate that the gap between blacks and whites had widened. The neonatal mortality rate was nearly twice as high for blacks as whites. This indicates that, although there has been significant progress in this area of infant mortality, whites appear to have received the greater benefits.

Some of the most startling infant mortality data are those for maternal mortality. There have been substantial reductions in maternal mortality over the last four decades. The maternal deaths shown in Table 2.2 reflect deaths per 1,000 live births from deliveries and complications of pregnancy, childbirth and puerperium. Although in 1980 the black mortality rate for this category was 3 percent of what it was in 1940, the difference in rates between white mothers and black mothers had increased from 2.4 times as high in 1940 to 3.2 times as high in 1980. In the years from 1977 to 1979 the maternal mortality rate stood four times higher than that of the white population of the United States.

Geographically, one might expect the region with the highest black infant mortality rates to be the South; however, in 1980 the East North Central region (which includes Ohio, Indiana, Illinois, Michigan, and Wisconsin) led the nation, with a black infant mortality rate of 24.4 deaths per 1,000 live births in 1980 (see Table 2.3). The state with the

Table 2.2
Infant, Neonatal, Fetal, and Maternal Mortality Rates,
by Race: 1940–80

Year	1940	1950	1960	1965	1970	1973	1974	1975	1976	1977	1978	1979	1980
Infant deaths	47.0	29.2	26.0	24.7	20.0	17.7	16.7	16.1	15.2	14.1	13.8	13.1	12.6
White	43.2	26.8	22.9	21.5	17.8	15.8	14.8	14.2	13.3	12.3	12.0	11.4	11.0
Black and other	73.8	44.5	43.2	40.3	30.9	26.2	24.9	24.2	23.5	21.7	21.1	19.8	19.1
Black	72.9	43.9	44.3	41.7	32.6	28.1	26.8	26.2	25.5	23.6	23.1	21.8	21.4
Ratio Black/White	1.7	1.6	1.9	1.9	1.8	1.8	1.8	1.8	1.9	1.9	1.9	1.9	1.9
Percent Difference	68.8%	63.8%	93.4%	94.0%	83.1%	77.8%	81.1%	84.5%	91.7%	91.9%	92.5%	91.2%	94.5%
Fetal deaths	—	19.2	16.1	16.2	14.2	12.2	11.5	10.7	10.5	9.9	9.7	9.4	9.0
White	—	17.1	14.1	13.9	12.4	10.8	10.2	9.5	9.3	8.7	8.5	8.4	8.0
Black and other	—	32.5	25.8	27.2	22.6	18.6	17.0	16.0	15.2	14.6	14.7	13.8	13.1
Black													
Ratio Black/White	—	1.9	1.8	2.0	1.8	1.7	1.7	1.7	1.6	1.7	1.7	1.6	1.6
Percent Difference	—	90.1%	83.0%	95.7%	82.3%	72.2%	66.7%	68.4%	63.4%	67.8%	72.9%	64.3%	63.8%
Neonatal deaths	28.8	20.5	18.7	17.7	15.1	13.0	12.3	11.6	10.9	9.9	9.5	8.9	8.5
White	27.2	19.4	17.2	16.1	13.8	11.8	11.1	10.4	9.7	8.7	8.4	7.9	7.5
Black and other	39.7	27.5	25.9	25.4	21.4	17.9	17.2	16.8	16.3	14.7	14.0	12.9	12.5
Black	39.9	27.8	27.8	26.5	22.8	19.3	18.7	18.3	17.9	16.1	15.5	14.3	14.1
Ratio Black/White	1.5	1.4	1.6	1.6	1.7	1.6	1.7	1.8	1.8	1.9	1.8	1.8	1.9
Percent Difference	46.7%	43.3%	61.6%	64.6%	65.2%	63.6%	68.5%	76.0%	84.5%	85.1%	84.5%	81.0%	88.0%
Maternal deaths	376.0	83.3	37.1	31.5	21.5	15.2	14.6	12.8	12.3	11.2	9.6	9.6	9.2
White	319.8	61.1	28.0	21.0	14.4	10.7	10.0	9.1	9.0	7.7	6.4	6.4	6.7
Black and other	773.5	221.6	97.9	83.7	55.9	34.6	35.1	29.0	26.5	26.0	23.0	22.7	19.8
Black	781.7	223.0	103.6	88.3	59.8	38.4	38.3	31.3	29.5	29.2	25.0	25.1	21.5
Ratio Black/White	2.4	3.6	3.7	4.2	4.2	3.6	3.8	3.4	3.3	3.8	3.9	3.9	3.2
Percent Difference	144.4%	265.0%	270.0%	320.5%	315.3%	258.9%	283.0%	244.0%	227.8%	279.2%	290.6%	292.2%	220.9%

Source: National Center for Health Statistics: Vital Statistics of the United States, 1983, Public Health Service, DHHS, Hyattsville, MD.

Table 2.3
Infant Mortality According to Race by U.S. Geographic Region,
1960, 1970, 1980

Race	White			Black			Ratio Black/White			Percent Difference		
Region/Year	1960	1970	1980	1960	1970	1980	1960	1970	1980	1960	1970	1980
United States	22.9	17.8	11.0	44.3	32.6	21.4	1.9	1.8	1.9	93.4%	83.1%	94.5%
New England	21.7	16.8	10.1	37.2	33.9	17.7	1.7	2.0	1.8	71.4%	101.8%	75.2%
Middle Atlantic	22.0	17.3	11.1	42.3	32.7	21.1	1.9	1.9	1.9	92.3%	89.0%	90.1%
East North Central	22.1	17.8	10.9	39.8	32.0	24.4	1.8	1.8	2.2	80.1%	79.8%	123.9%
West North Central	21.7	17.3	10.5	42.5	33.3	21.3	2.0	1.9	2.0	95.9%	92.5%	102.9%
South Atlantic	23.6	18.0	11.6	47.6	33.1	21.6	2.0	1.8	1.9	101.7%	83.9%	86.2%
East South Central	25.6	18.7	11.8	48.5	35.6	21.8	1.9	1.9	1.8	89.5%	90.4%	84.7%
West South Central	24.9	19.6	11.1	44.8	32.4	19.8	1.8	1.7	1.8	79.9%	65.3%	78.4%
Mountain	25.7	18.1	10.7	42.5	30.2	19.5	1.7	1.7	1.8	65.4%	66.9%	82.2%
Pacific	22.6	16.7	10.9	35.6	27.4	17.8	1.6	1.6	1.6	57.5%	64.1%	63.3%

Source: National Center for Health Statistics: Vital Statistics of the United States, 1983, Public Health Service, DHHS, Hyattsville, MD.

highest infant mortality rate in 1980 was not Mississippi or Alabama, as one might guess, but Delaware with 27.9 deaths per 1,000 live births. Delaware was followed by the District of Columbia with 26.7 deaths per 1,000 live births, Illinois with 26.3 deaths per 1,000 live births, and Mississippi with 23.7 deaths per 1,000 live births. The state with the lowest black infant mortality rate for 1980 was Massachusetts (16.8 per 1,000 live births), but even this rate was 66 percent higher than for the white population for that state.

LOW BIRTH WEIGHT

Low birth weight is the principal cause of death in the first week of life. A low-birth-weight infant may be defined as an infant born weighing less than 5½ pounds (2,500 grams). It has been reported that low-birth-weight infants are twenty times as likely to die in their first year as heavier infants.[5] Almost two-thirds of the infants that die are of low birth weight. The incidence of low birth weight in the United States in 1980 was 6.8 percent (Table 2.4). In the last decade (1970-80) the percentage of infants born with low birth weight has shown a gradual decrease. The racial differential in 1980 for low-birth-weight infants was more than twofold. Of the live births in 1980, nearly 13 percent of black infants born were of low birth weight; this compares with a rate of 5.7 percent for the white population. Risk factors associated with low birth weight include age, race, reproductive history, socioeconomic status, education, marital status, weight gain during pregnancies, cigarette smoking, drug use, alcohol consumption, and lack of prenatal care visits.[6]

There has been a substantial increase in the percentage of black mothers beginning prenatal care in the first trimester over the last decade, from 44.4 percent in 1970 to 62.7 percent in 1980 (see Table 2.4). The increase for whites was not as dramatic, ranging from 73.4 percent in 1970 to 79.3 percent in 1980. These data indicate an increasing awareness of the benefits of prenatal care and, in the case of the black community, utilization of the care made available to them during the 1970s.

The view that the racial differential in low-birth-weight incidence is partly a genetic one has been advanced.[7] However, analysis of birth-weight distribution according to socioeconomic status among homogeneous ethnic populations reveals a clear relationship between birth weight and social class; the birth weight of black infants of higher socioeconomic status is comparable to that of whites.

Moreover, a 1968 study conducted in New York City showed that when women at comparable risk with adequate medical care are compared, the low-birth-weight rates for blacks and whites are similar.[8] The Institute of Medicine has made the following comments on prenatal care:

Table 2.4
Live Births, According to Race and Beginning of Prenatal Care, Selected Years, 1970–80
(Data are based on the National Vital Statistics System)

Race and Characteristic	Year						
	1970	1975	1976	1977	1978	1979	1980
	Percent of live births						
TOTAL[1]							
Birth weight:							
2500 grams or less	7.94	7.39	7.26	7.07	7.11	6.94	6.84
1500 grams or less	1.17	1.16	1.15	1.13	1.17	1.15	1.15
Prenatal care began:							
First trimester	68.0	72.4	73.5	74.1	74.9	75.9	76.3
Third trimester	7.9	6.0	5.7	5.6	5.4	5.1	5.1
WHITE							
Birth weight:							
2500 grams or less	6.84	6.26	6.13	5.93	5.94	5.80	5.70
1500 grams or less	0.95	0.92	0.91	0.89	0.91	0.90	0.90
Prenatal care began:							
First trimester	73.4	75.9	76.8	77.3	78.2	79.1	79.3
Third trimester	6.2	5.0	4.8	4.7	4.5	4.3	4.3
BLACK							
Birth weight:							
2500 grams or less	13.86	13.09	12.97	12.79	12.85	12.55	12.49
1500 grams or less	2.4	2.37	2.4	2.38	2.43	2.37	2.44
Prenatal care began:							
First trimester	44.4	55.8	57.7	59.0	60.2	61.6	62.7
Third trimester	16.6	10.5	9.9	9.6	9.3	8.9	8.8

TABLE 2.4 (continued)

Race and Characteristic	Year						
	1970	1975	1976	1977	1978	1979	1980
RACIAL DIFFERENCE	Percent of live births						
Birth weight:							
2500 grams or less	7.02	6.83	6.84	6.86	6.91	6.75	6.79
1500 grams or less	1.45	1.45	1.49	1.49	1.52	1.47	1.54
Prenatal care began:							
First trimester	-29.0	-20.1	-19.1	-18.3	-18.0	-17.5	-16.6
Third trimester	10.4	5.5	5.1	4.9	4.8	4.6	4.5

1 Includes all other races not shown separately.

Source: United States Department of Health, Education, and Welfare, Health United States: 1979.

The women at high risk of having low birthweight infants make least use of the health care system during pregnancy. Are these women at high risk because they do not have early and complete prenatal care and advice, or are the very conditions that interfere with the mothers' willingness and ability to use health care services the same conditions that place infants at high risk? Regardless of this distinction, prenatal care has beneficial effects.[9]

VACCINATION STATUS AMONG CHILDREN

The vaccination status of children one to four years of age in 1976 and 1981 can be seen in Table 2.5. In this five-year period the percentage of children vaccinated increased for rubella and mumps. Measles, diptheria-tetanus-pertussis (DPT), and polio vaccinations showed a slight reduction. The percentage of nonwhite children receiving vaccinations for these diseases increased for all categories except DPT. The percentage of white children vaccinated increased for measles, rubella, and mumps, but declined for polio and DPT. These data indicate that less than 50 percent of nonwhite children are receiving vaccinations for polio and mumps. The greatest racial differential occurs for DPT and polio, 19 percent and 21 percent, respectively. Because the percentage of non-

Table 2.5
Vaccination Status of Children 1–4 Years of Age
According to Race: United States, 1976 and 1981

	Measles	Rubella	DPT[1,2]	Polio[2]	Mumps
1976					
Total	65.9	61.7	71.4	61.6	48.3
Race					
White	68.3	63.8	75.3	66.2	50.3
All other	54.8	51.5	53.2	39.9	38.7
1981					
Total	63.8	64.5	67.5	60.0	58.4
Race					
White	65.7	66.6	71.0	63.8	60.5
All other	55.3	55.2	52.0	42.7	49.1

Source: U.S. Department of Health, Education, and Welfare, Health United States: 1983.

white children vaccinated is lower for each disease, one might expect that, should an epidemic occur, the nonwhite population would pay a higher price in disability or death than the white population. These immunization patterns may be attributed to a number of factors, among them the lack of a public campaign on the ill-effects which these diseases can cause and, more probably, the availability of medical care.

LIFE EXPECTANCY

Table 2.6 presents life expectancy for the total U.S. population, for whites and nonwhites, from 1920 to 1980. There has been a significant improvement in life expectancy for both race groups. A gain of approximately twenty years for whites and twenty-four years for nonwhites was observed during this time period. Female life expectancy was greater than that of males in both groups. The racial differential declined from 9.6 percent in 1920 to 4.9 percent in 1980. Although the number of years of life gained for nonwhite males from 1920 to 1980 was significant, the racial differential has not changed significantly.

MORTALITY IN THE BLACK COMMUNITY

In general, mortality rates for all Americans have decreased since the turn of the century. Table 2.7 shows the age-adjusted death rates by race and sex for 1960, 1970, and 1980. Since 1960, the mortality rate for black males has declined but it still was 50 percent higher than white males and twice the rate of white females. Furthermore, black females' mortality rate was much less than that of black males. Social improvements in sanitation, nutrition, housing, and education contributed to the decline. Likewise, advances in medical care, such as immunization and the use of antibiotics, are associated with the decline in mortality rates.

Heart Diseases

Diseases of the heart continue to be the leading cause of death in the United States, exerting a predominant influence on total mortality (see Table 2.8). Although there has been a decrease in the mortality rate for deaths from coronary heart disease, the mortality rate for black males remains approximately 50 percent higher than for white males. The difference in mortality rates between black and white males for this category of death has shown an increase since 1960. Although mortality rates in general for this category of death have been declining, the percentage difference between white male and black male rates has been increasing. Black females showing a 29 percent higher mortality rate for

Table 2.6
Life Expectancy at Birth, 1920–80

Sex and Age

| | Year and Race | | | | | | | | | | | |
| | White Male | | | White Female | | | Black Male | | | Black Female | | |
Sex and Age	1960	1970	1980	1960	1970	1980	1960	1970	1980	1960	1970	1980
All ages, adjusted	917.7	893.4	745.3	555.0	501.7	411.1	1246.1	1318.6	1112.8	916.9	814.4	631
Under 1 year	2694.1	2113.2	1230.3	2007.7	1614.6	962.5	5306.8	4298.9	2586.7	4162.2	3368.8	2123
1–4 years	104.9	83.6	66.1	85.2	66.1	49.3	208.5	150.5	110.5	173.3	129.4	84
5–14 years	52.7	48.0	40.9	34.7	29.9	22.9	75.1	67.1	47.4	53.8	43.8	30
15–24 years	143.7	170.8	171.3	54.9	61.6	55.5	212.0	320.6	209.1	107.5	111.9	70
25–34 years	163.2	176.6	171.3	85.0	84.1	138.2	402.5	559.5	407.3	273.2	231.0	150
35–44 years	332.6	343.5	257.4	191.1	193.3	138.2	762.0	956.6	689.8	568.5	533.0	323
45–54 years	932.2	882.9	1728.5	458.8	462.9	372.7	1624.8	1777.5	1479.9	1177.0	1043.9	768
55–64 years	2225.2	2202.6	1728.5	1078.9	1014.9	876.2	3316.4	3256.9	2873.0	2510.9	1986.2	1561
65–74 years	4848.5	4810.1	4035.7	2779.3	2470.7	2066.6	5798.7	5803.2	5131.1	4064.2	3860.9	3057
75–84 years	10299.6	10098.8	8829.8	7696.6	6698.7	5401.7	8605.1	9454.9	9231.6	6730.0	6691.5	6212
85 years and over	21750.0	20392.6	19097.3	19477.7	16729.5	14979.6	14844.8	14415.4	16098.8	13052.6	12131.7	12367

Source: United States Department of Health, Education, and Welfare, Health United States, 1983.

Table 2.7
Death Rates for All Causes, According to Race, Sex, and Age:
United States, 1960, 1970, 1980
(Data are based on the National Vital Statistics System)

Year	White			Black and Other			Racial Differential		
	Total	Male	Female	Total	Male	Female	Total	Male	Female
1920	54.9	54.4	55.6	45.3	45.5	45.2	9.6	8.9	10.4
1930	61.4	59.7	63.5	48.1	47.3	49.2	13.3	12.4	14.3
1940	64.2	62.1	66.6	53.1	51.5	54.9	11.1	10.6	11.7
1950	69.1	66.5	72.2	60.8	59.1	62.9	8.3	7.4	9.3
1960	70.6	67.4	74.1	63.6	61.1	66.3	7.0	6.3	7.8
1970	71.7	68.0	75.6	65.3	61.3	69.4	6.4	6.7	6.2
1980	74.4	74.4	78.1	69.5	65.3	73.6	4.9	9.1	4.5
Years gained 1920 to 1980	19.5	20.0	22.5	24.2	19.8	28.4			

Source: United States Department of Health, Education, and Welfare, Health United States, 1983.

33

diseases of the heart in 1980, but, unlike males, the percentage difference between the rates for women has shown a decline (see Table 2.8). The mortality rate for diseases of the heart in the black population was 29 percent higher in 1980 when compared to the white population for both sexes combined. There has been a steady increase in the percentage difference in rates from 1960 (18.8%) to 1980 (29.4%). In 1960 the mortality rates for diseases of the heart in black males (381.2 per 100,000) was about the same as that of white males (375.4 per 100,000). In 1970 the difference was 8 percent, and by 1980 the difference had risen to 18 percent. Mortality from diseases of the heart for black females has remained 50 percent higher than for white females since 1960 (see Table 2.8).

Racial differences in heart disease mortality, especially for men at younger ages, are large. For each five-year age group, 25 to 39 years of age, heart disease mortality for black men was more than twice as high as for white men in 1980. For each five-year age group 40 to 64 years of age and over, the relative difference decreased. For persons 65 years of age and older, mortality was lower for black men. Racial differences in heart disease mortality were greater for women than for men, especially at younger ages.

Nonwhites have higher prevalence and death rates from cardiovascular diseases and lower hospitalization rates for those conditions. Whatever the causes of the higher prevalence, the higher death rate may be due to inadequate health care. That some of this inadequate health care has stemmed from lack of access, owing to financial limitations, is hinted at by the downward step function in death rate, which occurred a few years after the inception of Medicaid.

Cancer (Malignant Neoplasms)

Mortality from malignant neoplasms is the second leading cause of death in the United States. In 1980 the age-adjusted mortality rate was 132.8 deaths per 100,000 population; this represents almost a 6-percent increase from 1960 (see Table 2.8). From 1960 to 1980 the age-adjusted cancer mortality rate increased 23 percent for white men and 82 percent for black men. For the female population there was a decline for both black and white women of 2 percent and 10 percent, respectively. For all malignant neoplasms, the racial differential in the mortality rates increased from 15 percent in 1960 to 33 percent in 1980. The black male percentage difference increased from 11.9 percent in 1960 to 43.2 percent in 1980. Black female rates increased from a 16.7 percent difference in 1960 to a 20.4 percent difference in 1980. Malignant neoplasms of the respiratory system, the leading cancer problem, increased from a 5.8 percent difference in 1960 to a 41.2 percent difference in 1980. For black females the mortality rate remained at 7 to 8 percent from 1960 to 1980. Malignant neoplasms of the digestive system followed a similar pattern. The percentage difference in mortality rates for black females also increased from 10.6 percent to approximately 40 percent in 1980. Breast cancer mortality for black females was below that of white females in 1960 and 1970; in 1980 breast cancer mortality rates for black females surpassed those of white females.

Data from the National Cancer Institute indicate that for most cancer sites, cancer in whites is more likely to be localized (rather than systemic) at diagnosis.[10] It can be postulated from this observation that blacks do not receive medical attention as early as whites or that the diagnosis of cancer is not made in the early evaluations of blacks.

Cerebrovascular Disease

The third leading cause of death in the United States in 1980 was cerebrovascular disease or stroke. Cerebrovascular mortality rates have been on the decline for both blacks and whites since 1960. For both sexes combined, blacks' rates have decreased slightly, from a level 89 percent higher than whites in 1960 to 80 percent higher in 1980. Black male rates for 1980 were 85 percent higher than those of white males (see Table 2.8). For black males, despite a decrease in the mortality rate from cerebrovascular disease, there has been a steady increase in the percentage difference, from a 76-percent difference in 1960 to an 85-percent difference in 1980 (see Table 2.8). Although the disparity appears to be increasing for males, mortality owing to cerebrovascular disease and the percentage difference for females have been declining. Black female rates declined from 103 percent higher than those of white females in 1960 to 75 percent higher in 1980. Furthermore, females generally have lower rates than males. In part because they have higher blood pressure levels, black people experienced substantially higher cardiovascular mortality than whites for all age groups. Possible factors related to the decline include lowered incidence, improved management and rehabilitation of the stroke victim, and effective hypertension therapy (i.e., hypertension is a major risk factor for stroke).

Accidents and Adverse Effects

The fourth leading cause of death in the United States includes accidents and other adverse effects. This category is the leading cause of death for persons 1 to 34 years of age, with a mortality rate of 57.5 deaths per 100,000 persons. The major component of this category is motor vehicle accidents, which accounts for 50 percent of the total. Motor vehicle accident mortality decreased for black females from 10 deaths per 100,000 in 1960 to 8.4 deaths per 100,000 in 1980 (see Table 2.8). After a steady increase from the early 1960s mortality rates for black males was 31

Table 2.8
Age-Adjusted Rates for Selected Causes of Death, According to
Race and Sex: United States, 1960, 1970, 1980
(Data are based on the National Vital Statistics System)

Year/Cause of Death	1960	1970	1980	Difference 1960 to 1980
All causes	760.9	714.3	585.8	-23.0%
Diseases of the heart	286.2	253.6	202.0	-29.4%
Cerebrovascular diseases	79.7	66.3	40.8	-48.8%
Malignant neoplasms	125.8	129.9	132.8	5.6%
Respiratory system	19.2	28.4	36.4	89.6%
Digestive system	41.1	35.2	33.0	-19.7%
Breast	22.3	23.1	22.7	1.8%
Pneumonia and influenza	28.0	22.1	12.9	-53.9%
Chronic liver disease and cirrhosis	10.5	14.7	12.2	16.2%
Diabetes mellitus	13.6	14.1	10.1	-25.7%
Accidents and adverse effects	49.9	53.7	42.3	-15.2%
Motor vehicle accidents	22.5	27.4	22.9	1.8%
Suicide	10.6	11.8	11.4	7.5%
Homicide and legal intervention	5.2	9.1	10.8	107.7%

Race Year/Cause of Death	White			Black			Ratio Black/White			Percent Difference		
	1960	1970	1980	1960	1970	1980	1960	1970	1980	1960	1970	1980
All causes, male	917.7	893.4	745.3	1246.1	1318.6	1112.8	1.4	1.5	1.5	35.8%	47.6%	49
Diseases of the heart	375.4	347.6	277.5	381.2	375.9	327.3	1.0	1.1	1.2	1.5%	8.1%	17
Cerebrovascular diseases	80.3	68.8	41.9	141.2	122.5	77.5	1.8	1.8	1.8	75.8%	78.1%	85
Malignant neoplasms	141.6	154.3	160.5	158.5	198.0	229.9	1.1	1.3	1.4	11.9%	28.3%	43
Respiratory system	34.6	49.9	58.0	36.6	60.8	82.0	1.1	1.2	1.4	5.8%	21.8%	41
Digestive system	47.5	41.9	39.8	60.4	58.9	62.1	1.3	1.4	1.6	27.2%	40.6%	56
Pneumonia and influenza	31.0	26.0	16.2	70.2	53.8	28.0	2.3	2.1	1.7	126.5%	106.9%	72
Chronic liver disease and cirrhosis	14.4	18.8	15.7	14.8	33.1	30.6	1.0	1.8	1.9	2.8%	76.1%	94

TABLE 2.8 (continued)

Race Year/Cause of Death	White 1960	1970	1980	Black 1960	1970	1980	Ratio Black/White 1960	1970	1980	Percent Difference 1960	1970	1980
Diabetes mellitus	11.3	12.7	9.5	16.2	21.2	17.7	1.4	1.7	1.9	43.4%	66.9%	86
Accidents and adverse effects	70.5	76.2	62.3	100.0	119.5	82.0	1.4	1.6	1.3	41.8%	56.8%	31
Motor vehicle accidents	34.0	40.1	34.8	38.2	50.1	32.9	1.1	1.2	0.9	12.4%	24.9%	-5
Suicide	17.5	18.2	18.9	7.8	9.9	11.4	0.4	0.5	0.6	-55.4%	-45.6%	-39
Homicide and legal intervention	3.9	7.3	10.9	44.9	82.1	71.9	11.5	11.2	6.6	1051.3%	1024.7%	559
All causes, female	555.0	501.7	411.1	916.9	814.4	531.1	1.7	1.6	1.3	65.2%	62.3%	29
Diseases of the heart	197.1	167.8	134.6	292.6	251.7	201.1	1.5	1.5	1.5	48.5%	50.0%	49
Cerebrovascular diseases	68.7	56.2	35.2	139.5	107.9	61.7	2.0	1.9	1.8	103.1%	92.0%	75
Malignant neoplasms	109.5	107.6	107.7	127.8	123.5	129.7	1.2	1.1	1.2	16.7%	14.8%	20
Respiratory system	5.1	10.1	18.2	5.5	10.9	19.5	1.1	1.1	1.1	7.8%	7.9%	7
Digestive system	33.9	28.1	25.4	37.5	34.1	35.4	1.1	1.2	1.4	10.6%	21.4%	39
Breast	22.4	23.4	22.8	21.3	21.5	23.3	1.0	0.9	1.0	-4.9%	-8.1%	2
Pneumonia and influenza	19.0	15.0	9.4	43.9	29.2	12.7	2.3	1.9	1.4	131.1%	94.7%	35
Accidents and adverse effects	25.4	27.2	21.4	35.9	35.3	25.1	1.4	1.3	1.2	41.3%	29.8%	17
Motor vehicle accidents	11.1	14.4	12.3	10.0	13.8	8.4	0.9	1.0	0.7	-9.9%	-4.2%	-31
Suicide	5.3	7.2	5.7	1.9	2.9	2.4	0.4	0.4	0.4	-64.2%	-59.7%	-57
Homicide and legal intervention	1.5	2.2	3.2	11.8	15.0	13.7	7.9	6.8	4.3	686.7%	581.8%	328

Source: United States Department of Health, Education, and Welfare, Health United States, 1983.

percent higher than for white males; for black females compared to white females the rate was 17 percent higher.

Homicide and Legal Intervention

Mortality from homicides and legal intervention is seven times higher for black males than for white males (see Table 2.8). There has been a 60-percent increase in mortality for this cause of death since 1960 for black males and a 36-percent increase for white males. In 1980 black female mortality rates were four times higher than those of white females.

Pneumonia and Influenza

Pneumonia and influenza, the fifth leading cause of death in the United States in 1980, have continued to decline for both blacks and whites over the last two decades. However, in 1980 there remained a 72-percent difference in mortality between black males and white males and a 35-percent difference in mortality between black females and white females (see Table 2.8).

Diabetes Mellitus

Diabetes mellitus was the sixth leading cause of death in the United States for 1980. The racial differential in mortality from diabetes for black males has increased steadily form a rate 40 percent higher than white males in 1960 to a rate 86 percent higher in 1980. The diabetes mortality rates for black males increased from 16.2 per 100,000 population in 1960 to 17.7 deaths per 100,000 in 1980 (see Table 2.8). White males' rates, on the other hand, decreased 8.4 percent in the same time period. Black females were three times more likely to die from this cause as white females in 1980. There has been a 47-percent decline in mortality rates for white females since 1960, but black females have retained nearly the same rates.

Chronic Liver Disease and Cirrhosis

The seventh leading cause of death in the population of the United States is chronic liver disease and cirrhosis. The difference in mortality rates for blacks and whites in 1960 was negligible (2.8 percent), but by 1980 the racial difference in mortality rates had risen to 94 percent. The mortality rate for black males increased 200 percent from 1960 to 1980 and 35 percent for white males. In 1980 black males exhibited a rate twice that of white males (see Table 2.8).

SUMMARY OF MORTALITY DIFFERENTIALS

The mortality differential between white and black Americans is one of the largest and most consistent. While U.S. death rates for black people are almost always higher than comparable rates for whites, the differences vary a great deal depending on the specific population group. For instance, in 1980 black girls 5 to 14 years of age experienced a death rate about four times higher than that for the comparable white group. Black women 45 to 54 years of age experienced death rates approximately double those for comparable white women, but black women over 75 years of age experienced lower rates than white women in the same age grouping.

The greatest racial differentials are found among men. Ratios of 2.3 to 1 and higher are seen in the rates reported for black males 25 to 44 years of age compared to white males of comparable ages. The major cause of differences during the young adult years is the homicide rate. For instance, black men 25 to 29 years of age had a homicide rate more than twice that of white men in 1980. This accounts for about half of the excess black deaths in that age group. The ratio of black to white deaths for cirrhosis of the liver was approximately 5 to 1, but this cause is too rare to account for a major portion of the differential in the total rate. A wide variety of causes, ranging from heart disease to cancer, made up the remainder of the difference between whites and blacks in this age group. For the 15 to 19 year age group, black males had nearly the same death rate as white males in 1980. White teenagers, because of their higher socioeconomic status, have greater access to automobiles than do black teenagers. In 1980 the death rate for motor vehicle accidents for white males 15 to 19 years of age was twice as high as for blacks in the same age group. On the othr hand, the mortality rate for black homicide was several times higher than that experienced by whites.

For middle-aged men, the toll of cardiovascular diseases outweighed accidental deaths. Although homicide still accounted for 25 percent of the difference between white and black males 35 to 39, cardiovascular disease were a close second with 20 percent. Hypertension was a major contributory factor to mortality from circulatory diseases, and black people had about twice the rate of hypertension as did whites.

Obviously, lifestyle differences contribute to the differentials between black and white mortality. Various forms of violence contribute to the rate for young males. For older age groups, chronic diseases account for a vast majority of the deaths. Even there, lifestyle differences are important; a larger proportion of black people smoke than white people, and obesity is far more prevalent among black middle-aged women.[11] Furthermore, blacks may be exposed to more occupational hazards than whites, since most blacks work non-union jobs in the secondary job market. However, the differences in access to high-quality health care probably also account for some of the mortality differential. Blacks receive considerably fewer preventative services, on the average, than do white people.[12] Treatment is more frequently delayed until later stages among black people than among white people; consequently, blacks with a diagnosis of cancer do not survive as long as whites, even if the same stage of diagnosis is taken into account.

Although there has been a decline in mortality for most causes of death over the past two decades, there is still a wide racial differential to be overcome. Access to medical care is not the whole reason for this racial differential. Numerous factors contribute to mortality, ranging from genetic disorders to lifestyle, and for this reason the medical care system cannot be held entirely responsible for the differences in health status in the United States. The causes of poor health are complex and cannot be easily explained. Mortality and morbidity data can provide an indicator of health status for the U.S. black population and therefore of the progress that remains to be achieved. Understanding these measures is essential to the intelligent interpretation of health care problems.

In the preceding discussion the health status of blacks was compared to that of the white population. The mortality statistics used are unquestionably an indicator of health status. The health status of the black population can give some indication of the amount of health care needed. Comparisons of rates over time or between population groups may suggest changes in health status and health needs over time. The poor health status of the black population may reflect the accessibility of the health care system to all segments of the population served by the system. If health status is ameliorated as a result of improvements in the health care system, then evidence of better health status would accompany these improvements. Under these circumstances, all attempts should be made to improve health care, especially for population sectors with known health disadvantages. Increased access to medical care would probably improve the death rates for blacks, particularly if coupled with a healthier lifestyle.

NOTES

1. W. C. Baldwin, "Adolescent Pregnancies and Childbearing: Growing Concerns for Americans," *Population Bulletin* 31, no. 2 (1976): 3-37.

2. Helen C. Chase, *Trends in Low Birth Weight Ratios, United States and Each State, 1960-1968*, U.S. Department of Health, Education and Welfare, Health Services and Mental Health Administration, Maternal and Child Health Service (Washington, D.C.: Government Printing Office [GPO], June 1973).

3. Allen C. Naylor and Ntinos Myrianthopolous, "The Relationship of Ethnic and Selected Social Factors to Human Birth Weight," *Annal of Human Genetics* 31 (1967): 71-83.

4. H. Rudolph Melvin and Nancy Santangelo, *Health Status of Minorities and Low-Income Groups*, DHEW Publicaton No. (HRA) 79-627 (Washington, D.C.: GPO, 1979).

5. Samuel Shapiro and Marie C. McCormick, "Relevance of Correlates of Infant Deaths and Significant Morbidity at 1 Year of Age," *American Journal of Obstetrics and Gynecology* 136 (1980): 363-373.

6. U.S. Department of Health, Education and Welfare, *Healthy People: The Surgeon General's Report on Health Promotion and Disease Prevention, Background Papers*, DHEW Publication No. 79-55071A (Washington, D.C.: GPO, 1979).

7. U.S. Department of Health, Education and Welfare, "Characteristics of Births: United States 1973-1975," *Vital and Health Statistics*, ser. 21, no. 30, DHEW Publication No. (PHS) 78-1908 (Washington, D.C.: GPO, 1979).

8. Institute of Medicine, *Infant Death: An Analysis of Maternal Risk and Health Care* (Washington, D.C.: National Academy Press, 1973).

9. Institute of Medicine, *Health Care in the Context of Civil Rights* (Washington, D.C.: National Academy Press, 1981).

10. Lillian M. Axtell, Ardyce Asire, and Max H. Myers, eds., "Cancer Patient Survival," Report No. 5 from the Cancer Surveillance, Epidemiology and End Results Program, DHEW Publication No. 77-992 (Washington, D.C.: GPO, 1977).

11. Melvin and Santangelo, *Health Status of Minorities and Low-Income Groups*, p. 30.

12. Joseph S. Gonnella, Daniel Z. Louis, and John J. McCord, "The Staging Concept: An Approach to the Assessment of Outcome of Ambulatory Care," *Medical Care* 14 (1976): 13-21.

3. Risk Factors Associated with the Health Status of Black Women in the United States

Nancy R. Cope and Howard R. Hall

In spite of advances in medical technology during this century, blacks continue to show significant disparities relative to whites on certain indices of health in the United States. This chapter will examine the leading causes of death among black women, explore factors associated with these outcomes, and suggest policy recommendations to address these issues.

As a result of twentieth-century health care practices, the life expectancy for blacks has increased.[1] For example, in 1900 black women were expected to live an average of only 33 years, but by 1982 their life expectancy had increased substantially—to 73 years. White women at the turn of the century had an expectancy rate of 48 years at birth compared with 78 years today. The data for males show that white men lived an average of 48 years in 1900 versus 71 years now. Black men lagged behind all race-sex groups, with a comparatively low rate of 32 years in 1900 and 64 years in 1982. In 1970 black women surpassed the life expectancy rates of white men and continue to maintain a consistent lead.[2] When other data are examined, however, a less optimistic picture is evidenced.

Mortality figures in the United States indicate that the five leading causes of death among black women in 1981 were heart disease, cancer, cerebrovascular disease, accidents, and diabetes. Each of these will be discussed separately. It should be pointed out that, in general, men have higher mortality rates than women. The data show that in the death rates for all causes, black men were ranked first, followed by white men, black women, and white women (see Chapter 2).

HEART DISEASE

Similar to other groups, the leading cause of death for black women in the United States is heart disease. The incidence of heart disease has been decreasing in the overall population since 1950. For example, during this time the death rate for diseases of the heart among black women was 349 per 100,000, whereas white women died at a lower rate of 224. Black men during this period had the highest death rate of 415 versus a rate of 381 for white men. In 1980 the mortality rate for this disease in black women had dropped to 201, whereas for white women the rate was only 134. There was also a drop for black and white men, to 327 and 277 deaths, respectively.[3] In spite of substantial declines in the death rate for heart disease, black women and men continue to have higher rates than whites.

The risk factors associated with heart disease include hypertension, stress, dietary habits, family history, obesity, smoking, Type A behavior patterns, and high blood cholesterol levels. Each factor will be discussed in detail, using current research findings.

Hypertension

It has been noted that hypertension or high blood pressure is a risk factor for heart disease.[4] It has been implicated in the etiology of strokes and in kidney and eye disorders.[5] It is also widely accepted that high blood pressure is more prevalent among black Americans than whites. Recent estimates indicate that the number of blacks diagnosed with hypertension is between 20 to 30 percent compared with 10 to 15 percent for whites.[6] Saunders and Williams note that the condition generally strikes blacks earlier, with greater severity, and often results in death at an early age from stroke or coronary disease.[7] Myers et al. point out that the most common hypertension syndrome is "essential" hypertension.[8] According to Saunders and Williams, this condition affects 95 percent of black patients with high blood pressure.[9] The incidence of hypertension in black women heading households has been reported to be as high as 43 percent.[10] Although there are a variety of causes, some researchers note that "essential" hypertension is considered to be primarily psychophysiological in nature.[11] The condition has been associated with stress, dietary habits, and familial history.[12]

Stress

There is evidence that stress may be a contributing factor in the development of hypertension, and the literature indicates that black women are under considerable stress.[13] Stressful conditions of black women are a result of many life events. Black women have historically found themselves at the bottom of the socioeconomic ladder.[14] Today, an alarmingly high percentage of black families are headed by black women,[15] many of whom are living below the poverty level under conditions of overcrowding, a factor that exacerbates stress.[16] In 1983 it was reported that approximately 297 per 1,000 black women were divorced compared with only 78 per 1,000 in 1960.[17] It was also reported that black women were divorced at twice the rate of white women. Even more disturbing in these data was the positive correlation demonstrated between years of post-college attainment and higher divorce rates. Collins observes that part of this problem may stem from the lower number of black men with comparable educational achievements.[18] Moreover, as Jackson notes, "female excessiveness"—the outnumbering of women to men—has become a pervasive problem for black women.[19] In 1980 there were approximately 1.5 million more black women living in the United States than black men. Black women in the 15 to 34 age group exceeded black men by an astounding 430,000.

There has been some speculation that the small but growing number of blacks entering high-status, high-paying professional careers may be at more risk for developing stress-related disorders.[20] Although this hypothesis has not been substantiated, many black women have complained about the stress they feel in attempting to deal with the frustrations of their new positions. It has been observed that some of the problems include challenges to their authority,[21] subtle and overt put-downs,[22] exclusion from participation in the informal network where many decisions are made, and cultural alienation.[23] Many black women also find that a great deal of energy is expended fighting sexual discrimination and harassment, while at the same time they find themselves unable to identify with the feminist movement.[24]

Dietary Habits

Dollery notes that high salt intake has been linked to elevated blood pressure.[25] Only a small amount of salt—220 milligrams (one-tenth of a teaspoon of salt)—is needed per day by the average adult to maintain good health. However, blacks have been reported to consume more than 7 grams of sodium daily.[26] Saunders and Williams point out that many of the foods traditionally consumed by black Americans contain an excess of salt.[27] Interesting as a point of comparison is the fact that certain African tribes eat very little salt and have little or no incidence of hypertensive disease.

Family History

In many cases, a strong family history of hypertensive disease is evident. Although little is known about the formation of the genetic link and more medical research is needed, most medical authorities agree that several genes are involved in the process.[28]

Obesity

In addition to hypertension, another risk factor for heart disease is obesity. On the average, black women between the ages of 20 and 44 weigh more than white women. The difference becomes greater for black women in the 44 to 55 age category. Thus, weight may account for some of the higher incidence of heart disease in black women when compared with white women.[29]

Smoking

Increased risks for heart disease have been associated with cigarette smoking, and recent data indicate that men tend to smoke more heavily than women. For example, in 1980, 45 percent of black men compared with 37 percent of white men still smoked, whereas only 30 percent of black women and about 29 percent of white women smoked.[30] Research indicates that the risk of heart attacks increases with the amount of cigarettes smoked.[31] Furthermore, low-tar, low-nicotine cigarettes have not been found to lower the risk significantly. Unfortunately, most methods generally employed to stop smoking have been found ineffective.[32] However, the cessation of smoking is currently viewed as the best preventive measure.

Type A Behavior

Clark and Harrell, as well as Grove, observe that Type A behavior has been implicated as a risk factor in the development of hypertension[33] and coronary disease, respectively. Individuals displaying the Type A dimension are said to be anxious, impatient, hard-driving, and highly achievement-oriented. Research on behavioral and cognitive behavioral programs focusing on the promotion of less stressful life experiences and thinking patterns is promising, but further studies are needed.[34]

High Blood Cholesterol Levels

Studies have found that high levels of cholesterol contribute to arteriosclerosis and heart attacks.[35] It has been noted that black women are more prone than white women to have high levels of serum cholesterol. High blood cholesterol may be lowered by modifying the diet.[36] Age is also a risk factor in coronary disease; the older a person becomes, the higher the incidence of heart problems. Markides points out that this is particularly true for middle-aged black women and men.[37] Furthermore, Moore argues that individuals with diabetes are twice as likely to develop heart disease and men are more likely than women to be afflicted with cardiovascular problems.[38]

CANCER

Data compiled by the National Center for Health Statistics show that the second largest cause of death among black women living in the United States is malignant neoplasms.[39] When specific anatomical sites are examined, the five leading causes of death, according to the American Cancer Society, are breast (ranked first), followed by colon and rectum, lung, uterus, and pancreas cancers. Over the past 25 to 30 years, the mortality rates of black women have been increasing for breast cancer by almost 20 percent. Colon and rectum cancer rates increased a startling 14 percent. Pancreas cancer rates increased 87 percent, but uterus cancer death rates decreased more than 58 percent.[40]

Hall and Bell have employed a model by Sandram Levey to examine possible direct and indirect risk factors associated with the initiation or progression of cancer among blacks.[41] Under direct effects for cancer initiation, Hall and Bell reported three risk factors. They note that tobacco use, alcohol consumption, and occupational exposure to carcinogens have been associated with increased risk for cancers of the lung, mouth, pharynx, esophagus, stomach, liver, and pancreas. The risk factors with possible indirect effects in cancer initiation are diets high in fat and stress. They also note that beginning sexual intercourse at an early age and having many sexual partners has been associated with increased risk for cervical cancer. Under the area of cancer progression, Hall and Bell report distress and coping as having possible direct effects. For indirect effects, they note delay in seeking medical diagnosis, knowledge about cancer, socioeconomic status, poverty, geographic location, and environmental temperature.

CEREBROVASCULAR DISEASE

According to the National Center for Health Statistics, the incidence of cerebrovascular disease in the United States has been decreasing steadily during the past 35 years. In 1980 the incidence of strokes in black women was nearly two times (61 deaths per 100,000) that of white women (35 deaths per 100,000). Black men evidenced the highest mortality rate of all race-sex groups, with age-adjusted levels at 77 per 100,000 compared with 41 deaths per 100,000 for white men (see Chapter 2).

There are several different kinds of stroke, including cerebral hemorrhages, cerebral embolism, and cerebral arteriosclerosis. Studies show that blacks, particularly men, are at greater risk than whites for developing cerebral hemorrhages. Strokes also occur at a younger age in blacks than whites, are more debilitating, and result in death more often. Blacks with sickle cell anemia are more susceptible to strokes, as are individuals who are overweight. In addition, women using oral contraceptives are at greater risk.[42] Interestingly, the large drop in strokes evident in black women between 1970 and 1975 has been associated with a decline in the use of oral contraceptives. Black women have decreased their use of the pill at twice the rate of their white counterparts.[43] The incidence of strokes also decreased for white women during the same period, but at a slower rate. The exact role of the pill in the decline of strokes, however, is far from clear. Other risk factors associated with stroke are diabetes and meningitis. Persons in the lower socioeconomic groups are also at increased risk for cerebrovascular accidents.

ACCIDENTS

Accidents, as reported by the American Cancer Society, are ranked fourth among leading causes of death in black women. Within the 1 to 14 age cohort, accidents are the major cause of death for black females. The incidence of deaths from accidents is also high in the 15 to 34 age group (ranked second) and for black women between the ages of 35 and 54 (ranked third).[44] Although accidental deaths have been declining for black women, the mortality rate remains high. In 1981, 25 deaths per 100,000 were reported for black women compared with a startling 82 per 100,000 for black men. The rates for white men were 62 per 100,000, and white women evidenced the lowest mortality rates (21 per 100,00). Blacks, however, had an advantage over whites in the motor vehicle category. For car accidents, only 8 black women per 100,000 died compared with 12 deaths per 100,000 for white women. Similarly, black men had a mortality rate of 32 per 100,000, whereas white men died at a rate of 34 per 100,000. This difference has been linked to the lower socioeconomic status of many blacks. That is, because of their low-income status, blacks have more difficulty purchasing automobiles.[45]

The high percentage of accidental deaths among blacks may reflect their econoimc status. A disproportionate percentage of black women,

men, and children live in poverty under conditions that may increase the risk of accidents. However, Aldridge notes that the high percentage of accidental deaths among blacks may be somewhat inflated because many suicides are frequently labeled accidental deaths.[46] A similar observation may be made regarding deaths from automobile accidents and drugs.

DIABETES

Mortality due to diabetes in the United States has been decreasing in the general population since 1950, when 841 people died per 100,000. Recent figures reveal that the mortality rate has dropped substantially, to 556 deaths per 100,000 in 1982. However, a somewhat different trend is apparent in the black population. Although the rate for diabetes mortality has decreased for white men and women, the rate for black women has remained virtually unchanged during the past 35 years. Black women had the highest age-adjusted death rate (22 per 100,000) of any other race-sex group in 1981. They also had the highest rate in 1950. Furthermore, the rate of death for black women was almost three times the mortality rate of their white counterparts (8 per 100,000). The rates for diabetes mortality in black males rose during the 1960s and is currently 17 per 100,000. A comparatively lower rate of 9 deaths per 100,000 for white males was recorded in 1981.[47]

The greater propensity of black women to be overweight may be a factor in their increased susceptibility to diabetes. It has been reported that more than half of those who become diabetic are initially plagued with weight problems. Diabetes is also a risk factor for other disorders involving the circulatory system, such as strokes and disorders of the eyes and feet.[48]

PNEUMONIA AND INFLUENZA

Although pneumonia and influenza are not among the leading causes of death in black women, they do represent major health concerns. At the turn of the century, pneumonia and influenza were major causes of death in the United States. Although great strides have been made in reducing the mortality rate for this disease, black men continue to have higher mortality rates in this category (see Chapter 2). The American Cancer Society points out that in 1978 pneumonia and influenza ranked fifth among the leading causes of death for black women 75 years of age and older. It was the sixth leading cause of death for black women in the 55 to 74 age cohort. In 1980 black men had the highest mortality rate (28 per 100,000) compared with other race-sex groups. However, on the whole, black women displayed a more favorable outlook than black or white men (28 versus 12 per 100,000). This represents a substantial decline in mortality for black women who died from pneumonia and influenza at a rate of 50 per 100,000 35 years ago. White women continue to have the lowest death rate—9 per 100,000.[49]

A 1974 study found that a large percentage of black families had not received the standard immunizations. This study also noted that many blacks in the lower socioeconomic groups cannot afford preventive health measures such as immunizations and yearly physical examinations. Jackson observes that elderly black women experience these problems, for the majority of them live alone and in poverty.[50]

CIRRHOSIS OF THE LIVER

The mortality rate for chronic liver disease and cirrhosis in black women was a relatively low 5 deaths per 100,00 in 1950. The rate increased steadily until 1970, when 30 deaths per 100,000 were reported. The current rate has declined to 13 per 100,000. In 1981 black men died at a rate of 30 per 100,000 compared with 15 and 7 deaths per 100,000 for white men and women, respectively.

Alcohol abuse has been identified as the leading cause of liver disease in blacks.[51] It has been variously reported that excessive drinking may be more prevalent in blacks than in whites. Higher rates of cirrhosis tend to occur in blacks from lower socioeconomic groups, and this may occur as a result of poor dietary habits and higher incidence of hepatitis in poverty-stricken areas.[52] Jackson notes that there may be a relationship between the scarcity of males and alcohol abuse in female-headed households. Compounding this problem is the poor attendance reported of blacks in standard treatment programs for alcoholism such as Alcoholics Anonymous.[53]

SUICIDE

Black women had the lowest death rate of all race-sex groups in this category. Age-adjusted rates reveal that 2 deaths per 100,000 occurred in black women during 1980, which was only slightly higher than the rate recorded in 1950. Peak periods of suicide in black women took place between 1970 and 1979 when the rate was approximately 3 deaths per 100,000. The largest mortality rate appeared in the 35 to 44 age cohort. White males had the highest rate of suicide (18 per 100,000), followed by black men (11 per 100,000) and white women (5 per 100,000) (see Chapter 2).

In discussing upwardly mobile black women, Campbell implicates the synergistic effect of racism and sexism along with unfamiliar and stressful work experiences as risk factors in the development of depression and suicide. The isolation many black women feel as a result of unsuccessful personal relationships has also been discussed as a possible factor in suicide.[54] Some studies have found the problem to be very high among married women, while others report higher suicide rates among black women who have been separated, divorced, or widowed.[55] Helms hypothesizes that the oppressive stereotypes of super-strength or sexual prowess imposed on black women by society trigger depression or anger. Dumas asserts that such beliefs often leave black women disenchanted and occasionally unable to cope with the demands of high-pressured occupations.[56] As stressors Helms also cites the decline of the church and other social problems such as unemployment.[57] Aldridge, however, questions some of the often-mentioned risk factors of black female suicide such as the double-jeopardy phenomenon of being black and female, and instead warns that there is more of a need to examine possible psychosocial stressors contributing to the problem.[58]

MATERNAL MORTALITY

A dramatic decline in maternal mortality has taken place during this century. In 1915 a total of 608 deaths per 100,000 live births were reported for the overall population; in 1978 this figure dropped dramatically to only 9 deaths per 100,000. However, black women are still three times as likely to die while pregnant than are white women.

Among black women, 65 percent received prenatal care during the first trimester compared with 80 percent of white women in 1980. Nearly 80 percent of black women received little or no care at all in the final trimesters.[59] Toxemia in pregnancy occurs more often in black women, possibly because blacks tend to develop hypertensive disorders at an early age.[60]

HOMICIDE

Important racial disparities are evident in the data for homicide mortalities in the United States. In 1980 homicide was the leading killer of black women and men between the ages of 15 and 34. The death rate for black women was three times that of white women (13.7 versus 3.2 per 100,000). Black men had a striking rate of 71.9 deaths per 100,000 compared with 10.9 deaths per 100,000 for white men (see Table 2.8).

Blacks have suffered as a result of their disadvantaged economic and political position in the United States.[61] One manifestation of this phenomenon is crime. Gordon asserts that blacks are overrepresented as agents and victims of crime, and the result has been devastating to the black community. In fact, because of the high number of suicides in one American city, the life expectancy of black males dropped three years during the last decade. Most at risk, according to Gordon, are young black males between the age of 15 and 30.[62]

IMPLICATIONS AND CONCLUSION

This chapter has attempted to explicate an amalgam of factors imping-
ing on the health of black women. This preliminary investigation high-
lights the need to reexamine health care priorities in the United States.
Some of the responsibility must also be placed on black women, who are
challenged to alter their perceptions of and behaviors toward health and
health care.[63] A sense of urgency lists for health care systems to
examine those indices displaying marked racial differences in mortality.
For black women, this is especially needed in three areas: hypertension,
cancer, and maternal mortality.

Saunders and Williams suggest that the identification and early
screening of hypertension is a major goal in health care.[64] They also
recommend that prudent measures be taken to educate blacks about the
risks of hypertension and the importance of preventive measures such as
physical exercise and diet. However, Rodgers-Rose notes that many
blacks may be unable to afford the foods recommended by nutritionists
and physicians for better health.[65] Many food stamp programs, while
assisting lower income black women, do not provide enough assistance
to allow them a diet consisting of fresh vegetables, fruits, fish, and
poultry. For example, during 1984, food stamps provided only an average of $46 per recipient per month. In addition, Groves suggests that
more research is needed in developing effective behavioral measures to
control the risk factors for heart disease such as cigarette smoking and
obesity.[66]

Black women have been found to be noncompliant in following hypertension preventive measures. For example, a study conducted in 1974
found that only 25 percent of black female hypertensives obtained consistent treatment.[67] Negative and uncaring physician attitudes, along
with long waiting periods at health care facilities, have been cited as part
of the problem. Such conditions only serve to reinforce the negative
impressions many blacks have of the health care system. More black
female health providers are needed. Such professionals may have more
credibility with some black women, as well as the ability to empathize
with the cultural characteristics and special concerns of black women.

As mentioned earlier, in their cancer study Hall and Bell recommended further research to explore direct risk factors (tobacco use,
alcohol consumption, occupational exposure, distress, and coping) and
indirect factors (diets high in fat, stress, delay in seeking medical diagnosis, socioeconomic status, poverty, geographic locations, and
environmental temperature). They suggest that these factors may contribute to increased cancer rates among blacks. Such research will also
provide answers regarding increased cancer rates among black women
in the United States. Hall and Bell also mention the need for more

research on traditional as well as newer psychological and behavioral approaches to cancer treatments for blacks.[68]

Wynder and Kabat have outlined prevention strategies aimed at reducing cancer rates among blacks. These authors suggest anti-smoking programs to reduce lung cancer rates, sexual-hygiene education to lower cervix cancer rates, and decreases in dietary fats and increases in vegetables to lower the risk of nutritionally related cancers. Wynder and Kabat also provide recommendations for prevention strategies in the work setting that have direct implications for reducing cancer rates among black female employees. These include medical screening with Pap smears and training in breast self-examination.[69]

In 1983 maternal and child health programs received 23 percent less federal funding than in the previous year. At the same time, the National Center for Health Statistics noted that early and improved prenatal care for black women was a major objective for lessening differentials in maternal and infant mortality. Such a goal will be difficult to accomplish without adequate federal funding for the health care services of black women in lower socioeconomic groups.

NOTES

1. For a more general discussion on this point, see Emily C. Moore, "Women and Health," *Public Health Reports* 95 (Supplementary to September-October 1980 issue): 14-15.

2. See National Center for Health Statistics, *Health: United States and Prevention Profile—1983*, DHHS Publication No. (PHS) 84-1232 (Washington, D.C.: GPO, 1983), p. 181.

3. Ibid., pp. 187-190.

4. See Irene Lewis, "Hypertension Treatment Compliance: A Study on Blacks and Minorities," *Western Journal of Black Studies* 4 (1980), 33.

5. See Elijah Saunders and Richard Allen Williams, "Hypertension," in Richard Allan Williams, ed., *Textbook of Black-Related Diseases* (New York: McGraw-Hill, 1975), p. 354.

6. See Maurice Sokolow, "Heart and Great Vessels," in Marcus A. Krupp and Milton J. Chatton, eds., *Current Medical Diagnosis and Treatment* (Los Altos, Calif.: Lange Medical Publications, 1979), p. 192.

7. Saunders and Williams, "Hypertension," p. 336.

8. Hector F. Myers, Rochelle T. Bastien, and Ralph E. Miles, "Life Stress, Health, and Blood Pressure in Black College Students," *Journal of Black Psychology* 9 (1983): 2.

9. Saunders and Williams, "Hypertension," p. 338.

10. See James D. McGhee, "A Profile of the Black Single Female-Household," in *The State of Black America—1983-1984* (Washington, D.C.: National Urban League, 1984), p. 47.

11. See, for example, Gerald Groves, "Stress Disorders," in Samuel M. Turner

and Russell T. Jones, eds., *Behavior Modification in Black Populations: Psycho-social Issues and Empirical Findings* (New York: Plenum Press, 1982), p. 283.

12. See Ernest A. Bates, "Neurology," in Williams, ed., *Textbook of Black-Related Diseases*, p. 597; Lewis, "Hypertension Treatment Compliance," p. 34; and Saunders and Williams, "Hypertension," p. 341.

13. See, for example, Saunders and Williams, "Stress and Strains on Black Women," *Ebony* 24 (1974), 33.

14. See La Frances Rodgers-Rose, "Some Demographic Characteristics of the Black Woman: 1940-1975," in La Frances Rodgers-Rose, ed., *The Black Woman* (Beverly Hills, Calif.: Sage, 1980), p. 35.

15. For a general discussion on this point see McGhee, "A Profile of the Black Single Female-Household," p. 43.

16. See Lewis P. Clopton, "The Impact of Ecological Influences on the Mental Health of Urban Black Communities," in Lawrence E. Gary, ed., *Mental Health: A Challenge to the Black Community* (Philadelphia: Dorrance, 1979), p. 205.

17. See Bebe Moore Campbell, "To Be Black, Gifted, and Alone," *Savvy* 5 (December 1984): 74; and James D. McGhee, "The Black Family Today and Tomorrow," in *The State of Black America 1985* (Washington, D.C.: National Urban League, January 1985), p. 3.

18. Patricia Hill Collins, "Third World Women in America," in Barbara Harber, ed., *The Women's Annual—1981: The Year in Review* (Boston: G. K. Hall, 1982), p. 92.

19. Jacquelyne Johnson Jackson, "Urban Black Americans," in Alan Harwood, ed., *Ethnicity and Medical Care* (Cambridge, Mass.: Harvard University Press, 1981), p. 43.

20. See Bebe Moore Campbell, "Black Executives and Corporate Stress," *New York Times Magazine*, December 12, 1982, pp. 101-102.

21. See Rhetaugh Graves Dumas, "Dilemmas of Black Females in Leadership," in Rodgers-Rose, ed., *The Black Woman*.

22. See Patricia Bell Scott, "Moving Up the Institutional Hierarchy: Some Suggestions for Young Minority and Women Professionals from the Notebook of a Novice," *Journal of the National Association for Women, Deans, Administrators, and Counselors* 43 (Winter 1979): 35.

23. See John P. Fernandez, *Racism and Sexism in Corporate Life: Changing Values in American Business* (Lexington, Mass.: D. C. Heath, 1981), pp. 53-56.

24. See Joan L. Griscom, "Sex, Race, and Class: Three Dimensions of Women's Experience," *The Counseling Psychologist* 8 (1979): 10-11.

25. C. T. Dollery, "Arterial Hypertension," in James B. Wyngaarden and Lloyd H. Smith, eds., *Cecil Textbook of Medicine*, Vol. 1 (Philadelphia: W. B. Saunders, 1982), p. 267.

26. See Lewis, "Hypertension Treatment Compliance," p. 34.

27. Saunders and Williams, "Hypertension," p. 341.

28. See Dollery, "Arterial Hypertension," p. 267.

29. See George Berkley, *On Being Black and Healthy* (Englewood Cliffs, N.J.: Prentice-Hall, 1982), p. 26.

30. See National Center for Health Statistics, *Health: United States and Prevention Profile—1983*, p. 211.

31. See David Burns, "Tobacco and Health," in Wyngaarden and Smith, eds., *Cecil Textbook of Medicine*, p. 47.

32. See Groves, "Stress Disorders," p. 294.

33. Vernessa R. Clark and Jules P. Harrell, "The Relationship Among Type A Behavior: Styles Used in Coping with Racism, and Blood Pressure," *Journal of Black Psychology* 8 (1982): 89.

34. See Groves, "Stress Disorders," p. 294.

35. See John P. Kane, "Diet and Arteriosclerosis," in Wyngaarden and Smith, eds., *Cecil Textbook of Medicine*, p. 38.

36. Ibid.

37. Kyriakos S. Markides, "Mortality Among Minority Populations: A Review of Recent Patterns and Trends," *Public Health Reports* 98 (May-June 1983): 254-255.

38. Moore, "Women and Health," pp. 17-18.

39. National Center for Health Statistics, *Health: United States and Prevention Profile—1983*, p. 188.

40. American Cancer Society, *Cancer Facts and Figures for Minority Americans* (New York: American Cancer Society, 1983), p. 12.

41. Howard Hall and Xyna Bell, "Increase in Cancer Rates Among Blacks," *Journal of Black Psychology* 12 (1985): 1-14.

42. Genell J. Subak-Sharpe, Morton Bogdonoff, and Rubin Bressler, eds., *The Physicians' Manual for Patients* (New York: New York Times Book Co., 1984), p. 68.

43. See Moore, "Women and Health," p. 50.

44. See the American Cancer Society's publication, *Cancer Facts and Figures*, which lists the ten leading causes of death among blacks by age group and sex.

45. See National Center for Health Statistics, *Health: United States—1982*, DHHS Publication No. (PHS) 83-1232 (Washington, D.C.: GPO, 1982), p. 20.

46. Delores P. Aldridge, "Black Female Suicides: Is the Excitement Justified?" in Rodgers-Rose, ed., *The Black Woman*, p. 274.

47. See National Center for Health Statistics, *Health: United States and Prevention Profile—1983*, pp. 187-188.

48. See Berkley, *On Being Black and Healthy*, p. 66.

49. National Center for Health Statistics, *Health: United States and Prevention Profile—1983*, pp. 187-188.

50. Jacquelyne Johnson Jackson, "Aged Black Americans: Double Jeopardy Re-examined," in Williams, ed., *The State of Black America 1985*, pp. 150-151, 155.

51. See Carroll M. Leevy, "Digestive Diseases and Malnutrition," in Williams, eds., *Textbook of Black-Related Diseases*, p. 630.

52. See Alvin F. Poussaint, "The Mental Health Status of Blacks—1983," in Williams, ed., *The State of Black America—1984*, p. 219.

53. See Jackson, "Urban Black Americans," pp. 43-44.

54. Bebe Moore Campbell, "Stresses and Strains on Black Women," *Ebony* 24 (1974): 25.

55. See Robert E. Staples, "Black Family Life and Development," in Lawrence E. Gary, ed., *Mental Health: A Challenge to the Black Community* (Philadelphia:

Dorrance, 1979), p. 84; anbd Janet E. Helms, "Black Women," *The Counseling Psychologist* 8 (1979): 41.

56. Dumas, "Dilemmas of Black Females in Leadership," p. 208.

57. See Helms, "Black Women," p. 44.

58. Aldridge, "Black Female Suicides," pp. 273, 283.

59. See Joel C. Kleinman, Margaret Cook, Steven Machlin, and Samuel S. Kessel, "Variation in Use of Obstetric Technology," in National Center for Health Statistics, *Health: United States and Prevention Profile—1983*, p. 64.

60. Leroy R. Weekes, "Obstetrics and Gynecology," in Williams, ed., *Textbook of Black-Related Diseases*, p. 104.

61. For a more detailed discussion on this point, see Alphonso Pinkney, *The Myth of Black Progress* (Cambridge, Mass.: Cambridge University Press, 1984).

62. Thomas A. Gordon, "The Black Adolescent," in Gary, ed., *Mental Health*, p. 129.

63. See Haynes Rice and LaRah D. Payne, "Health Issues for the Eighties," in James D. Williams, ed., *The State of Black America 1981* (New York: National Urban League, 1981), p. 137.

64. Saunders and Williams, "Hypertension," pp. 354-355.

65. La Frances Rodgers-Rose, "Some Demographic Characteristics of the Black Woman: 1940 to 1975," in Rodgers-Rose, eds., *The Black Woman*, p. 31.

66. Groves, "Stress Disorders," p. 294.

67. See Jackson, "Urban Black Americans," p. 104.

68. Hall and Bell, "Increase in Cancer Rates Among Blacks, p. 3.

69. E. L. Wynder and G. C. Kabat, "Opportunities for Prevention of Cancer in Blacks," in C. Mettlin and G. P. Murphy, eds., *Cancer Among Black Populations: Progress in Clinical and Biological Research*, Vol.. 53 (New York: Alan R. Liss, 1981), pp. 237-252.

PART II

Health Policy, Politics, and the Black Community

4. Congress and Black Health: Dynamics and Strategies

K. Robert Keiser

The Congress, in attempting to meet its responsibilities as a policymaking institution, has been neither an ardent champion of progressive reform nor a diehard supporter of reactionary obstructionism. Its rate of legislative productivity has tended to vary in accordance with political and economic conditions. Thus far, it has continued to maintain a dual system of health and welfare—one for the middle class and another for the poor. Despite its actions concerning Medicare and Medicaid, it has not been able to agree on national health insurance. And although it has expanded nutritional and health care programs, it still has been less than forceful in attacking disease and disability in the ghetto. This chapter examines the dynamics of congressional decision-making concerning black health and suggests strategies for the future.

DETERMINANTS OF CONGRESSIONAL POLICYMAKING

A transformation in the Congress has enabled it to engage in more activism in health policy, but the modest nature of the metamorphosis has tended to diminish the substance of the actions it has taken. Much of congressional government is committee government. The significant committees in the health area are the House Committee on Energy and

Commerce and its Subcommittee on Health and the Environment, the House Ways and Means Committee, the Senate Committee on Labor and Human Resources, the Senate Committee on Finance, and the two Committees on Appropriations and their Subcommittees on Labor, Health and Human Services, and Education.

Changes in the composition and the procedures of Congress, which occurred in the 1960s and 1970s, have led this committee system to work more on behalf of public health. A Northern Democrat such as Senator Edward Kennedy (D-Mass.), for instance, was able to accumulate enough seniority to become the chairman of the Senate Committee on Labor and Human Resources. In the House, Representative Henry Waxman (D-Calif.) was selected as chairman of the Health and Environment Subcommittee of the Committee on Energy and Commerce, despite the fact that he had less seniority than a moderate Southerner who was competing for the job.[1] The chairs have tended to use these leadership positions to gain a reputation of accomplishment both inside and outside the legislature. Senator Kennedy's standing as "Mr. Health" in the Senate further enhanced his potential as a presidential candidate. Even Representative Paul Rogers (D-Fla.), chairman of the Subcommittee on Health and the Environment and a representative of a conservative-leaning district, considered most expansions of health policy to be safe enough for him to lend his support.[2]

Four major influences on congressional decision-making are party, cue-taking, ideology, and constituency. Even though American political parties are notable for their organizational weakness and absence of discipline, they still predict legislative behavior better than the characteristics of the members' constituencies do. The differences in roll-call votes are more likely to reflect the representatives' membership in either the Democratic or Republican party rather than differences in the median income or ethnic composition of the districts.[3]

A related influence on congressional voting is the practice of cue-taking. Members of Congress simply do not have the time to make an independent collection and assessment of the information relevant to the hundreds of issues on which they must vote in each legislative session. In order to cope with their enormous burden of decision-making, they learn to rely on certain trusted sources of advice and direction. In the largest number of cases, the representatives will vote with the state party delegation to which they belong. Other cue-givers include the party leaders, the party majority, the majority of the House, and committee chairs.

The way a member of Congress makes up his or her mind tends to vary with different types of legislative issues.[4] When the legislators must vote on highly controversial and visible issues, most of them base their decisions on both their own personal philosophy and their constituents' preferences. On more routine measures on which the members have standing records, they are inclined to vote along ideological lines. They take their cues from committee members with whom they are in agreement on complicated issues and from constituencies on federal grants to local communities. And they vote with the congressional majority or the consensus on nonvisible legislation.

As a general matter, ideology has both direct and indirect effects on the public policies Congress makes. It has a direct impact on controversial and routine measures. In addition, it exerts an influence over the precise kind of cue-taking behavior the members practice. They tend to depend on committee members and to pay attention to constituents with whom they share values.

A key factor in the responsiveness of Congress in any session is the relative strength of the conservative coalition. The coalition appears when a majority of Republicans vote with a majority of Southern Democrats against a majority of Northern Democrats. Joining together infrequently in the 1930s, the Republicans and Southern Democrats came together more regularly in the 1940s. In more recent times, the mean appearance rate has stabilized at a range between 20 percent and 40 percent of nonunanimous votes.[5] When the coalition does appear, it tends to win. At the peak of its strength in the late 1940s and early 1950s, the right-wing bloc achieved victory in the overwhelming majority of their contests with the Northern Democrats. In the 1960s and 1970s their success rates were reduced, but they continue to block congressional reform. They are not powerful enough to pass a right-wing agenda, but they are influential enough to limit the scope of other initiatives.

CONGRESSIONAL BLACK CAUCUS

The Congressional Black Caucus was created in 1970 to fill the leadership vacuum within the civil rights movement. When the black members of Congress requested a visit with President Richard Nixon, they were at first rebuffed. Later, when it was pointed out that numerous other groups had been given the opportunity to send delegations to the White House, the president agreed to a meeting at which he listened to the caucus's demands. The event and the controversy that surrounded it managed to place the caucus in the national limelight.

At a time when the civil rights movement was in a state of transition between protest action and electoral politics, the caucus acted as more than a legislative faction and undertook initiatives outside of the Congress. Representative Charles Diggs (D-Mich.), the chair of the caucus, joined with Mayor Richard Hatcher of Gary, Indiana and poet-activist Imamu Baraka in calling for a National Black Political Convention. The caucus as a whole, however, refused to endorse the political assemblage, and it disassociated itself from the platform of the convention when the delegates voted for positions that opposed school busing and criticized the state of Israel.[6] In the aftermath of these events, the caucus decided to concentrate on legislative politics. It hired a professional staff which it was able to finance with funds raised at an annual dinner. It established a working relationship with organizations such as the Leadership Conference on Civil Rights, the Urban League, the League of Women Voters, and Common Cause. It also established communications with local black leaders in congressional districts with large numbers of black voters.[7]

The members of the caucus tend to vote alike, but they also vote much the same way as do other Democrats from urban, Northern districts. The group is more an independent source of initiative within the liberal coalition than it is a distinct voting bloc. It has given high priority to and helped to pass legislation promoting full employment and guaranteeing a percentage of federal contracts for minorities. Health legislation has not received the same level of attention as issues of economic advancement. The caucus has also lobbied with other Democrats and negotiated with the House leadership for first-rate committee assignments. Members of the caucus serve on the most powerful and prestigious committees, including Rules, Ways and Means, and Appropriations. Black representatives are more likely to be attracted to committees such as Judiciary and Education and Labor, which have jurisdiction over civil rights and issues concerning equality of educational and economic opportunity.

The issue of health has not been neglected, however. In 1984 Representative Charles Rangel (D-N.Y.) and Representative Harold Ford (D-Tenn.) were part of the Ways and Means Subcommittee on Health. Representative Mickey Leland (D-Tex.) was on the Energy and Commerce Subcommittee on Health and Environment, and Representative Louis Stokes (D-Ohio) was a member of the Appropriations Subcommittee on Labor, Health and Human Services.

CONGRESSIONAL ACTIVISM

During the 89th Congress (1965-66), a liberal majority was able to defeat the conservative coalition consistently, and the result was a decisive breakthrough in American legislative history. The concept (even if not the reality) of the guarantor state, which ensured a minimum level of well-being for all, was extended to issues of health. The newly adopted measures only altered a segmented system of health services, but they greatly expanded the role of the public sector. After years of legislative stalemate, the Medicare and Medicaid programs were passed. Altogether, fifteen different bills affecting health services were enacted into law.

Although President Lyndon Johnson devoted much of his time and resources to legislative leadership, the Congress was willing to expand the scope of health policy even more. The House Ways and Means Committee decided to recommend that Medicare cover doctors' fees as well as hospital bills. And as part of its consensus-building process, the committee introduced the Medicaid program to assist the states in providing care to the medically indigent and poor.[8]

In a last-ditch attempt to stop the passage of Medicare, the American Medical Association proposed that the benefits and coverage of the Kerr-Mills program be expanded. The Kerr-Mills bill had been enacted in 1960 as a way to assist with the worst problems of the elderly who were poor. The federal commitment under the act was fairly strong. But the extent to which the states participated in the program varied a great deal. Even though the industrial states of California, New York, Massachusetts, Michigan, and Pennsylvania had only about one-third of the elderly population, they received about 90 percent of the funds. The elderly in many other states were less likely to benefit.

The Republicans and the American Medical Association often had been in agreement on health care issues in the past, but this time the Republican legislators decided that the political situation demanded a different approach. The ranking Republican member of the Ways and Means Committee, Representative John Byrnes (R-Wisc.), introduced a voluntary health insurance plan that would cover doctors' fees as well as hospital costs and that would be financed largely out of general revenues.

Representative Wilbur Mills (D-Ark.), chairman of the Ways and Means Committee, decided to incorporate all of these proposals into one legislative package. The final version of Medicare consisted of two parts: under Part A, hospital insurance for the elderly would be financed through the Social Security system and payroll taxes; Part B was a modification of the Byrnes proposal concerning voluntary insurance for doctors' services. In addition, Kerr-Mills was expanded into Medicaid to include coverage for the nonelderly poor and indigent.

While Medicare is a social insurance program administered by the federal government, Medicaid is a public assistance program managed by the state governments. The federal government helps to finance Medicaid expenses through matching grants. It also establishes minimum requirements concerning the eligibility of recipients and the scope of benefits. The states must include in the program all the needy in families with dependent children as well as all the categorically needy among the aged, blind, and disabled. Federal funds are also extended to the states which decide to assist the aged, blind, disabled, or families with dependent children who are classified as medically needy.

Among the basic services that states must include are hospital care, physicians' services, family planning, laboratory tests, nursing care, and screening and treatment of children. If they wish to, the states can also provide for clinic care, emergency hospital care, and other benefits. At the same time, they can limit the amount of basic services and reimburse doctors at low rates. As a result, there are many gaps in Medicaid coverage. Many poor people do not qualify. Single individuals and childless couples are not eligible, and most two-parent families are unable to obtain assistance. Those who do qualify may receive only minimal services, or they may be treated only by those providers who will accept less reimbursement.

While Medicare and Medicaid were simply financing schemes, the community or neighborhood health center program, initiated under the Economic Opportunity Act, was an attempt to bring a new kind of health care approach to the poor and minorities. The initial projects sought not only to deliver high-quality medical care, but also to alter the nonmedical factors that could have an influence on health. In 1966 the Congress indicated its support for these projects by granting specific authorization for the development of health centers. Subsequently, the Partnership for Health Amendments of 1967 funded community health centers which would be adminstered through the Department of Health, Education and Welfare.[9]

The centers sought to establish health facilities which would be located closer to where low-income patients resided, to end discriminatory practices in the treatment of minorities, and to promote adequate counseling and explanations of treatments. The use of a team of health professionals to treat patients was an important innovation in the provision of quality care. Unfortunately, the funding levels and congressional restrictions on reimbursements limited the number of centers that were created and the extent of services that were provided.

Even after Richard Nixon replaced Johnson in the White House, Congress proceeded to take more steps in the health field. The 92nd Congress in 1971-72 was particularly productive, with much of the legislation directed at specific diseases and health problems. It included the National Heart, Blood Vessel, Lung and Blood Act, which supported new centers for research and treatment of cardiovascular and pulmonary diseases, and the National Sickle Cell Anemia Control Act, which authorized funds for research and screening and counseling of victims. Representatives from the Department of Health, Education and Welfare and the Office of Management and Budget testified against much of this legislation. But once Congress acted, President Nixon did not use his veto power to prevent the measures from becoming law. Both branches of the government acted as if health was a politically popular issue with which to be associated. In contrast, once Gerald Ford assumed the presidency, he attempted to curtail federal spending for health. He successfully pocket-vetoed a health services bill that would have cost more than a billion dollars over what the administration had recommended. In his other efforts to veto health legislation, however, he was overridden. Not only did large majorities of both houses support a 1975 health services measure after a presidential veto, but even a majority of Republican members joined in the override.[10]

As economic growth lagged during the 1970s, Congress turned more of its attention to holding down the costs of health care. Yet, even in these inauspicious times, large majorities in Congress voted for a major expansion of the food stamp program. The Carter administration successfully proposed the elimination of the purchase requirement for food stamps—which had mandated that recipients pay cash for a portion of the stamps. The advocates of free stamps wanted to ensure that the program would reach the very poor. The votes split along party lines, but many Republicans voted with the Democrats to approve the revision. Congress also authorized new legislation that led to further expansion of community health centers. More assistance was provided for rural health centers, and in addition, demonstration projects were established for the reimbursements of paraprofessionals in urban communities. In the places where they have been in operation, the centers have increased access to high-quality care for poor and minority patients.

A related reform made it more possible for residents in the inner cities to benefit from the National Health Service Corps. The corps has supplied doctors and other professionals to communities without adequate service from private medicine. The revision in the legislation altered the definition of a Health Manpower Shortage Area. Under the previous language, entire cities and counties were the unit of analysis. As a result, smaller neighborhoods without physicians which were part of an urban center with many doctors were ineligible for assistance. The new law allowed more corps personnel to be placed within these urban communities.[11]

THE REAGAN YEARS (1981–82)

In the 1980 election the Republicans obtained majority control of the Senate for the first time since 1952. They also gained 33 seats and their highest vote totals in the House of Representatives since 1956. As a result, the power of the conservative coalition in Congress was stronger than it had been in years. Its strength was indicated on the vote on budget targets that were proposed by Phil Gramm (D-Tex.) and Delbert

Latta (R-Ohio). Because Democrats of all persuasions agreed that they did not possess the votes seriously to oppose Reagan's budget reductions, Jim Jones (D-Okla.), chairman of the House Budget Committee, led the deliberations on the budget resolution in the spirit of cooperation. Although the committee contended that it granted the administration most of what it had requested, the administration refused to compromise. The Gramm-Latta substitute proposal was devised by Representative Gramm and by David Stockman, Director of the Office of Management and Budget.

As Table 4.1 illustrates, the budget targets, which were approved by a vote of 253 to 176, marked a significant victory for the conservative coalition of Republicans and Southern Democrats. The unanimity of the Republican party was a critical factor in the budgetary process. A number of Democrats voted on the conservative side only when it was clear that a Republican victory was certain.[12] On later decisions to make the budget stick, the margin of victory was much closer.

It would be an oversimplification to suggest that the cutbacks in social spending were so sharp just because of the composition of the Congress. In addition, the White House had greater resources than the Democratic leadership for mobilizing interest group and constituency support for its proposals. It contacted campaign contributors who had given to both Reagan and a Democratic member of Congress and requested that the contributors put pressure on the legislators. The volume of mail was so heavy that the House post office could not handle it all.[13] As a consequence, federal spending for Medicaid was cut back about $1 billion a year, food stamps for the near poor were almost eliminated, and subsidized school lunches were sharply reduced. Still, Congress managed to resist some of the administration's proposals. In the House, members refused to place a cap on federal spending for Medicaid. In the Senate, more moderate and liberal members of the Labor and Human Resources Committee balked at removing federal regulations over community health centers which provided primary care in low-income neighborhoods.[14]

In 1982 the Congressional Black Caucus introduced an alternative budget proposal that would have substantially enhanced federal appropriations for public health. As could be expected, the Republicans and Southern Democrats overwhelmingly opposed the motion, but a majority of Northern Democrats also voted against the proposal. The consensus of this Congress was that social spending on matters such as health should be given a lower priority.

At the same time, overwhelming legislative majorities could be mobilized for modest measures for which widespread public support could be anticipated. By voice vote, the House passed legislation to restore funds to programs designed to improve child nutrition. On another voice vote, the House authorized federal grants and tax credits toward the develop-

Table 4.1
Selected House Votes on Health, 1981-82

1981	Voting Pattern	Northern Democrats	Southern Democrats	Republicans	Pro-Health Outcome
Budget targets	Coalition	17-144	46-32	190-0	--
Budget resolution	Party conflict	4-157	23-55	189-0	--
1982					
Budget substitute	Consensus	78-79	8-66	0-177	--
Transfer of child nutrition programs	Consensus				+
Health promotion	Consensus				+
Orphan drugs	Consensus				+

Source: Congressional Quarterly Almanac, 1981-1982.

ment of drugs for the treatment of rare diseases. This piece of legislation included requirements that the government should fund at least ten research centers for the investigation of sickle cell disease.[15]

AFTER THE MIDTERM

After the midterm elections, the balance of power in the Senate remained much the same, but the relative strength of the Republicans in the House was diminished. The conservative coalition did not appear in roll-call votes concerning health (illustrated in Table 4.2). The major initiatives which the House supported failed to gain passage in the Senate. The Democratic majority in the House, for instance, voted to extend health insurance to the unemployed; but in the debate over how to finance the scheme, conservatives threatened to filibuster and succeeded in blocking the proposal.

The congressional response to the public controversy over hunger illustrates the inhibited approach which the members had adopted. As unemployment spread during the recession, more individuals and families sought help from soup kitchens and food distribution centers. Interviews with volunteers and victims were reported in the media. Organized groups such as the Food Research and Action Center and the U.S. Conference of Mayors asserted that more families had little to eat and were suffering from malnutrition.[16]

By voice vote, Congress ordered that federally owned commodities, such as cheese, dry milk, honey, and wheat, be distributed to the charitable groups assisting the poor. It also authorized the allocation of federal monies for the expenses incurred in the distribution of the commodities. This subsidy to charitable organizations was justified on the grounds that bulk commodities had to be repackaged or reprocessed before they could be distributed.

As Congress and the media focused more attention on the issue, the White House appointed a presidential task force which argued that no widespread undernutrition existed in the United States. Once Congress authorized emergency action to alleviate the problem, it declined to take any large steps concerning hunger and nutrition. The House did pass a bill that would have increased the levels of financial support for federally funded meals for children, but the Senate failed to act on the measure. When the unemployment rate stopped increasing, the issue of hunger began to slide off the legislative agenda.

A similar pattern of behavior can be discerned on the issue of medical care for children.[17] Although infant mortality rates in the United States have improved in recent years, there is still a greater proportion of infant deaths in this country than in a number of other industrialized nations. In addition, mortality rates are twice as high in the black com-

Table 4.2
Selected House Votes on Health, 1983

1981	Voting Pattern	Northern Democrats	Southern Democrats	Republicans	Pro-Health Outcome
School lunch and nutrition amendments	Party conflict	169-0	84-4	53-110	+
Emergency fund	Consensus	161-0	86-2	142-6	+
Unemployment health insurance	Party conflict	170-3	45-42	37-129	+

Source: Congressional Quarterly Almanac, 1983.

munity as in the rest of the nation. The Children's Defense Fund has led the coalition of groups that has supported more federally funded care for mothers and children. One of its concerns is that the relative numbers of low-weight babies has not declined at the same rate as has infant mortality. Low-weight offspring are more likely to be born to mothers who are young and poor. In later life, they are more prone to developmental problems that affect academic performance.

Members of Congress who spearheaded the drive to expand federal support argued that preventive care was cheaper than the accumulated expenses associated with low-weight babies. Representative Henry Waxman (D-Calif.), chairman of the Subcommittee on Health, introduced a bill to extend federal funding for maternity care to pregnant women who would qualify for Medicaid after the birth of a child. Waxman's proposal would also have provided Medicaid for women and children in intact families whose principal wage-earner was unemployed. The proposal cleared the committee, but a floor fight over procedures stymied the legislation. Finally, in 1984 the Congress did make some funds available to provide Medicaid for pregnant women and children in intact and indigent families.[18] As part of this process, some states have expanded their Medicaid coverage. Except for these modest changes in federal policy, the energies of health activists in Congress were depleted in defensive actions against cutbacks in ongoing programs.

The House did complete action on a bill to provide health assistance to the unemployed, but it never came to the floor of the Senate for a vote. What the House authorized were block grants to the states for insurance and for hospitals that provided care for the uninsured. It also established requirements concerning private insurance to assist those who might lose their jobs in the future. These actions were taken in response to information that a majority of the unemployed lost their health insurance shortly after they had been dismissed from their jobs. The issue tended to be an emotional one, beset with political pressures. A moderate-to-liberal majority defeated a more conservative minority. Almost all the Northern Democrats voted in favor of the extension of health protection, and a little over 50 percent of the Southern Democrats supported it. On the other side of the aisle, the overwhelming majority of the Republicans voted in opposition to the measure.

The size of the black constituency did not directly affect the vote. As Table 4.3 indicates, the behavior of the Northern Democrats, Southern Democrats, and Republicans did not vary with the concentration of the black population within their districts. While all the Northern Democrats who represented districts in which blacks made up 20 percent or more of the population voted in favor of health insurance, only half the Southern Democrats who represented such districts with large numbers of black

Table 4.3
Black-Populated Districts and Support for
Unemployment Health Insurance

	Black Population	
	20% or more	Less than 20%
Northern Democrats	100.0% (25)	98.0% (148)
Southern Democrats	50.0 (42)	53.3 (45)
Republicans	0.6 (16)	0.7 (150)

Source: Focus, September 1982, pp. 4-5.

constituents supported the program. The Republicans who were elected from such districts still voted with other Republicans in opposition.

Southern Democrats represented the largest number of districts which contained heavy concentrations of black voters. These legislators tended to vote for the extension of health insurance when they served more urban districts in which black support could be joined with blue-collar votes or other ethnic-group support. Representative Ben Endreich, for example, was elected in Birmingham and Jefferson County, Alabama, garnering a large proportion of his vote from the black and working-class communities. Representative Jack Brooks (D) represented Texas's Ninth District, which includes the urban areas along the coast in east Texas. The labor movement, the large black population, and the addition of other ethnic groups has made it a more liberal district on most welfare issues. Another supporter of the measure, Representative Martin Frost (D), gained most of his votes from the black and Hispanic residents in the south side of Dallas.[19]

Those legislators representing large black constituencies who voted against the health bill tended to come from more rural areas in which the black minority could find few allies in the electoral process. Representative Charles Hatcher was elected in Georgia's Second District, which is mostly rural and agricultural. Although policies in south Georgia have entered a period of instabilty, traditionally it has been conservative.

Another state whose party delegation mostly opposed the proposal was North Carolina. Representative Charles Whitley represents North Carolina's Third District, which consists of small towns and small farms. Whitley has voted with the Democratic leadership on some key votes, but the voters in his district have supported the right-wing politics of Jesse Helms when he has campaigned for the Senate. Representative Tim Valentine was elected over a black opponent in the Second District. The residents of the city of Durham are part of the district, but the majority of the voters live in small towns and rural communities. There are possibilities for change, but events are still developing.

FUTURE STRATEGIES

Since the election of 1964, neither a liberal majority nor the conservative coalition has been able to maintain firm control over Congress for any length of time. By and large, it has charted a relatively moderate course. The members have not sought to stage a revolution in public health, but they have been disposed to expand health programs in times of economic growth and to protect previous advances in times of scarcity. While continuing to maintain a dual system of entitlements for the middle class and charity services for the poor, they have sought to make some improvements in that system.

The representatives have been united only on certain health issues. For example, there has been a consensus in favor of some governmental promotion of sustenance and well-being, especially among the most dependent members of the population, such as children and the elderly. However, ideological and partisan conflict has arisen over issues related to redistribution. Thus far, Congress has failed either to bring all members of the society into the mainstream of medicine and health or to finance adequately separate structures of care and support for the less advantaged members.

The important breakthrough in innovative legislation on behalf of health care for the poor occurred during a period when politics resembled "responsible party government." Much of the Great Society legislation was originally introduced and publicized by activist Democrats in cooperation with interest groups such as the AFL-CIO, the National Education Association, and the United States Conference of Mayors.[20] When John F. Kennedy and Lyndon Johnson took charge of the executive branch in 1960, they had a fairly clear and consistent party program to guide their efforts. Once the Democrats gained overwhelming control over the 89th Congress, they carried out the party's promises in one of the most productive legislative sessions in U.S. history.

A similar movement of legislative activism would help the black community make sizable progress toward solving its health and survival problems. The best way to bring about such a course of events is to pursue a polarizing party strategy. The goal of this strategy would be to become part of the governing coalition in both the executive and legislative branches and to isolate the conservative coalition within the Congress. The black community should follow a party strategy because the redistributive policies in its interests tend to divide the legislature along party lines. A polarizing strategy is required because these redistributive issues tend to activate supporting and opposing ideological blocs.[21]

Both black leaders and black voters have already committed themselves to this kind of political approach. All the members of the Congressional Black Caucus are also members of the Democratic party. About 80 percent of the black electorate has expressed a preference for the Democratic party, and only less than 10 percent have identified with the Republican party.[22] Little interest has been shown for supporting most Republican candidates. The black community is not an interest group seeking some narrow benefits that can be dispersed by either party. Because it is demanding large-scale reallocation of resources, it will have to exert enormous pressure to make even one party respond. It should be expected that a large proportion of the other party will be in opposition.

A polarizing party strategy does not mark a stark transition from protest to politics. The social policies of the Kennedy and Johnson administrations were passed in the midst of political turbulence. The civil rights movement put pressure on the party politicians to assign a higher priority to the needs of minorities and the poor. It helped to intensify the ideological conflict that characterized the election of 1964. The catalyst for partisan polarization does not necessarily have to be street protest, however. An open primary system, as Jesse Jackson has illustrated, can be used to exert pressure on a party from within. One goal of this type of campaign is to increase the number of blacks who are registered to vote. Even if additional numbers of registered blacks who would vote Democratic are counterbalanced by additional numbers of registered whites who would vote Republican, the electoral base of the Democratic Party would be altered. Another possibility is third-party politics. The most successful third party in American history was organized over the issue of race. Even though third parties have not had a decisive impact in the twentieth century, they have still been used for purposes of protest. A minority which is growing in strength can use third-party tactics to demonstrate its new power to the major parties.

Once a power base has been established within a progressive coalition, the black community must mobilize its resources both inside and outside the Congress to pass legislation that will meet its special needs and concerns. An inside-outside strategy was developed in 1973 by Representative Walter Fauntroy (D-D.C.) in an effort to obtain home rule for the District of Columbia.[23] Fauntroy contacted black elected officials and other prominent blacks in Southern districts which contained large black populations in order to initiate grass-roots pressure on members of

Congress. Inside the legislature, Fauntroy and the Congressional Black Caucus asked the representatives from the targeted districts to support the proposed measure. A similar approach could be used to improve and expand the Neighborhood Health Centers and other programs that have a disproportionate impact on the health of minorities.

The polarizing party strategy is likely to reap benefits when both political and economic circumstances are auspicious. Political conditions are favorable when the conservative coalition is weak in both the executive and legislative branches of the government; economic conditions are favorable for expanding the scope of health policies in periods of economic growth when the costs of redistribution are less painful. Both sets of conditions existed when the health legislation of the Great Society was passed. The large Democratic majorities in the Congress reduced the political obstacles to reform, and the fiscal dividend generated by economic growth softened the opposition to new expenditures in the health field. A similar fortuitous combination of factors would allow the black community to make further substantial gains.

In more recent times, however, both political and economic conditions have been unfavorable. They were particularly disadvantageous during the first term of the Reagan administration. The right wing of the Republican party had captured control over the executive branch and put together a working coalition in the legislative branch. After another oil crisis, double-digit inflation and negative growth had imposed fiscal constraints on governmental action. In such predicaments, the programs on which minorities and low-income groups depend are most vulnerable. The Congressional Black Caucus was not able to reverse the Reagan administration's budget-cutting plans.

The best strategy for such difficulties is to prepare for them in advance. During these years entitlement programs suffered much less than did means-tested programs. Reductions in Social Security and Medicare were not nearly as deep as were the budget cuts for food stamps and Medicaid. Thus, it is important to seek to expand the scope of social insurance. If more blacks are included in entitlement programs when political and economic conditions permit such legislation, then their interests can be more easily protected under more trying circumstances.

In more ambiguous situations when political conditions are favorable at the same time that economic conditions are unfavorable, bold new policies are improbable but limited revisions of existing programs are possible. For example, during the Carter administration, on the political front large Democratic majorities were elected in both houses of Congress. On the economic front, however, stagflation and economic instability tempered any enthusiasm for new governmental expenditures. Comprehensive proposals concerning welfare reform and national health insurance made little headway, but existing programs such as food stamps and the Neighborhood Health Centers were improved in order to better serve minorities and the poor.

A critical element in the strategy of policy refinement is the presence of legislative activists who are willing to play the role of "fixer."[24] This oversight actor carefully monitors the implementation of a policy to ensure that it produces the intended results. The fixer corrects problems that develop by amending the original legislation or by influencing bureaucratic behavior. Senators Edward Kennedy and Warren Magnuson took special interest in the National Health Service Corps beginning in 1972 and sponsored further legislation to improve and expand its operations. Few legislators spend much energy on fixing because it can be dreary and unglamorous work. There are more incentives to advocate the introduction of new programs or simply to lambast the bureaucracy. This shortage in the supply of fixers opens up some political opportunities for black legislators. When other possibilities are blocked, they might seek to make existing programs work better for their constituents.

In other times when political conditions are unfavorable but economic conditions are favorable, little immediate action might be taken, but an agenda for the near future can be created and promoted. During the 1950s and early 1960s, political conditions did not facilitate the passage of new health legislation. The executive branch was resistant in the Eisenhower years, and the legislative branch was an obstacle in the Kennedy years. Economically, there was enough prosperity to support the argument that more Americans should share in it. Although the government tended to be deadlocked, organized labor and Democratic activists promoted health insurance for the elderly and made it a leading campaign issue in 1960 and 1964.

If the economy improves in the late 1980s and 1990s, a new agenda for health policy might be created. Specifically, a more comprehensive version of national health insurance could be reintroduced. In the early 1970s, when the nation was beset with severe economic difficulties, even a Republican president endorsed the idea of expanding health insurance. Now that the severity of the nation's economic problems has eased, serious debate on the issues of the nation's health should be renewed.

After the 1980 election, there was speculation about a conservative realignment in American politics. The proliferation of business-sponsored political action committees created the possibility that conservative challengers could draw on a rich supply of campaign funds to compete against congressional incumbents. The American right appeared to have reached new heights in political organization and sophistication. By 1984, however, the picture had changed. Despite the reelection of Ronald Reagan, the conservatives failed to win control of Congress. In fact, the newly elected members of the Senate were more moderate or liberal than their predecessors, and the Republican senators who ran ahead of the president in their states tended to more moderate.[25] In the lower house, the conservative forces remained a minority.

Mobilization of the black vote would further weaken the conservative coalition. In the aftermath of the Voting Rights Act of 1965, Southern Democrats in Congress have sided with Northern Democrats on social welfare issues.[26] Increasingly, members representing districts with black constituencies have more often voted in opposition to the conservative coalition.[27] The political actions of the black community are increasingly capable of quickening the tempo of change when conditions are favorable and limiting the extent of backsliding when conditions are unfavorable.

NOTES

1. Barbara Sinclair Deckard, *Majority Leadership in the U.S. House* (Baltimore: Johns Hopkins University Press, 1983), p. 9.

2. Eric Redman, *The Dance of Legislation* (New York: Simon and Schuster, 1973), pp. 88-90.

3. Randall B. Ripley, *Congress* (New York: W. W. Norton, 1983), pp. 138-145, 311-319.

4. David C. Kezak and John D. Macartney, eds., *Congress and Public Policy* (Homewood, Ill.: Dorsey Press, 1982), pp. 313-328.

5. Mack C. Shelley II, *The Permanent Majority* (University, Ala.: University of Alabama Press, 1983), pp. 23-41.

6. Charles P. Henry, "Legitimizing Race in Congressional Politics," *American Politics Quarterly* 5 (April 1977): 149-176.

7. Marguerite Ross Barnett, "The Congressional Black Caucus," in Harvey C. Mansfield, ed., *Congress Against the President* (New York: Praeger, 1975), pp. 34-50.

8. Theodore R. Marmor, *The Politics of Medicare* (Chicago: Aldine, 1973), pp. 62-70.

9. Karen Davis and Cathy Schoen, *Health and the War on Poverty: A Ten Year Appraisal* (Washington, D.C.: Brookings Institution, 1978), pp. 161-173.

10. *Congressional Quarterly Almanac* (Washington, D.C.: Congressional Quarterly, 1975), pp. 598-599.

11. Fitzhugh Mullan, "The National Health Service Corps and Health Personnel Innovations," in Victor W. Lidel and Ruth Lidel, eds., *Reforming Medicine* (New York: Pantheon Books, 1984), pp. 189-190.

12. Deckard, *Majority Leadership in the U.S. House*, pp. 191-192.

13. Ibid., pp. 193-194.

14. *Congressional Quarterly Almanac*, 1981, pp. 483-488.

15. *Congressional Quarterly Almanac*, 1983, pp. 490-493.

16. Ibid., pp. 412-416.

17. Ibid., pp. 419-420.

18. Linda E. Demkovich, "Hospitals That Provide for the Poor Are Reeling from Uncompensated Costs," *National Journal*, November 24, 1984, p. 2249.

19. Michael Barone and Grant Ojifusa, *The Almanac of American Politics* (Washington, D.C.: National Journal, 1984).

20. James L. Sundquist, *Politics and Policy* (Washington, D.C.: Brookings Institution, 1968), pp. 389-414.

21. On polarizing strategies, see R. Douglas Arnold, *Congress and the Bureaucracy* (New Haven, Conn.: Yale University Press, 1979), p. 44.

22. Hanes Walton, Jr., *Invisible Politics* (Albany: State University of New York Press, 1985), p. 146.

23. Marguerite Ross Barnett, "The Congressional Black Caucus: Illusions and Realities of Power," in Michael B. Preston, Lenneal J. Hennderson, Jr., and Paul Puryear, eds., *The New Black Politics* (New York: Longman, 1982), pp. 39-40.

24. Frank J. Thompson, *Health Policy and the Bureaucracy* (Cambridge, Mass.: MIT Press, 1981), p. 24.

25. Charles E. Jacob, "The Congressional Elections," in Gerald Pomper, ed., *The Election of 1984* (Chatham, N.J.: Chatham House, 1985), pp. 121-123.

26. Shelley, *The Permanent Majority*, pp. 55-56.

27. Charles S. Bullock III, "Congressional Voting and the Mobilization of a Black Electorate in the South," *Journal of Politics* (August 1981): 662-682.

5. Health Policy Design: Implementation Politics of Child Health and Family Planning Programs

Malcolm L. Goggin

In recent years, the health status of children and women of childbearing age has been profoundly affected by several federally and state-funded child health and family planning programs. Blacks make up a substantial proportion of eligible beneficiaries of at least two of these programs—the Early and Periodic Screening Diagnosis and Treatment (EPSDT) program for poor children and youth under Medicaid, and the family planning services program for former, current, and potential welfare recipients under Title IV-A (then Title XX) of the Social Security Act. Both programs apply a strict means or incomes test in determining eligibility for services.

Two other child health and family planning laws, the State of California's Child Health and Disability Prevention (CHDP) Act of 1973 and the federal Family Planning and Population Research Act of 1970, have also affected the health status of women and children. Yet, their more liberal eligibility requirements have meant that blacks have been a much smaller percentage of the pool of eligible beneficiaries. Neither the CHDP nor the Title X family planning law applies a strict means test to determine eligibility.

The implementation of some of these programs was more political than others. The State of California represents a good example of the politics involved in these programs owing to the racial diversity and the political economy of the state. Because of these features, as well as the fact that California is the nation's most populous state, California is used as a case study in this chapter to provide insights into the politics of health policy design and implementation. The chapter examines the implementation of two family planning laws and two child health laws in the state.

In California, the two family planning laws were implemented more successfully than the two child health laws. And in the two programs with the lowest percentage of blacks among eligible clients, CHDP and Title X family planning, implementation was more successful, when compared to the implementation of counterpart programs with higher percentages of black eligibles, that is, EPSDT and the family planning program specifically designed for welfare recipients, respectively. These differences in implementation experiences are puzzling, for the four programs are similar in size, policy domain, time period, and impact on the state's political economy.

It is useful, therefore, to consider some of the reasons why implementation within the State of California might have varied as it did across these four programs. One plausible explanation, which is examined in this chapter, is that implementation politics varied systematically with policy design. On the basis of a comparison of differences in implementation experiences with differences in policy design—program philosophy, benefits, beneficiaries, and incentives for compliance—we can see how "policy determines politics."[1] In addition, interviews with implementing actors and documentary and statutory evidence will be used to argue that policy content influenced implementation results. More specifically, this chapter will show that differences in the racial composition and incomes of the eligible clients help explain why the two programs that were for poor people were not implemented as successfully as the two programs that were for both poor and nonpoor.

FOUR CASES OF IMPLEMENTATION

The four cases of implementation are similar with respect to policy type (transfer), policy domain (social), size (moderate), state (California), and time frame (mid-1970s). They differ in how they were implemented (see Table 5.1). First, the time required to introduce these new programs varied from *prompt* (a few months) to *delayed* (several years). Second, changes in program content ranged from minor (a few insignificant changes in means) to major (significant modifications in program philosophy and goals, benefits, beneficiaries, or incentives).

The cases also differed along the theoretically relevant dimensions of program philosophy, benefits, beneficiaries, and incentives. By recon-

Table 5.1
A Typology of the Politics of Implementation

| | Timing | |
	Prompt	Delayed
Minor	Title X	Title IV-A
Scope of Change		
Major	CHDP	EPSDT

structing the process from the enactment of each law until the first services were delivered in the states, what Alexander George calls "process-tracing," co-variations between the four policy content variables and the two process variables of delay and change yield evidence of the plausibility of each of the hypotheses.[2] A brief description of each of the cases of implementation will illustrate how they are similar and comparable.

EPSDT

The Early and Periodic Screening, Diagnosis, and Treatment (EPSDT) program is an example of a "conflictual" type of implementation politics; it was delayed in its implementation, and its program philosophy and scope of beneficiaries were changed during the course of implementation. EPST was established as a program in 1967 when Congress passed PL 90-248, an amendment to Title XIX of the Social Security Act. The law required states to provide comprehensive, preventive health services to children under 21 years of age who were members of families eligible for welfare benefits. It took California seven years to make the program operational, and the program's implementation was marked by conflict, delay, and major changes in the content of the law.

Title X Family Planning

The Family Planning and Population Research Act of 1970 is a good example of a "consensual" type of implementation politics: this amendment to Title X of the Public Health Service Act was implemented within six months of its adoption; and policy goals were not reformulated during the initial "take-off" period. The law provided grants to California's Department of Health and to private, nonprofit agencies like Planned Parenthood in order to pay for the delivery of comprehensive, voluntary family planning services. There were no eligibility requirements for services, but priority was to be given to low-income individuals. The implementation of the Title X Family Planning law in California was straightforward and uninhibited. Regulations were approved, money appropriated, and project grants awarded so that services were delivered promptly around the state.

CHDP

The California Child Health and Disability Prevention Program (CHDP) was both conflictual and consensual in its implementation. CHDP was more conflictual than Title X family planning, but less conflictual than its federal counterpart, EPSDT. Major changes were made in the scope of the program, as the number of beneficiaries dwindled with modifications in eligibility requirements. In spite of difficulties in getting regulations approved during the first months following the CHDP law's enactment, the first services were delivered in a few of California's counties within a year. The CHDP law was passed by the California legislature and signed by Governor Ronald Reagan in October 1973. It provided for free child health screening and referral services to all California children as a condition for school entry. The purpose of the program was to identify childhood disabilities at an early age. CHDP was primarily conflictual in the early years of its implementation. As compromises were worked out among public health officials, welfare administrators, state politicians, and consumer and provider advocates, implementation began to resemble the smoother, consensual type.

Title IV-A Family Planning

The family planning amendments to Title IV-A of the Social Security Act, like CHDP, were mixed in their mode of implementation. There were few changes in policy content. At first, implementation was delayed, and proponents of family planning services at the state and local level could not reach an accommodation with Governor Reagan and his appointees. Eventually, a political bargain was struck, and the process was quickly transformed from a conflictual to a consensual one. The family planning provisions of that law provided for grants to the California Department of Social Services (the Welfare Department in the state) in order to pay for family planning services for former, current, and potential recipients throughout the state.

A PLAUSIBILITY PROBE OF A CANDIDATE THEORY

In the case of social policy, program philosophy can be either consistent or inconsistent with dominant beliefs and behaviors. In these particular cases, there was also a significant difference in how implementing actors perceived the programs and in what they were designed to accomplish. The benefits structure across these four cases differed with respect to scope and acceptability. The scope of benefits is a function of the number and type of services to be delivered; benefits can be either narrow or comprehensive in scope. Acceptability refers to the attitudes of those who participated in the law's implementation, and the attitudes toward benefits ranged from acceptable to questionable.

Beneficiaries differed with respect to income, age, social class, and the exent to which they were motivated to demand the program's services. Eligibility requirements were either exclusive or inclusive, with the exclusive including only the poor among the beneficiaries and the inclusive both the poor and nonpoor.

Incentives that were incorporated or were later added to these programs were either positive rewards or negative sanctions. They ranged from effective to ineffective, depending on the extent to which they were certain and severe. Effective incentives were those that resulted in compliance, whereas ineffective incentives were those that did not lead to compliant behavior.

Program Philosophy

The two child health and the two family planning programs differed with respect to how well they fit with the existing health and medical care system. EPSDT represented the most radical departure form the status quo: it was the government's first attempt to go beyond the mere financing of welfare medical services, for example, Medicaid. One indication of the innovative nature of the program were the words of President Lyndon Johnson, when he told Congress of the use of "new types of health workers" who would be providing "New patterns of health services" through the EPSDT program.[3]

The EPSDT program, according to its program manager, California, was a duplicate system that competed with the established, traditional system of private pediatric care. In California, the program was originally sold to state legislators as a "mass screening" approach to childhood disabilities. It would rely on paraprofessionals to give screening examinations for potentially handicapping disabilities in the public schools. The idea of mass screening was attractive to politicians who were trying to put a cap on state spending for welfare medicine. In their zeal for fiscal responsibility, they set a fee of $12 per screen—on screening examinations which one doctor described as "not necessarily an exquisitely detailed and comprehensive examination, but limited in scope and depth and predicated on seeing a large number of children."[4]

The program philosophy of mass screening was anathema to pediatricians, who saw themselves as the only professionals capable of "treating the whole child." Pediatricians in northern California organized a local chapter of the American Academy of Pediatrics (AAP), whose national chairman at the time described EPSDT as "screening without meaning." The academy's biggest complaint was that their California members would be by-passed as primary providers in the new child health screening program. This was a particularly distasteful prospect for medical doctors in the San Francisco Bay Area who were already in competition with newcomers. As one politically active pediatrician in the state testified in Sacramento, "The emotional idea that a simple test will result in a productive citizen, without using the medical profession, is unrealistic."[5]

An inexpensive screening of a large number of school-age children for hearing, vision, and nutritional deficiencies, as well as other potentially disabling diseases, was politically attractive. However, the county health departments lacked the capacity to carry out the state plan, and new health workers were not available. Therefore, the state health bureaucracy needed the cooperation of pediatricians in private practice. Needless to say, providers in private practice were reluctant to embrace a program that by-passed them in favor of paraprofessionals, that set up a competitive health care delivery system, and that gave them less than what they were already receiving for screening patients under the Medi-Cal program or for a private fee for service.

The Child Health and Disability Prevention Program was the California state legislature's solution to the problems of EPSDT. Perplexed over the welfare image of EPSDT and bogged down with delays in setting up a services delivery system because they could not entice private pediatricians to sign up as providers, the Children's Lobby, a national philanthropic organization that lobbies for the cause of children, pressured San Francisco Assemblyman Willie Brown to introduce in the Assembly a law that would establish a state-funded and -administered CHDP program. As introduced, the law was to provide screening and referral services to all California children, regardless of income. In drafting the bill, Brown's aide was careful to avoid tainting the bill with either the welfare image or the idea of "mass screening." The new state legislation stressed "health assessment" instead. The bill was also worded so that it would win the support of the state's private pediatricians; it included the phraseology, "first source of referral shall be the usual source of health care."[6] This seemed to include only pediatricians, and not paraprofessionals or nurse practitioners.

When the bill passed in the state legislature and, to everyone's surprise, was signed by then Governor Reagan on October 1, 1973, the CHDP law provided not only for a "regular source of care" but also for "continuity of care" under the watchful eye of a medical practitioner. The Children's Lobby, the American Academy of Pediatrics, key members of the state legislature, and the state health bureaucracy finally had a law that made the pediatrician the lynchpin of the services delivery system. The initial start-up delays, which were due in large part to the providers' caution in light of their experiences with EPSDT, gave way to cooperation at about the same time that the fees for a screening service were increased substantially.

The reconstruction of the California implementation of the Family Planning Services and Population Research Act of 1970 reveals a completely different portrait of the politics of implementation. The law was enacted in December 1970 with the objective of offering women who had been identified as wanting but not having access to family planning services the advice and devices they needed in order to determine the timing, number, and spacing of their children. This 1970 amendment to Title X of the Public Health Services Act gave health officials a vehicle for enticing women to enter the health and medical care system. These officials used the new program to build a positive attitude toward preventive health and the habit of periodic health maintenance.

The family planning amendment to Title IV-A of the Social Security Act, on the other hand, was adopted for social as well as health reasons. It was part of a cafeteria of social services to assist the needy to get off welfare and to prevent them from becoming totally dependent on government subsidies. It was managed by the welfare rather than the health department at both the federal and state levels of government.[7]

One factor that distinguished the family planning programs from the child health programs was the way in which the family planning programs were integrated with the system. Both of the family planning programs under investigation fit comfortably with existing health and welfare practices. They utilized traditional medicine, traditional professionals, and an established delivery system to provide needed services.

Unlike the pediatricians and the EPSDT and CHDP programs, obstetricians and gynecologists were enthusiastic about the Family Planning Services and Population Research Act because it expanded the existing system and offered part-time work for some of the younger doctors while posing no threat to the others. It did all this with no increased financial burden to the state: the federal government paid all the bills. Even the abortion issue may have helped break down resistance to family planning services programs; abortion diffused some of the moral and religious opposition to contraception, which probably seemed a preferable alternative to abortion for members of the Pro-Life movement.

Thus, it is plausible that a program's philosophy does affect the way it will be implemented. Table 5.2 shows the program philosophy and politics of implementation of these four policies. The implementation of policies that were perceived as part of the welfare apparatus, for example, EPSDT and Title IV-A family planning services, were not as smooth in their implementation as counterpart programs which were viewed as having health goals associated with them, for example, CHDP and Title X family planning services. EPSDT and Title IV-A suffered from the stigma of welfare. More importantly, the family planning services programs received widespread support and provider cooperation because they fit with existing structures and practices. EPSDT and CHDP did not receive the same measure of support because, in the words of one county health and welfare director, "They were countercurrent programs."

Table 5.2
Program Philosophy and the Politics of Implementation

Type of Politics	Fit	Type	Concept
Consensual			
Title X	Consistent	Health	
Mixed			
Title IV-A	Consistent	Welfare	N.A.
CHDP	Inconsistent	Health	Health Assessment
Conflictual			
EPSDT	Inconsistent	Welfare	Mass Screening

The support and cooperation which the family planning services program received, boosted by an enthusiastic and powerful member of the state legislature (then State Senator Anthony Beilenson), hastened the implementation of family planning programs in the state and discouraged the conflict controversy which eventually leads to delay and modifications in programmatic content.

Program Benefits

The benefits written into these four laws differed in scope and acceptability. The programs with the broadest range of benefits were those with formula financing, where both the state and federal government contribute a share of the funding. The programs with benefits that were the most acceptable were the family planning programs, partly for the reasons discussed in the previous section.

The program with the narrowest range of benefits was the Title X family planning program. The only services written into that law were financial and technical assistance to institutions that provide family planning services at the local level. The CHDP program was also narrow in its scope; its benefits were limited to outreach and health education services, health screening, referral, and follow-through.

EPSDT benefits were much more comprehensive. They included screening; a physical examination; blood and urine tests; hearing, vision, and tuberculosis tests; an assessment of a child's nutritional, dental, and developmental status; diagnostic studies; referral to an appropriate provider of treatment; and followup. Treatment and followup were, of course, available only to those children who were diagnosed as having handicapping disability. Like EPSDT, the Title IV-A family planning benefits were comprehensive. The law provided for minimum services such as medical treatment and medical contraceptive services, information and educational services, as well as social services such as child care and free transportation to and from the clinic. States were free to add to this "basic" set of family planning services.

In general, the family planning services were viewed positively by the medical profession. Some pediatricians, however, considered child health screening services as neither good medicine nor good economics. Obstetricians in private practice apparently welcomed the government provision of family planning services. Pediatricians, on the other hand, organized to lobby against some of the provisions of the child health screening laws in California. For example, they actually succeeded in deleting the Denver Development test from the program. Opponents of the test considered it unreliable and concluded that the costs of stigmatizing a child on the basis of equivocal results of the test outweighed its benefits.

Medical doctors also rejected the idea of using paraprofessionals to screen children in the schools for disabilities. Members of the northern California chapter of AAP not only criticized the substance of policy, but they also complained about the procedures—for example, the paper

work involved, the lack of confidentiality of medical records, and the
state's demands for data collection. Their main complaint, however, concerned the amount of compensation received for providing screening
services.

Fiscal conservatives in the Reagan, and then the Brown, administration and in the state legislature questioned the advisability of both child
health screening programs, arguing that the cost of screening far outweighed the benefits. Financial analysts in the Department of Finance in
Sacramento were particularly critical of what they perceived were
excessively high administrative expenses. Because of the high administrative cost per screen, the Department of Finance in both the Reagan
and Brown administrations was skeptical about the programs and the
benefits they provided. Underlying this skepticism may have been the
fear that if many disabilities were uncovered, the state legislature would
be pressured to appropriate more funds for treatment. This fear of a run
on the state treasury was one reason why the EPSDT program met with
so little enthusiasm in the state capitols around the country when the
law was first passed.[8]

If the child health laws were viewed with caution because of the
possible negative effects on the state's health budget, the family
planning programs were warmly received because they were seen as
having the capacity to save the state money. The state's Office of Family
Planning (OFP) made a convincing argument that for every dollar spent
on family planning services, the state could save $8.52 in welfare
services.[9] Later, OFP made a more modest estimate that $2 could be
saved from every dollar spent on family planning services. The argument was based on what the MediCal program would save by not paying
the expenses of either an abortion or a delivery as a result of an
unwanted pregnancy, as well as saving in child welfare subsidies.

Providers and Public Health officials liked family planning services
programs because they made women aware of the need for routine
health examinations and regular contact with the health and medical
care system.[10] Politicians had a positive attitude toward the Title IV-A
law especially because it was seen as one way to cut the welfare rolls.
The only dissenting voices were heard from the black community, which
viewed family planning as a form of genocide.[11] Other groups were
opposed to the idea of government-sponsored and -financed family planning on religious or moral grounds. How did differences in the scope and
acceptability of program benefits relate to differences in the mode of
implementation?

Table 5.3 summarizes the difference in benefits across cases. The one
program that was implemented in a timely fashion was Title X family
planning. This law provided for a narrow range of benefits that were
accepted by those involved in implementation. The policy was perceived

Table 5.3
Program Benefits and the Politics of Implementation

Politics	Scope	Acceptability	Fiscal Impact
Consensual			
Title X	Narrow	Acceptable	Cost Savings
Mixed			
Title IV-A Savings	Comprehensible	Acceptable	Cost
CHDP	Narrow	Questionable	Cost Creating
Conflictual			
EPSDT	Comprehensive	Questionable	Cost Creating

as sound medical practice and good social policy. Moreover, it could save taxpayers money. According to one state health official, part of the reason for the program's popularity was that it focused on a single problem, and the services or benefits to be provided were accepted as a solution to the problem. The benefits could also be easily demonstrated to the client: when a woman of childbearing age who did not want to become pregnant used a contraceptive, she did not usually become pregnant. The use-effectiveness of contraceptives was extremely high, that is, in the range of 90 percent for most birth control devices.

In contrast, the EPSDT program, which experienced the longest delays in implementation, provided the broadest range of benefits. Rather than saving the taxpayers money, child health screening programs resulted in added expenses to the state—especially when diagnosed conditions had to be treated at the state's expense. EPSDT was not targeted for a single disease, for no fewer than seven tests for different disabilities were included among the program's services. Consequently, because of the lack of focus and because it was a program of preventive health, no single disease-focused group mobilized to give political support to the program.

The benefits of the EPSDT program could not be easily demonstrated.

Many of the children who came into the clinics for screening were seemingly well; they had no apparent symptoms. Yet, when the tests turned up a potentially handicapping disability, parents and children were suddenly faced with the realities of a disability and the prospects of unexpected medical expenses. Mothers were not highly motivated to sign up for services, partly because of the nature of the program's benefits. In many cases, the welfare eligibility workers had to convince parents that they should make appointments for the children so that they could be screened. In order for the program to be successful, welfare workers had to engage in aggressive outreach. Yet, the EPSDT program was administered by the Department of Health and not by the Department of Social Services. This was another reason for delays in initial start-up.

Both child health laws were changed as they were implemented. Part of the explanation for this lies in the fact that the program was questioned by donors, providers, administrators, or clients. At the risk of oversimplification, child health program changes were largely carried out to appease disgruntled implementing actors, individuals who were not consulted during the policy design stage of the policy cycle. The EPSDT law was changed when the eligibility requirements were changed. An "eligible" population of clients was narrowed to a much smaller pool of "targeted" clients when the age limit was reduced from 21 to 6. The CHDP law was changed in two ways: age restrictions were imposed, and a "means" test was applied, with free services offered only to those family incomes that were below 200 percent of the poverty level. The net effect of these changes in eligibility requirements was that the state had to "prioritize" various segments of the childhood population with potentially handicapping disabilities.

The California Department of Finance recommended that only enough funds be allocated in the state budget to screen 11,000 of the 2.8 million California children who were eligible under the original law's benefits provisions. This administrative decision forced the Department of Health to concentrate its screening efforts only on five and six year olds in families where incomes were below twice the poverty level.[12]

Former Program Director Ed Melia identified the state's failure to devise regulations as the principal cause of delay and program modification.[13] However, it is clear that even these failures can be traced to the pediatricians' reluctance because of their unhappy experiences with EPSDT, and to the very nature of the CHDP program.

The comparative analysis of the reconstructed implementation processes in these four cases indicates that the hypothesis linking the narrow scope of benefits to implementation politics which results in delay and program change is not very plausible. In fact, these four cases demonstrate quite the opposite. Moreover, what appears to be much more important than the scope of benefits is whether implementing actors perceived services as "health" or "welfare" benefits, and whether the services were seen as saving or costing the state money. Therefore, the hypotheses that should be included in any future research should posit a positive correlation between welfare-type benefits and cost-creating services, on the one hand, and delay and change during implementation on the other.

Program Beneficiaries

The programs with benefits that were comprehensive, questioned by participants in the implementation process, perceived as welfare, and as costing the taxpayers money were the most conflictual in their implementation. In general, programs delivering child health services emerged as the more difficult to implement. To compare the effects of eligibility requirements on implementation, we must examine the matched pairs by analyzing differencs between programs in each of the two categories: child health and family planning.

The most exclusive eligibility requirements were in the EPSDT and Title IV-A laws: the only people who were eligible for benefits were those who lived in families whose incomes fell below the poverty level, namely, those who were eligible for welfare payments. The CHDP program was intended as an inclusive program, with no restrictions on income in the original law. The most inclusive eligibility requirements could be found in the Title X family planning law. Although it required administrators to give preference to low-income clients, it gave them considerable discretion to set eligibility requirements. In practice, all who wanted family planning services under Title X had access to them.

Upon closer examination of each matched pair of programs, a pattern of implementation emerges: the programs that applied a strict means test and that, by definition, were welfare programs, took longer to implement and experienced more changes than counterpart programs that included both the poor and the nonpoor among the beneficiaries. For example, the politics associated with implementation of the Title IV-A program were much more conflictual than the politics that characterized implementation of the Title X law. The implementation was also much more conflictual compared to CHDP. Similarly, the implementation of EPSDT was much more delayed and more changes were made during implementation, when compared to CHDP.

At first glance, these comparisons add to the credibility of Foltz's and Brown's observation that a categorical aid program like EPSDT might succeed if only its eligibility requirements were made more inclusive. If more socioeconomic groups were included among the beneficiaries, they argue, then the program might receive more political support.[14] Policy designers in California followed Foltz's and Brown's advice and made the CHDP program more inclusive than the EPSDT program. According to one of the participants, eligibility requirements were purposely made inclusive in order to "broaden the constituency and, therefore, broaden the support." What is puzzling is that this modification apparently did little to make CHDP's initial implementation politics more consensual. Income of the beneficiary does not in itself seem to be a good predictor of the type of politics one can expect during program implementation. Besides income, did other characteristics of the beneficiaries have a significant impact on the way these policies were implemented?

One possible crucial difference is the socioeconomic class of the clients for child health and for family planning services. Sexually active adolescents are among the beneficiaries of the Title IV-A-funded family planning services program. While young adults who have declared their independence from their parents may not be able to pass a "means" test, many come from families that are in the middle and upper classes. In contrast, the children who are eligible for child health services through the EPSDT program are part of the lowest socioeconomic class.

Another difference may lie in the extent to which potential clients are supported by organized interests. Although it is true that the Children's Lobby, the Children's Defense Fund, and other lobbyists supported the idea of child health screening programs, these organizations are not as politically powerful as Planned Parenthood of America and the Population Council. Because more than 1 million sexually active teenagers become pregnant each year, unwanted pregnancies are seen as a national problem. Therefore, there is popular sympathy for the teenager who seeks free family planning services. The black welfare mother with a child who *might* have a disability gets neither publicity nor sympathy.

Finally, there were attitudinal differences among the clients of these four programs. These psychological differences might account for variations in the implementation mode. Those who seek family planning services are highly motivated to come to a family planning clinic for an initial physical examination and a prescription, and then continue with regular visits as a prerequisite for free birth control devices. These clients actively demand services, and many who come to the clinics are aware of the connection between practicing birth control and satisfying the personal goal of avoiding an unwanted pregnancy. In contrast, few blacks actively seek child health screening services. Either they are uninformed about the availability of services or they have children with no evidence of a disability. Thus, the welfare eligibility worker has to coax many black welfare recipients to bring their children in for screening.

Table 5.4 summarizes the differences in beneficiaries. Differences in income do seem to affect the level of support a program is likely to

Table 5.4
Program Beneficiaries and Implementation Politics

Type of Politics	Eligibility	Support	Attitudes
Consensual			
Title X	Inclusive	High	Motivated
Mixed			
Title IV-A	Exclusive	High	Motivated
CHDP	Inclusive	Low	Uninformed
Conflictual			
EPSDT	Exclusive	Low	Uninformed

receive. For example, programs that are inclusive and that service both the poor and nonpoor seemed to be easier to implement than comparable programs targeted for the poor, especially the black poor. As expected, there was more conflict over redistributive programs like EPSDT and Title IV-A. The evidence from these cases indicates that the beneficiary's socioeconomic class is positively related to the extent to which the client's problems are known and are given sympathy. Support of organized interests also seems stronger for programs that have more inclusive eligibility requirements, and more support usually means fewer delays —but can result in more changes if different supporters have different priorities. Finally, the client's own attitudes and motivation can affect the mode of implementation: highly motivated clients who want and demand services are likely to get them faster than clients who either do not know about the availability of service or who have no way of knowing that they actually need them, or have other, more pressing needs, such as food and shelter.

Program Rewards and Penalties

Public laws and court decisions require particular patterns of consensual behavior at the state and local levels of government in order for federal mandates to be carried out as planned. To assist state and local implementing actors, lawmakers and judges frequently incorporate incentives into their decisions. They take the form of rewards for compliance and penalties for noncompliance. In spite of the fact that positive incentives seem to work better than negative ones, authorities relay heavily on penalties.[15] When incentives do not lead to the desired behavior, consumer advocates may intervene by filing lawsuits against individuals, groups, or agencies in order to force them to comply with the law.

Such was the case with the child health laws in California. Consumer advocates used the courts to force the state to speed up its implementation of EPSDT and to motivate the Health and Welfare Agency to become more aggressive in finding eligible clients for CHDP services. The first legal move against the Department of Health was *California Welfare Rights Organization v. Brian*. The case, and other class action suits like it throughout the country, never went to trial.

Steve Fleischer of the Youth Law Center in San Francisco filed another suit against the Department of Health (*Telles v. California Health and Welfare Agency*). The case languished in the courts for eighteen months until a pre-trial conference was arranged when a new judge was assigned to the case. In attempting to negotiate a consent decree, consumer advocates wanted the Department of Health to agree to screen a set number of eligible children each month. Fleischer wanted monthly quotas, but the program director, according to Fleischer, "just stonewalled it." Without definite commitments to the number of people to be screened, the spokesman for the plaintiff saw any other agreement as only procedural. The judge ruled in favor of Telles and other eligible clients but stopped short of ordering the Department of Health to set and reach monthly quotas.

To the consumer advocates the victory seemed hollow, but from the perspective of the Region IX office of the Department of Health, Education and Welfare (DHEW), the consent decree had a "major impact" on the training of eligibility workers in local field offices of the Department of Social Services. In the eyes of the DHEW regional office, it was undoubtedly used by the state's program manager to get child health screening off the ground in California.

In 1972 the U.S. Congress decided to impose a 1-percent penalty on Aid to families with Dependent Children (AFDC) funds for states that were not in compliance with the EPSDT law. In California, this translated in to an annual bill of $8 million. According to a program consultant at the time, the annual penalty was considered a real threat at the time and was the thing that really got the child health screening program going. The federal EPSDT regulations stipulated that the Department of Health had to reach every eligible child and inform them of the availability of services. Screening services were to be provided within 60 days of the initial interview with the welfare department's intake worker. Two federal compliance officers traveled from county to county, checking records for performance, and offering technical assistance for those counties having trouble meeting the federal criteria. DHEW legal counsel determined that California would be noncompliant if even one record drawn at random from county records indicated that services were not provided within the two-month time limit. The penalty seemed to work at first, but HEW never deducted the funds. Once state health and welfare officials realized that the penalty was neither certain nor severe, the sanctions were not taken as seriously and were therefore ineffective.

Congress also imposed a penalty on states that failed to comply with the Title IV-A family planning provisions. There was one crucial difference in the way the Title IV-A penalty was administered, when compared to EPSDT. In the case of Title IV-A, no state had ever been found to be out of compliance with the family planning law. According to one regional family planning administrator, this made it difficult for regional federal bureaucrats to compel state and local officials to carry out the federal mandate.

On the positive side, incentives were offered to the state for full compliance with the law. The principal reward was federal matching funds: 50 percent, and later 75 percent, federal funding for selected outreach services in the case of EPSDT; and 75 percent, later increased to 90 percent, for family planning services under Title IV-A. Bill Cook of the California Office of Family Planning said in a personal interview that the change to 90 percent federal financing meant that "we had extra money, and we were able to expand the program gradually but steadily. We always had plenty of money for the program. No other state puts that kind of general revenue money into family planning."

Statutory provisions for rewards and penalties were important, but only when implementing agents perceived them as being credible. Obviously, child health officials took seriously the threats of consumer advocates, but only after they had been taken to court for noncompliance. Table 5-5 points out the penalties and rewards for the four programs.

In sum, the class action suit filed by consumer advocates on behalf of welfare children inspired a state program that reached into the middle class and the working poor. Designers of the CHDP program seemed to be reacting to pressure from consumer advocates and hoped that with a more broadly based constituency CHDP would have more success than EPSDT had. Progam administrators apparently used the *Telles* decision to pressure those who were blocking the program's implementation into cooperation.

The 1-percent penalty which Congress imposed on AFDC funds was important to state welfare officials, who were in charge of finding potential beneficiaries and persuading them to be screened. The 1-percent

Table 5.5
Program Incentives and Implementation Politics

Politics	Penalty	Reward	Effectiveness
Consensual			
Title X	None	100% funding	Effective
Mixed			
Title IV-A	1% penalty	75% funding	Effective reward
CHDP	Consent Decree	None	Effective penalty
Conflictual			
EPSDT	1% penalty	50% funding	Ineffective

penalty hung like the sword of Damocles over the head of the child health screening program administrator until he finally realized it was probably only a paper transaction. By the time the penalty lost its credibility, momentum for compliance was already building. On balance, it appears that positive rewards work better than penalties, especially when the penalties lack credibility.

CONCLUSION

A comparative analysis of two child health and two family programs indicates that within the State of California, family planning program implementation was more successful than child health program implementation. This is because child health implementation was more conflictual or political. A reconstruction of the four implementation experiences, especially regarding the time it took to get each program off the ground and the extent and direction of modifications in program content during implementation, also shows that the programs for the poor and black people did not fare as well as the programs that included among their clients both the poor and nonpoor. Evidence from the four case studies, as suggested by Ripley and Franklin, indicates that redistributive programs are harder to implement than either distributive or regulatory ones.[16]

Child health programs failed in their implementation in part because they were preventive health programs which, if successful, would have identified disabilities that would have required additional state funding if they were to be treated at state expense. Family planning laws, however, were implemented more successfully in California for a variety of reasons, the most important of which was that family planning was sold to the state legislature as a cost-savings program. One could reasonably argue that race played a role in this argument: legislators who supported family planning might have done so because they believed that a successfully implemented program would have reduced the birth rate among AFDC blacks.

What is most striking about the California experience is that the two means-tested, or redistributive, programs were marred by inordinate delays and substantial modifications in program content during the course of their implementation. Because blacks were overrepresented among the clients of these redistributive programs, one interpretation is that race helps to explain the extent to which implementation is political: the higher the percentage of blacks and other minorities among the group that is eligible for services, the more likely implementation will be political and, therefore, delayed and modified. Clearly, the characteristics of the people who were to be served by the program affected that program's implementation. Whether it is the clients' poverty, their race, their lack of political resources, their attitudes toward health services and their utilization, or some combination of these factors is debatable and subject to empirical verification. What is clear from this analysis is that the child health and family planning programs that serve them underperformed when compared to similar programs with eligible beneficiaries that included a higher percentage of white and more affluent women, children, and youth.

NOTES

1. See Theodore J. Lowi, "American Business and Public Policy: Case Studies and Theory Development," *World Politics* 16 (July 1964): 677-715; and Theodore J. Lowi, "Four Systems of Policy, Politics, and Choice," *Public Administration Review* 32 (July/August 1972): 298-310. For a commentary on and critique of the "policy determines politics" schema, see George D. Greenberg et al., "Developing Public Policy Theory: Perspectives for Empirical Research," *American Political Science Review* 61 (December 1977): 1532-1543.

2. See Alexander L. George, *Presidential Decision-Making in Foreign Policy: The Effective Use of Information and Advice* (Boulder, Colo.: Westview Press, 1980), pp. 31-39.

3. U.S. Presidents, *Public Papers of the Presidents of the United States* (Washington, D.C.: Office of the *Federal Register*, National Archives and Record Service, 1964-67, Lyndon B. Johnson, 1967), p. 254.

4. California Legislature, Assembly Committee on Health, *Transcript re: Hearings on Child Health and Disability Program*, San Jose, November 3, 1975, p. 26.

5. Ibid.

6. California Legislature, Assembly Committee on Health, "Analysis of AB 2068 (Brown)," Sacramento, June 11, 1973 (Mimeo).

7. One of the main goals of the California Department of Social Services during these years was to hold down welfare spending. One of the principal objectives of the Department of Health, however, was to improve the health status of Californians. The contradictory agency objectives created implementation problems.

8. John K. Iglehart, "Health Report: HEW's Child Health Failures," *National Journal Report* 6 (June 29, 1974): 969-974.

9. State of California, Department of Health, Office of Family Planning, "The Cost Benefit of Family Planning in California," Sacramento, n.d. (Typewritten).

10. Interview with R. Auder.

11. Andrew Billingsly, "Black Educator Attacks Planned Parenthood," *San Francisco Chronicle*, October 27, 1971, 2:1; and Gerald Fraser, "Blacks Condemn Mixed Adoptions," *New York Times*, April 10, 1972, 1:21.

12. California Legislature, Senate Committee on Health and Welfare, *Transcript of Proceedings: Hearings on Child Health and Disability Prevention Program*, Sacramento, February 11, 1976, p. 62.

13. California Legislature, Assembly Committee on Health, *Hearings*, November 3, 1975, p. 26.

14. Ann Marie Foltz and Donna Brown, "State Response to Federal Policy: Children, EPSDT, and Medicaid Muddle," *Medical Care* 13 (August 1975): 641.

15. John Brigham and Don W. Brown, eds., *Policy Implementation* (Beverly Hills, Calif.: Sage, 1981).

16. Randall B. Ripley and Grace A. Franklin, *Bureaucracy and Policy Implementation* (Homewood, Ill.: Dorsey, 1982), ch. 7.

6. Public Policy Compliance/ Enforcement and Black American Health: Title VI of the Civil Rights Act of 1964

Mitchell F. Rice[1] and Woodrow Jones, Jr.

It is well documented that black Americans as a group have been and continue to be recipients of what has been called "second-class medicine" in the United States. Differential health status between blacks and whites is reflected in nearly every set of federal government health care indexes. These indexes indicate that blacks are less healthy and receive less health care than white Americans and most other ethnic groups. Recent government figures show that:

1. Whites outlive blacks by an average of nearly six years—75.1 years to 69.3 years.
2. The black infant mortality rate is nearly *twice* as high as that for the white race—21.4 deaths per 1,000 births to 11.0 deaths per 1,000 births.
3. The black maternal mortality rate is over *three* times higher than the white rate—26.0 per 100,000 live births to 7.7 per 100,000 live births.
4. The total health care expenditures in 1982 comprised about 10.5 percent of the Gross National Product or about $322.4 billion, an average of $1,365 per capita.

Given the conditions of the American health care system, why do health status disparities between blacks and whites continue to remain so large, especially when a number of general and specific public policies exist that should directly or indirectly improve the overall health status of the general population? For example, Title VI of the Civil Rights Act of 1964 has a direct relationship to the provision and delivery of health care services. The Office of Civil Rights (OCR) in the U.S. Department of Health and Human Services (DHHS) (formerly the Department of Health, Education and Welfare) is charged with enforcing the statutory obligations of Title VI. This chapter examines the role and compliance/enforcement activities of OCR with the Title VI provision as it relates to health service delivery. Compliance/enforcement activities including legal activity are key elements in the implementation of public policy. These activities at the policy implementation stage determine the intended or unintended consequences of public policy.

TITLE VI AND THE DEPARTMENT OF HEALTH AND HUMAN RESOURCES

After the historical decisions in *Brown v. Board of Education*, several litigation efforts ensued challenging segregated health facilities in the South.[2] These efforts, however, did not deal with the broader issue of access of minorities to health care. The passage of the Civil Rights Act of 1964 provided legal impetus for desegregation efforts in health care. Section 601 of Title VI reads as follows: "No persons in the United States shall on the grounds of race, color, or national origin, be excluded from participation, or be denied benefits of, or be subjected to racial discrimination under any program or activity receiving Federal financial assistance."[3]

In short, Title VI prohibits discrimination on the basis of race, color, or national origin in federally assisted programs and activities. Title VI primarily prohibits exclusion from services and different treatment programs, including segregation and denials of comparably effective services. DHHS provides federal financial assistance to a large number of health and human services recipients who, in turn, provide a wide variety of services. For example, DHHS provides funds to more than 6,800 hospitals, 13,700 outpatient and primary care facilities, various state and local public health agencies, 8,000 day care centers, and 37,000 local service agencies and programs such as halfway houses and private social service agencies which contract with government agencies to provide services. In total, there are more than 43,000 DHHS recipients serving more than 93 million beneficiaries.

Primary recipients, such as a state's welfare agency, receive financial assistance indirectly (subrecipients). One example is a local welfare agency which receives a portion of the funds originally granted to a primary recipient. Still other welfare agencies may receive federal funds based on a contractual arrangement with other primary or sub-recipient organizations which serve as vendors for specific services. Whether a primary, subrecipient, or recipient vendor, every organization receiving federal funds is obligated to make its services and programs available in a nondiscriminatory manner. Congress clearly intended for the Title VI provision to apply to health facilities.[4] The provision also required federal agencies to implement the policy by issuing regulations that called for termination of federal funds for noncompliance.

The Office of Civil Rights (OCR) is charged with the enforcement function of Title VI. DHEW issued the first set of interpretative regulations and enforcement programs with effects standards in 1965.[5] Although no funds were appropriated for Title VI enforcement, DHEW did proceed with some enforcement activities.[6] However, at the time DHEW was also occupied with aggressive litigation in the educational arena and, as a result, could not principally focus its enforcement activities on Title VI.

With the enactment of Medicare and Medicaid programs, Titles XVII and XIX, respectively, of the Social Security Act of 1965, DHEW increased its enforcement activities under Title VI. Hospitals became covered under the Title VI nondiscrimination language. DHEW visited and obtained Title VI assurances of nondiscrimination from over 3,000 hospitals and a few nursing homes.[7] Yet, many of these same hospitals and nursing homes were later found to have segregated practices that were in violation of Title VI. In fact, many health care institutions attempted to circumvent the Title VI mandate and maintain segregated facilities by rearranging wards and multiple-bed facilities into private rooms.[8] Because of these problems, DHEW (OCR) issued specific Title VI regulations and guidelines that were applicable to hospitals and nursing homes.[9] The Institute of Medicine has noted that these hospital and nursing home regulations and guidelines remain the only available official interpretation of Title VI in a health care context. The Institute has further noted that despite congressional intent and the interpretative regulations issued by DHEW in 1965 and again in 1973,[10] the DHEW regulations did not apply to general health care delivery.[11]

OCR ENFORCEMENT, COMPLIANCE, AND TITLE VI IN HEALTH CARE

It was not until the late 1970s that OCR began to show increasing concern for civil rights issues in health. After DHEW was reorganized in 1978 as the Department of Education (DOE) and DHHS, OCR began to become more active in civil rights activities in health. As previously noted, OCR had concentrated most of its efforts in education.[12] OCR has now expanded its enforcement activities in health to include other recipients of DHHS funds, including day care centers, state medical agencies, nursing homes, family health centers and clinics, health planning agencies, mental health centers, nutrition programs and the like.

The primary mission of OCR is "to eliminate unlawful discrimination and to ensure equal opportunities for the beneficiaries and potential beneficiaries of Federal financial assistance by DHHS."[13] OCR enforces several statutory provisions including Title VI.[14] In the area of health service delivery under Title VI, OCR is responsible for ensuring that beneficiaries are not treated differently, denied access or admission to services or facilities, and are not required to meet different standards or conditions for services. In short, OCR is authorized to establish whether beneficiaries are granted equal opportunity to health care and treatment. OCR cannot deal with issues regarding the quality of care and professional medical decisions. Moreover, Title VI protection extends to employees in cases where discrimination against the employee adversely affects the delivery of services and programs to beneficiaries.

OCR is managed by a director who reports to the Secretary of DHHS. The director also serves as the Secretary's Special Assistant for Civil Rights and is responsible for the overall management of DHHS civil rights activities. OCR has regional offices for implementing a comprehensive compliance and enforcement program consistent with statutory and regulatory requirements. OCR consists of an overall staff of 300 (a decrease from over 700 in the late 1970s). The statutes and regulations under OCR's authority mandate that the Office engage in certain types of compliance activities, including complaint investigations, compliance reviews, pre-grant reviews, and monitoring activities.

Under Title VI a complainant must make an oral or written allegation to OCR within 180 days of the last act of alleged discrimination "unless the time limitation is waived for good cause by the designated OCR official." Oral allegations must be reduced to writing. The filing day limitation is not applicable to complainants who allege continuing violations or to Hill-Burton community service complainants. OCR regional offices have 195 calendar days from the date of receipt of a complete complaint to make a compliance determination or, when necessary, to forward to OCR Headquarters on enforcement recommendation. OCR's ability to comply with policy requirements, as with most agencies charged with enforcement and compliance, is dictated by the complexity of the complaint issues, current case load, available staff resources, and staff expertise and training.

For recipients who are found to be in noncompliance, OCR seeks voluntary compliance.[15] If voluntary compliance is not obtained, OCR has two courses of enforcement action: it can initiate administrative proceedings to suspend, terminate, refuse to grant or continue federal financial assistance to the recipient, or it can initiate judicial proceedings against the recipient by referring the case to the U.S. Department of Justice. The director of OCR determines which option to pursue.[16] The decision to terminate funds, however, must be approved by the Secretary of DHHS and other high-ranking officials. Hill-Burton enforcement per regulatory mandate goes directly to the U.S. Department of Justice.

Beginning with an administrative agency, like OCR, may be more economical for complainants—who are usually modest to low-income individuals. OCR conducts its own investigation and develops and compiles the data and studies necessary to the investigation.[17] However, once a recipient receives an official letter of findings from OCR which shows the recipient to be in noncompliance, he or she must be accorded full due process. This means that the recipient must be given full opportunity to refute or disprove OCR's findings. From 1980 through fiscal year 1983, OCR received 5,851 complaints; 964 were filed under Title VI and 92 were filed under the Hill-Burton regulations.[18] More than 2,400 were alleged violations of Section 504 of the Rehabilitation Act of 1973. However, whereas OCR has been more active and has initiated several investigations, most have been initiated by private lawsuits.[19]

CASE OUTLINES OF OCR INVESTIGATIONS

The following two hypothetical case outlines are representative of the kinds of cases OCR investigates relative to discrimination in health service delivery. Note that both cases relate to employment discrimination that affects the delivery of services to beneficiaries (patients). The first case illustrates facts and evidence of a complete OCR investigation of employment discrimination in a hospital facility. The second case illustrates an OCR investigation after an employment discrimination decision by the U.S. Equal Employment Opportunity Commission.

Case 1: Maxwell v. County General Hospital

Background. Complainant is a black male employed by the recipient hospital as the assistant comptroller. Complainant filed on behalf of all black employees, alleging employment violation contrary to Title VI of the Civil Rights Act of 1964. Complainant specifically alleges that employment discrimination against black hospital employees has existed at the facility since 1974, at which time the facility was merged with another predominantly white facility to accommodate integration necessary to receive federal financial assistance. Complainant states that prior to 1974 the two were segregated hospitals. At the time of the merger, the recipient assured all employees that positions would be awarded based on experience, prior performance, and the facility's needs. Complainant alleges that the recipient has not adhered to its stated policies of equal treatment of all employees or equal employment opportunities. The complainant alleges that black employees are paid lower wages for the same or comparable positions, and that blacks are terminated from positions for alleged rule infractions while whites are disciplined less severely for similar or more serious rule infractions. He also alleges that blacks are denied access to the recipient's grievance procedures, while less qualified whites are promoted to positions for which more highly qualified blacks have applied and been denied. He also alleges that whites are appointed to supervisory positions, while blacks with more education, training, and supervisory experience are denied such opportunities. The complainant concludes that the recipient maintains a pattern and practice of race discrimination against black employees.

Statement of OCR's jurisdiction and investigative authority. The allegations cited in this complaint are covered by Title VI of the Civil Rights Act of 1964 and its implementing regulation found at 45 CFR 80.3 (c) (3). Regulation 45 CFR 80.3 (c) (3) prohibits discrimination against employees where such discrimination would adversely affect the delivery of service to beneficiaries. The Title VI provision is applicable to employment discrimination and sanctions OCR's investigation of employment discrimination allegations where such allegation identifies a pattern and practice of discrimination against employees or where the allegation leads OCR to conclude that beneficiaries would be discriminated against if the facts and evidence supported the allegations. The allegations cited in this complaint meet both criteria referenced above.

A search of OCR records regarding federal financial assistance to this recipient established that the hospital receives both Medicare and Medicaid program funds. Medicare and Medicaid funds constitute federal financial assistance as defined by Title VI of the act. Based on the specifics of the complaint allegations and the hospital's receipt of federal financial assistance, it is established that OCR has authority and jurisdiction to investigate the allegations cited in this complaint.

Statement of issues. The issues as seen from OCR regulations would be as follows:

1. *45 CFR 80.3 (a) (iv)*—Whether this recipient subjects its black employees to treatment different than that afforded its white employees.
2. *45 CFR 80.3 (c) (3)*—Whether, as a result of discriminatory treatment afforded black employees, beneficiaries (patients) using the recipient's facility are denied services and treatment different from or of lesser quality than that required.

Investigative approach/differential treatment of employees. The allegations in this complaint indicate that black employees are treated differently and are subjected to discriminatory treatment because of their race. The allegations also indicate that because of the discriminatory treatment afforded black employees, patients who enjoy the recipient's services are adversely affected. Title VI requires that OCR focus its primary attention on the effect of the alleged discriminatory treatment against employees or beneficiaries. In order to establish whether beneficiaries are being adversely affected, OCR must first establish whether the alleged discriminatory treatment against employees is established by the facts. If the facts support the allegation, OCR must then determine which employees are subjects of discrimination.

If the facts establish that black employees holding beneficiary services and care, for example, administrators and supervisors, are being discriminated against, OCR must establish whether the discrimination against these employees detracts from the delivery of services to patients and how such detractions occur. If OCR establishes that such detractions occur, OCR must find that the recipient has violated Title VI and that corrective actions are required to ensure compliance with the regulatory requirements.

If OCR determines that black employees are not being discriminated against, OCR must make a finding of no violation and close the case. Likewise, if OCR determines that black employees are being discriminated against but that the discrimination has no adverse effect on beneficiary services and treatment, OCR must also make a finding of no violation of Title VI. OCR, however, must transfer its discrimination findings to the Equal Employment Opportunity Commission for appropriate action under Title VII of the Civil Rights Act of 1964.

Investigative data. In order to establish the facts relative to the allegations, OCR requires the following data and information.

1. Number of recipient employees by race, positon held, and tenure of each employee in his or her respective position.
2. Copies of recipient's personnel policies, including policies applicable to hiring, promotion, discipline, termination, affirmative action program, salaries and wage determinations for each position, and grievances.
3. Copies of recipient's procedures for hiring, promotion, disciplines, terminations, salary and wage determinations for all positions, and employee grievances.
4. Descriptions of each position within the facility, including required duties and responsibilities, and the credentials necessary for each position.
5. Policies and procedures for evaluating employees in the various positions.
6. Copy of hospital organizational structure and administrative procedures and policies.
7. Records of all hirings, promotions, terminations, demotions, and disciplinary actions against all employees for the past three years, by the race of each

employee affected. Terminations should be categorized according to whether they were voluntary or involuntary and the reasons for each. If possible, records should be organized according to categories of employees, by employees, by employee type, for example, nurses or doctors.

8. Records of the salary/wage history of all employees by race and positions held for a period covering the last three years.

9. Access to employee personnel files. Specific files to be reviewed include randomly selected files of both black and white employees, as well as those files of employees specifically identified during the investigation (based on interviews) as persons who have been afforded different treatment because of their race. (This latter group will include the files of black and white employees.)

10. Information detailing the emergency room, outpatient and inpatient census for the facility for the past three years. The information should detail the race of the patient population by patient status and service, average length of stay per service, and mortality rate by service.

11. The assignment of hospital staff by position and according to the race of the employee. (Employees who rotate on a regular basis should be grouped separately from employees with regularly assigned duty stations.)

12. Other data as required, subsequent to interviews of hospital administrative staff and patient care staff and support staff.

Interviews. The following persons will be interviewed during the course of the investigation:

1. Recipient Chief Executive Officer
2. Affirmative Action Officer
3. Administrator for each hospital operating unit
4. Supervisors for various service units within the hospital, especially those units identified in the complaint document
5. Recipient Personnel Staff
6. Employee Union Representatives
7. The Complainant
8. Injured Parties listed in the complaint document

Special need. Prior to the initiation of the on-site aspect of this investigation, OCR will consult with hospital administrative specialists with background and experience in facilities with characteristics similar to those of the facility under investigation. This consultation will establish a base of understanding of standard procedures that should be in effect relative to providing patient care and service.

On-site activities. While on-site, OCR will seek to determine indicators of possible different treatment of employees that affect patient care. Some of the indicators include:

1. Whether patients are segregated within the facility.
2. Whether hospital staff are assigned to patient units according to the race of the patients and employees.
3. Whether, as a result of the treatment afforded employees, patients are required to wait longer for services or not afforded services as needed.
4. Whether, as a result of the treatment afforded black employees, costs to the patients for services are more than the average for similar services at other facilities.
5. Whether, as a result of the treatment afforded black employees, patients are not afforded continuity in services and treatment.

Case 2: Weeks v. University of State Hospital Background

Complainant is a black male formerly employed by the recipient as the Assistant Director of Administration. Complainant alleges that he was terminated from his position because of his race. He also alleges that, prior to being terminated, he was denied a salary comparable to those afforded his white counterparts who held positions comparable to his. Complainant alleges that the recipient engages in a systematic pattern and practice of employment discrimination against black hospital administrators, and that the actions of the recipient result in discrimination against beneficiaries. Complainant filed an individual discrimination complaint seeking personal redress through the U.S. Equal Employment Opportunity Commission (EEOC). The EEOC investigation concluded that the complainant had been discriminated against because of his race when he was denied a salary comparable to those of his counterparts. The EEOC made no ruling on whether he was terminated because of his race because the allegation was untimely filed.

The EEOC investigation revealed that subsequent to the complainant's request for comparable salary, he was asked to submit the resignation. Furthermore, in an effort to justify the request, the recipient informed the complainant that the resignation request was the result of a planned reorganization. He was also informed that as a result of the reorganization, his duties would be modified substantially. However, the resignation would not be effective until nine months after the reorganization, and, during the interim, the complainant was expected to continue his regular duties and responsibilities.

The EEOC investigation also revealed that subsequent to the complainant's involuntary resignation, none of the duties formerly assumed by the complainant were transferred to any other staff person. A review of EEOC's evidence revealed that the complainant's position included duties and responsibilities that involved more than 75 percent direct patient or patient-related services.

Statement of OCR's jurisdiction and investigative authority. The alle-

gations cited in this complaint are covered by Title VI of the Civil Rights
Act of 1964 and its implementing regulations found at 45 CFR 80.3 (c) (3).
Regulation 45 CFR 80.3 (c) (3) prohibits discrimination against employees where such discrimination would adversely affect the delivery of
services to beneficiaries. The Title VI provision sanctions OCR investigations of employment discrimination allegations, where such allegations identify a pattern and practice of discrimination against employees
or where the allegation leads OCR to conclude that beneficiaries would
be adversely affected if the facts and evidence supported the allegation.
One allegation in this complaint meets a criterion listed in the Title VI
provision, that is, a pattern and practice of employment discrimination.
The evidence secured by EEOC is acceptable as an indication of potential or actual adverse effects against beneficiaries.

A search of OCR records reveals that the recipient receives Medicare
and Medicaid funds, as well as other federal financial assistance for
purposes of maintaining and operating a medical training program.
Based on the specifics of the complaint allegations and the receipt of
federal financial assistance, OCR has the authority and jurisdiction to
investigate the allegations cited in this complaint.

Statement of issues. The issues as seen from OCR regulations would be
as follows:

1. *45 CFR 80.3 (a) (iv)*—Whether this recipient subjects black hospital administrators to treatment different from that afforded its white administrators.
2. *45 CF 80.3 (C) (3)*—Whether, as a result of discriminatory treatment afforded
   black hospital administrators, beneficiaries are denied services or treatment
   or are otherwise adversely affected.

Investigative approach. This complaint alleges that a segment of the
recipient's black employee population is treated in a discriminatory
manner because of their race. The allegations also indicate that, because
of this discrimination, beneficiaries are adversely affected. Title VI
requires OCR to focus primarily on the allegation of adverse effect
against beneficiaries. In order to establish whether beneficiaries are
being adversely affected, OCR must first establish whether employees
are being discriminated against. In this case, the findings established by
EEOC eliminate the need for OCR to establish employment discrimination. OCR, therefore, must seek to determine whether the established
discrimination had an adverse effect on beneficiaries. If the facts show
that beneficiaries have been discriminated against, OCR must find a violation of Title VI and seek corrective action. If the facts do not show that
the beneficiaries were discriminated against, OCR must make a compliance finding and close the case.

Investigative data. These include the following:

1. A complete copy of EEOC's investigative file.
2. Number of recipient's administrative positions, duties and responsibilities associated with those positions, and employees holding those positions by race.
3. Education, training, experience of the administrators, and their tenure in their positions.
4. Description of the complainant's former position, including a listing of all duties and responsibilities.
5. Copy of the recipient's personnel policies, procedures, and statement of how the policies and procedures are implemented, together with any evidence to support the statement.
6. Recipient's recruitment procedures for administrative positions, including its affirmative action plan, statement, and policy.
7. Detailed description of the distribution of all of the complainant's former duties since his involuntary resignation and recipient's reorganization.
8. Position and titles of all persons responsible for the complainant's former duties, as well as descriptions and official records of their training, education, and experience.

Interviews. OCR will interview the following persons:

1. The complainant
2. The recipient's Chief Administrative Officer
3. All persons currently responsible for complainant's former duties
4. All current administrators
5. All former administrators, if located
6. Recipient's Affirmative Action Officer
7. EEOC investigative staff
8. Recipient's personnel staff and recruiters

On-site activities. Based on in-depth interviews with the complainant and others regarding services provided patients prior and subsequent to complainant's involuntary resignation, OCR will seek to establish differences in quality and level of services afforded patients.

THE COURTS, TITLE VI, AND HEALTH CARE

A significant private lawsuit alleging violation of Title VI was the case of *Cook v. Ochsner*. In 1970 a group of black residents in New Orleans brought suit against ten private hospitals alleging a variety of discriminatory practices. A series of legal actions ensued.[20] In 1971 DHEW was also named as a party defendant. The plaintiffs and DHEW worked out a consent agreement in which DHEW agreed to conduct a review of eigh-

teen New Orleans area hospitals to ensure compliance with Title VI provisions.[21] During compliance review investigations, two of the hospitals
refused to provide data to DHEW and challenged DHEW's jurisdiction
under Title VI. After hearing motions for summary judgments by the
hospitals against the plaintiffs and by the United States for DHEW
against the hospitals, the district court granted DHEW's motion. In
1978 DHEW failed to obtain voluntary compliance with Title VI from
three of the original defendant hospitals. These hospitals also challenged
DHEW's jurisdiction. Repeating the action it took against the previous
hospital, the district court denied their motions.[22]

One important legal issue raised by the *Cook* litigation is, what
constitutes proof of racial discrimination in health care service delivery.
The focal point of this issue is whether *proof of discriminatory effect or
impact or proof of discriminatory purpose or intent is sufficient to establish a cause of racial discrimination in health care service delivery.*[23] In
general, discriminatory disproportionate impact occurs whenever official
procedures relating to selection or entitlement to benefits produce a less
favorable result for a protected group.[24] There must be an adverse
(negative) impact. Statistical or other empirical evidence is necessary to
show discriminatory, disproportionate, and adverse impact.

Purposeful or intentional discrimination means that a decision would
not have been made except for its differential impact on a racial
minority. The decision is made without regard to the interests of minorities.[25] A decision of this type may be referred to as a "race-dependent"
decision—"a decision that would have been different but for the race of
those benefited or disadvantaged by them."[26] Race-dependent decisions
can take three forms: racially motivated administration, racially motivated regulations, and racially selective indifference. The first involves
the discriminatory administration of a law or ordinance; the second
regulation adopted for a race-dependent motive and discriminatory
impact; and the third unconscious racial actions that lead to discriminatory impacts on minorities.[27]

Although in the language of the Title VI legislation Congress did not
specify prohibition in terms of discriminatory effect or discriminatory
purpose,[28] the Title VI regulations promulgated by DHEW require only
a *prima facie* case of discriminatory effect. The regulations provide that
"a recipient . . . may not . . . utilize criteria or methods of administraton
which have the effect of subjecting individuals to discrimination . . . or
have the effect of defeating or substantially impairing accomplishment
of the objectives of the program as respect individuals of a particular
race, color or national origin."[29] In *Cook* the three hospitals in question
provided regular inpatient services to patients of private physicians who
had been granted practicing privileges at the hospitals. Most of these
physicians had few black patients. Black patients and the poor were

directed to the charity hospital system in New Orleans. At that time New Orleans' population was 45 percent black, and prior to the late 1960s two of the hospitals had no black patients. The other hospital had, at best, served only a token number. Thus, the plaintiffs and DHEW alleged that the method of administration at these hospitals had the effect of denying them access to federally funded service benefits in violation of Title VI.[30]

Despite the impact standard specified in DHEW's Title VI regulations, the Supreme Court has interpreted Title VI as embracing both impact and intent. The Supreme Court found a Title VI violation based solely on disparate impact in *Lau v. Nichols*.[31] The plaintiffs in *Lau*, while acknowledging that all students in the San Francisco public schools received the same instruction, alleged that Chinese students were receiving "unequal educational opportunities" because of their lack of fluency in English. The Court agreed that this disparate effect was in itself enough to constitute a Title VI violation. The Court even stated the following:

Discrimination is barred which has the *effect* even though no purposeful design is present: a recipient may not . . . utilize criteria or methods of administration which have the effect of subjecting individuals to discrimination or have the effect of defeating or substantially impairing accomplishment of the objectives of the program as respect individuals of a particular race, color, or national origin.[32]

The case was remanded to the lower court in order to fashion appropriate relief. The Court in *Lau* also noted that Title VI was intended to put the power of the federal purse behind efforts to eliminate discrimination.[33] This was explicitly recognized by the Supreme Court in *Fullilove v. Klutznick*:[34] "Congress has frequently employed the Spending Power to further broad policy objectives by conditioning the receipt of federal monies upon compliance by the recipient with federal statutory and administrative directives."[35] After the *Lau* decision, Congress enacted virtually identical language in several additional statutes,[36] thus indicating congressional agreement with the disparate impact interpretation by administrative regulation and the *Lau* decision. If Congress had not intended for Title VI and its offspring to require disparate impact discrimination, these later policies would have been written differently.

In *Board of Regents v. Bakke*, a majority of the justices implied that the standard for determining a violation of Title VI was identical to the standard for determining a constitutional violation.[37] This position was interpreted to mean that purposeful or intentional discrimination was required for a Title VI violation.[38] The intent standard as a *prima facie* constitutional violation was articulated by the Court in *Washington v. Davis*[39] and reaffirmed and broadened in *Arlington Heights v. Metro-*

politan Housing Corp.[40] In these cases, the Court found that a law or official act was not unconstitutional solely because of disparate impact. An intent to discriminate on the basis of race must be present in order to find a constitutional violation.[41] By late 1979, however, the Court had not directly resolved the issue of whether impact or intent was necessary in order to establish a Title VI violation. In its decision in *Board of Education v. Harris*,[42] three dissenting justices argued that Title VI prohibits only intentional discrimination.[43] The majority opinion did not consider Title VI relevant to its decision and required proof of disparate impact.[44]

Because the Supreme Court has not established a clear and consistent decisional pattern with regard to what constitutes a Title VI violation, the lower courts have struggled in their applications of the Supreme Court's opinions. The lower courts' applications of discriminatory effect or discriminatory intent standards to Title VI in the area of health care service delivery are illustrative of this point.

In *Bryan v. Koch*, a class of local minority residents sought to prevent the closing of Sydenham Hospital located in their neighborhood because they claimed that the closing would violate Title VI.[45] New York City, in an attempt to reduce expenditures and increase the efficiency of its municipal service, decided to close the hospital for a number of economic reasons.[46] The plaintiffs contended that the decision to close the hospital was discriminatory in that the hospital's patients were 98 percent minorities as compared to 66 percent minorities served by the New York City hospital system as a whole. The plaintiffs further contended that New York City had other alternatives to closing the hospital which would have had a less disproportionate impact. The district court ruled in favor of the city:

The Government's approach proves that simplicity is not always a virtue. . . . Any recipient of federal funds, from any Title VI agency, could be required to justify reducing any service, even if overall service increased, where the service is utilized by a minority population proportionately greater than the minority population served by the system as a whole. . . . The standard would apply to any minority group, and since many ethnic groups tend to live in close geographic proximity, many decisions to modify virtually any form of service or facility would be affected. In fact, since we are speaking of Title VI, it is far from clear that the standard could be applied only to minorities; the Act prohibits discrimination against any race. . . . The fact is that almost any decision to close any federally funded facility or to reduce any federally supported service will adversely affect one group disproportionately more than some other group.[47]

The district court also made a distinction between the concepts of "adverse effect" and "racially disparate impact." The court inferred that adverse impact may exist whenever an inner-city hospital closes.

Disparate impact, however, that is probative of discriminatory motives requires more than proof of adverse effects.[48] Additional evidence of adverse effects was not substantiated by the court for two reasons. First, the city made *one* decision to close the hospital, not a series of independent decisions that could possibly establish racial discrimination. Second, since the city had taken steps to ensure alternative service that was equivalent to the service that was terminated, this more than eliminated any real adverse effects.[49] Thus, from the standpoint of intent, the district court found no violation of Title VI. The Second Circuit Court of Appeals affirmed the district court's decision, reasoning that under neither the purpose nor effect standard, particularly effect, was the closing unlawful because no actual adverse effect was shown.[50] The Second Circuit further noted that out of the four hospitals New York City sought to close, Sydenham Hospital was the best candidate for closure.

In *NAACP v. Wilmington Medical Center*, both intentional discrimination and disparate effect were alleged.[51] The Wilmington Medical Center, in Wilmington, Delaware, was faced with serious problems, including loss of accreditation, and had to reorganize (relocate and consolidate) its facilities. This reorganization plan would have decreased the Center's accessibility to various minority groups.[52] Blacks and other minority groups filed suit, alleging intentional discrimination which, if implemented, would have disparate, adverse effects on minorities, the handicapped, and the elderly. The plaintiffs maintained that the reorganization plan would violate Title VI. The hospital claimed that discriminatory intent or purpose was necessary to state a cause of action under Title VI.

The district court found no violation of Title VI and ruled in favor of the hospital. Specifically, the district court found that the plaintiffs could not prevail under either the intent or disparate impact standard. Furthermore, the district court expressly defined the effects standard as requiring that the plaintiffs prove discriminatory effect and initially carry the burden of proof. This action then shifted the burden of proof to the defendant.[53] The Third Circuit Court of Appeals affirmed, holding that proof of disparate impact is sufficient to establish a *prima facie* violation of Title VI and that ultimate burden of persuasion was on the plaintiffs, who had failed to meet their burden of proof.[54]

In conclusion, the *Medical Center* ruling should assist the courts in establishing a standard for disparate impact in racial discrimination cases arising under Title VI. Yet, the effects standard may not prevail because the Supreme Court has adopted an effects test in Title VII racial discrimination cases.[55] It has also enunciated the disparate treatment theory of discrimination in several cases.[56] Disparate treatment, unlike disparate impact, requires a finding of discriminatory purpose. Moreover, if the Supreme Court maintains its recent decisional patterns established in constitutional claims (Equal Protection Claims) challenging racial discrimination actions, a showing of discriminatory impact in statutory claims will not suffice.

CONCLUSION

This chapter has discussed the compliance/enforcement investigative activities of the Office of Civil Rights in the U.S. Department of Health and Human Services and legal issues as they relate to the health of black Americans. Compliance/enforcement activities in health associated with Title VI of the Civil Rights Act of 1964 are important variables in policy implementation and determine the success or failure of policy. This chapter describes what compliance/enforcement investigative steps OCR utilizes in its attempts to secure compliance with Title VI in health service delivery.

OCR's compliance/enforcement efforts have been at best modestly successful in both preventing and eliminating discrimination in health service delivery to beneficiaries (patients) of recipients receiving federal financial assistance. In the final analysis, compliance/enforcement in the policy implementative process must be viewed as part of the political environment that can influence the consequences of public policy. Future research in public policy, particularly public policy related to the nondiscriminatory provision and delivery of health care services, must be subjected to continued analysis and scrutiny if the health of black Americans is to improve.

NOTES

1. Research support provided by a 1984-85 National Research Council Rockefeller Foundation Postdoctoral Fellowship.

2. See *Brown v. Board of Education*, 347 U.S. 483 (1954) and 349 U.S. 294 (1955). Litigation following *Brown v. Board of Education* included *Rackley v. Board of Trustees of Orangebury Regional Hospitals*, 310 F. 2d 141 (4th Cir. 1962): *Coleman v. Aycock*, 304 F. Sup. 132 (N.D. Miss. 1969); and *Marable v. Alabama Mental Health Board*, 297 F. Sup. (N.D. Ala. 1969).

3. Public Law 88-352.

4. See *Hearings on Miscellaneous Proposals Regarding the Civil Rights of Persons Within the Jurisdiction of the United States Before Subcomm. No. 5 of the House Comm. on the Judiciary, Parts I, II, III, IV* (88th Cong., 1st Sess., 1963): 1830-46, 2485, 2776-2777.

5. See 30 *Federal Register* (1965): 35.

6. On this point, see H. R. Doc. No. 318, 88th Cong., 2nd Sess., 1964.

7. For a discussion of these enforcement efforts, see Kenneth Wing and Marilyn Rose, "Health Facilities and the Enforcement of Civil Rights," in Ruth

Roemer and George McKray, eds., *Legal Aspects of Health Policy: Issues and Trends* (Westport, Conn.: Greenwood Press, 1980); and Dorothy K. Newman et al., *Protest, Politics and Prosperity* (New York: Pantheon, 1978), p. 199.

8. See U.S. Commission on Civil Rights, *Title VI: One Year After* (Washington, D.C.: GPO, 1966).

9. See U.S. Department of Health, Education and Welfare, Office of Civil Rights, *Guidelines for Compliance of Hospitals with Title VI of the Civil Rights Act of 1964* (Washington, D.C.: GPO, revised, November 1964).

10. See 38 *Federal Register* (1973), 1979.

11. See Institute of Medicine, *Health Care in a Context of Civil Rights* (Washington, D.C.: National Academy Press, 1982), pp. 42-43.

12. According to Wing, prior to the division of DHEW into DOE and DHHS, OCR had investigated very few health care providers, and the Institute of Medicine has pointed out that "prior to 1980, as little as 10 percent of OCR's staff were committed to health . . . issues." See Kenneth Wing, "Title VI and Health Facilities: Forms Without Substance," *Hastings Law Journal* 30 (September 1978): 137-190; and Institute of Medicine, *Health Care in a Context of Civil Rights*, p. 143.

13. Presentation made by members of the Office of Civil Rights Staff at the Black Congress on Health, Law and Economics, New Orleans, Louisiana, July 29, 1984. Much of the following information is based on this presentation.

14. The other statutory provisions are: Title IX of the Education Amendment of 1973; Section 504 of the Rehabilitation Act of 1973; Age Discrimination Act of 1975 and Titles VII and VIII of the Public Health Service Act; Titles VI and XVI of the Public Health Service Act (Hill-Burton); and the Nondiscrimination Provisions of the Omnibus Budget Reconciliation Act of 1981 (the Block Grant Program).

15. There are more than 43,000 DHHS recipients who serve more than 93 million beneficiaries.

16. See note 12.

17. One observer notes that it might be advantageous to proceed directly to court because this approach gives the complaining parties the right to develop the evidence and does not influence the . . . judge with the views of an administrative agency which is supposed to be expert in the area but may be as much influenced by political forces as by legal theories." See Marilyn G. Rose, "Challenging the Relocation and Closure of Inner-city Hospitals—Analysis, Methodologies and Limitations," *Clearinghouse Review* 16 (June 1982), p. 105.

18. The majority of the complaints (2,420) were filed under Section 504 of the Rehabilitation Act of 1973. The remainder were filed under the other statutes OCR enforces.

19. On this point, see Institute of Medicine, *Health Care in a Context of Civil Rights*.

20. See Civ. No. 70-1969 (E.D. La. 1970); 319 F. Supp. 603-1970; and 559 F. 2d 968 (5th Cir. 1977).

21. The suits also alleged violations of Hill-Burton uncompensated care and community service obligations. The Hill-Burton causes were severed for separate trials, which resulted in a consent agreement with the hospitals in 1972. Contempt actions were later brought against six of the hospitals in 1974. See

Marilyn G. Rose, "Access for Minorities into Mainstream Hospital Care," *Clearinghouse Review* 13 (June 1979): 83-86.

22. For a more detailed account of these suits, see above.

23. The terms "discriminatory effect" and "discriminatory impact" dare used interchangeably in this chapter. These terms, along with "disproportionate impact," "disparate effect," and "adverse impact or effect," are taken to mean the same thing. Discriminatory purpose and intent are also used interchangeably.

24. See Michael J. Perry, "The Disproportionate Impact Theory of Racial Discrimination," *University of Pennsylvania Law Review* 125 (January 1979): 541-589.

25. Unlike purposeful or intentional discrimination, discriminatory impact may result from an action that could plausibly serve two distinct functions, one with a veiled function. Thus, discriminatory impact may be more difficult to determine. For example, a written exam for public employment may serve the function of racial selection, but it also serves the function of selecting a more skilled work force. See Perry, "Disproportionate Impact Theory," p. 554.

26. Paul Brest, "In Defense of the Antidiscrimination Principle," *Harvard Law Review* 90 (November 1976): 6.

27. Ibid., pp. 12-14.

28. On this pont, see Robert Belton, "Burdens of Pleading and Proof in Discrimination Cases: Toward a Theory of Procedural Justice," *Vanderbilt Law Review* 34 (October 1981): 12-5-1287. Furthermore, Congress did not include an exact definition of "discrimination" or a statement of its scope in the legislation.

29. 45 C.F.R. Section 80.3 (b) (2).

30. See Rose, "Access for Minorities into Mainstream Hospital Care," p. 30.

31. 414 U.S. 563 (1974).

32. Ibid. p. 569.

33. Ibid.

34. *Supreme Court* 100 (1980): 2758.

35. Ibid.

36. See, for example, the Revenue Sharing Act, 31 U.S.C. Section 242 (1976) and the Public Works Employment Act, 42 U.S.C. Section 6707 (1976).

37. 438 U.S. 265 (1978).

38. Ibid., pp. 297, 325.

39. *Washington v. Davis*, 426 U.S. 229 (1976). The case involved the District of Columbia's police department qualifying test known as "Test 21," which was developed by former Civil Service Commission members for general use through the federal service. The failure rate of black candidates was over four times higher than the failure rate of whites. Black plaintiffs charged that the test had a highly discriminatory impact in screening out black applicants.

40. *Arlington Heights v. Metropolitan Housing Corp.*, 429 U.S. 252 (1977).

41. For further discussion of these two cases as they relate to intent/effect controversy, see Mitchell F. Rice, "The Discriminatory Purpose Standard in Racial Discrimination Litigation: "From *Yick Wo* to *Arlington Heights*," *Southern University Law Review* (forthcoming), and "The Discriminatory Purpose Standard in Racial Discrimination Litigation: A Problem for Minorities," *Boston College Third World Law Journal* (forthcoming).

42. *Board of Education v. Harris*, 444 U.S. 130 (1979).

43. The impact or effects standard has been clearly articulated by the Supreme Court under Title VII. See, for example, *Griggs v. Duke Power Co.*, 401 U.S. 424 (1971), and *Teamsters v. U.S.*, 431 U.S. 324 (1977).

44. For a concise discussion of these cases as they relate to the effect/intent controversy, see David F. Chavkin, "Health Access and the Civil Rights Laws: The Smoking Gun and Other Sorrows," *Clearinghouse Review* 15 (November 1981): 561-566.

45. *Bryan v. Koch*, 492 Supp. 212 (S.D. N.Y. 1980).

46. Ibid., pp. 614-618.

47. Ibid., p. 235.

48. Ibid., p. 236.

49. Ibid., pp. 237-238.

50. *Bryan v. Koch*, 627 F. 2d 612 (2d Cir. 1980).

51. *NAACP v. Wilmington Medical Center*, 491 F. Supp. 290 (D. Del. 1980).

52. The plan included closing two hospitals in downtown Wilmington and building a new hospital in a suburban area because of increased population in the area. These closings and relocation would shift nearly 800 beds from the inner city to the suburban area. Ibid., pp. 302-308.

53. Ibid., pp. 313-315.

54. *NAACP v. Wilmington Medical Center*, 657 F. 2d 1322 (3rd Cir. 1981).

55. See, for example, *Griggs v. Duke Power Co.*, 401 U.S. 424 (1971).

56. See, for example, *McDonnell Douglas v. Green*, 411 U.S. 792 (1973), and *Furnco Construction Corp. v. Waters*, 438 U.S. 567 (1978).

7. Closing the Gap Between Black and White Infant Mortality Rates: An Analysis of Policy Options

Dorothy C. Howze

Recent evidence indicates that there has been a perceptible slowing in the decline of the U.S. infant mortality rate (IMR).[1] According to the U.S. Department of Health and Human Services, in 1983 and 1984 the drop in the infant mortality rate was well below what it had been in previous years,[2] falling by 2.7 and 2.8 percent, respectively. These declines were significantly below the average of 4.9 percent over the previous seven years. As noted by Dr. Edward Brandt, the former Assistant Secretary for Health, such slowing in the overall infant mortality rate "has not been observed since the plateau in infant mortality between 1955 and 1965."[3]

The IMR, an indicator of the health and welfare of a population, is expressed as the number of deaths to live births under one year of age per 1,000 live births. In 1982 the U.S. infant mortality rate was 11.5 deaths per 1,000 live births—a rate higher than that for fifteen other nations of the world.[4] In fact, year to year, the United States ranks between fifteenth and eighteenth in infant mortality, usually following such countries as Spain, Ireland, Japan, Canada, Australia, Hong Kong, and Singapore.[5]

Of major concern is the death gap between black and white infants. In 1982 the IMR for black infants was 19.6 per 1,000 live births, as compared to 10.1 for white infants.[6] What this means is that black infants born in the United States die at a rate almost twice that of white infants. There are reports, however, that infant mortality for black infants in some cities is more than two times that of whites.[7] A survey conducted in 45 cities in 1982 by Public Advocates of San Francisco showed the black infant mortality rate in some 32 cities was almost three times greater than that for white infants. In addition, it has been reported that the gap between black and white infant mortality rates, which narrowed somewhat in the mid-1970s, is widening.[8]

This concern about the differential in black-white infant mortality is generated by reports linking the economic cycles with federal cutbacks as contributing to this widening gap.[9] The black-white gap in infant mortality is a very important issue, for what is at stake is an erosion of major improvements in the overall infant mortality rates, which have been attributed to an increase in the availability and access to maternal and child health program elements.[10]

Concern about the black-white differential is also generated by evidence suggesting that the objective of reducing infant mortality by 1990, which was proposed in the 1980 Surgeon General's *Report*, will not be achieved if current trends persist.[11] In 1980 the Surgeon General set the following objectives for reducing the infant mortality by 1990:

1. To reduce the national infant mortality rate to no more than 9 deaths per 1,000 live births.
2. To ensure that no county and no social or ethnic group of the population has an infant mortality in excess of 12 deaths per 1,000 live births.
3. To reduce the neonatal death to no more than 6.5 deaths per 1,000 live births.[12]

It is estimated that at the current rate of progress, the United States will not achieve these objectives. Specifically, it is noted that 32 percent of the states will not meet the objective for reducing mortality rates among all children and 55 percent of the states will not meet their goals for nonwhite babies.[13]

The appropriate policy response to the problem of the disparity in black-white infant mortality rates is the subject of numerous debates occurring at the federal, state, and local levels. Out of these debates have emerged numerous policy proposals to address the problem of infant mortality in general and the black and white differential in particular. However, there is little consensus regarding which of these policy options should be pursued to resolve this problem. This chapter attempts to address the question of an appropriate policy response through a policy analysis approach, a technique designed to help make informed choices among policy alternatives. Policy analysis is employed because in this time of retrenchment politics, budgetary cutbacks, and overall concern with government spending, it seems wise to acknowledge that programs that reduce infant mortality will have to compete for funding both against other health and social programs and against nonsocial programs such as defense, energy, and transportation. Because the number of dollars available for new programs is finite and becoming smaller, those committed to eliminating the disparity between black and white infant mortality rates, and thus improving overall infant mortality, must be ready to set policy priorities and defend them.

This chapter uses the policy analysis approach proposed by Haskins and Gallagher.[14] In brief, this approach presents several criteria—equity, efficiency, preference satisfaction, right to privacy, avoidance of stigma, unintended consequences, and political feasibility—to assess policy alternatives. These general criteria are used to rate various alternatives proposed as means to eliminate the gap between black and white mortality rates.

LOW BIRTH WEIGHT AND INFANT MORTALITY

Any attempt to explain recent trends in infant mortality must focus on the relationship between low birth weight and infant mortality. Recent examinations of infant mortality have redefined the problem as that of low-birth-weight infants. According to recent reports, low birth weight is one of the major challenges to future decreases in infant mortality.[15] In addition, there is empirical evidence indicating that if a reduction in the black infant mortality rate is to occur, improvements are needed in the distribution of black low-birth-weight infants.[16]

Any infant born alive weighing 2,500 grams (5.5 pounds) or less is classified as an infant of low birth weight. There are two types of low-birth-weight infants: the truly pre-term infant, the infant born before 40 weeks; and the small-for-gestational-age infant (SGA), the infant born too small, a full-term baby. Low-birth-weight infants account for approximately two-thirds of all neonatal infant mortality deaths (deaths of infants under 28 days per 100 live births) and constitute 50 percent of all deaths in the first year of life.[17] If low-birth-weight babies survive, there is an increased likelihood that they will experience further hospitalizations and suffer developmental and physical complications. Numerous studies have associated low birth weight with increased occurrence of mental retardation, learning disabilities, birth defects, blindness, autism, cerebral palsy, epilepsy, visual and hearing disabilities, delayed speech, and chronic respiratory problems.[18] Unfortunately, blacks are twice as likely as whites to have low-birth-weight infants (under 2,500 grams) and two and one-half times more likely than whites to have very low-birth-weight infants (under 1,500). As shown in Table 7.1, the ratio

Table 7.1
Percentage of Live Births Less than 2,500 Grams and 1,500 Grams

	Percent Less than 2,500 Grams	Percent Less than 1,500 grams
White	5.7[a]	0.9[a]
Black	12.5[a]	2.4[a]
Chinese	4.9[a]	0.6[a]
Mexican-American	5.3[b]	0.9[b]
American Indian	6.9[c]	---

[a] National Center for Health Statistics: "Characteristics of Asian Births: United States, 1980." Prepared by S. Taffel. Monthly Vital Statistics Report, Vol. 32, No. 10 (supplement). Public Health Service. Washington, D.C.: U.S. Government Printing Office, February 1984.

[b] National Center for Health Statistics: "Births of Hispanic Parentage, 1979." Prepared by S. J. Ventura. Monthly Vital Statistics Report, Vol. 31, No. 2 (supplement). Public Health Service. Washington, D.C.: U.S. Government Printing Office.

[c] National Center for Health Statistics: "Factors Associated with Low Birthweight, 1976." Prepared by S. Taffel. Vital and Health Statistics, Series 21, No. 37. DHEW No. (PHS) 80-1915. Public Health Service. Washington, D.C.: U.S. Government Printing Office, April 1980.

of low birth weight for blacks to other nonblack groups is approximately 2.5 to 1. Furthermore, it has been noted that the low-birth-weight rates for whites have remained relatively consistent, but the gap between blacks and whites is widening.[19]

The low-birth-weight rate is often blamed for the poor international ranking of the United States in infant mortality. As previously noted, the United States ranks fifteenth to eighteenth in infant mortality ranking for industrialized countries. A comparison of selected countries shows that the United States rates third behind Hungary and Israel in the number of low-birth-weight infants and second in very low-birth-weight infants (see Table 7.2). Other data show that the low birth-weight rate for American blacks was approximately 1.5 percent higher than Hungary's, by far the highest rate on this table. However, white births showed somewhat better results, with the United States ranking fifth in low birth weight.[20]

The reasons why blacks are at increased risk of having low-birth-weight babies is the subject of much debate. In the past several years, numerous studies have been conducted to determine factors contributing to the black-white differences in infant mortality. Among the factors

Table 7.2
Percentage of Very Low Birth Weight (1,500 grams or less)
and Low Birth Weight (2,500 grams or less) Live Births in
Selected Developed Countries, 1980

Country	VLBW[1]	LBW
Austria	0.80	5.68
Canada[2]	0.84	6.10
Denmark	0.72	6.00
German FR	0.71	5.51
Hungary	1.71	11.79
Israel	0.99	7.16
Japan	0.39	5.18
New Zealand	0.65	5.27
Sweden[3]	0.49	4.03
U.S.	1.15	6.84

Source: United Nations, Demographic Year Book 1981.

[1] May represent underestimates if infants weighing less than 500 grams are excluded.

[2] Data for 1979.

[3] Data for 1978.

or reasons cited are that black mothers are more likely to have: (1) late initiation of prenatal care due to limited access or underutilization of medical services; (2) inadequate nutrition; (3) a higher proportion of teenage pregnancies and out-of-wedlock births, (4) low socioeconomic status, and (5) low educational level. The only conclusion that can be made from much of the research is that reasons for the relatively high low-birth-weight rate among black women are not fully understood and that there is a need for additional research to disentangle the relationship between low birth weight on the one hand and race and other factors on the other.

The failure to explain the black-white differential fully has led to attempts by some health scientists to attribute the differential in low birth weight, as well as that in infant mortality, solely to biological and genetic differences between ethnic and racial groups. However, these attributions are countered by evidence showing that countries inhabited by large numbers of racial and ethnic minorities (largely immigrants from other countries seeking employment) have rates of low birth weight and infant mortality approximating those reported for the indigenous population.[21] This view is further challenged by the history of poverty and social and medical neglect of blacks. The effects of years of adverse conditions are cumulative and, interacting with biological and genetic factors, play an important role in the observed black-white differential.

Despite the unanswered questions regarding the black-white differences in low birth weight, there is ample evidence suggesting that the black-white gap in low birth weight can be reduced. Especially in the area of prenatal care, we find evidence that supports effective intervention in reducing low birth weight among high-risk groups of women such as the poor and minorities.[22] In fact, the impact of prenatal care on pregnancy outcomes appears to be most substantial for black women and for black and white women who are poor.[23]

There is also consensus among some professionals that the federal government should have a role in ensuring access to prenatal care for these groups.[24] Cited most often in discussions of federal government responsibility is the elimination of financial barriers to accessing prenatal care. Although it is acknowledged that other barriers to care exist, it is also recognized that the federal government, by virtue of its enormous revenue-producing power, must assume ultimate responsibility for eliminating this chief barrier to prenatal care.

The following discussion details a selected number of policy proposals focusing on the financing of prenatal care. The review is limited to proposals addressing the issue of financing, inasmuch as the "high cost" of prenatal care has been cited repeatedly as a crucial barrier to accessing care for low-income women of all ages and ethnic groups. For example, Chao et al. found that among a group of poor urban women who obtained no prenatal care by the time of delivery, half mentioned their reason was lack of financial resources.[25] Similar findings were reported in a study of low-income women in the rural Southwest.[26] Of the 400 women interviewed, 87 percent stated they had not obtained prenatal care because they could not afford it.

ANALYSIS OF POLICY ALTERNATIVES

Five policy proposals to reduce the black-white gap in low-birth-weight rates by providing prenatal care are presented and analyzed below. They are:

1. Do nothing.
2. Expand Medicaid coverage.
3. Target selected groups for special services.
4. Provide access to comprehensive prenatal care for all pregnant women.
5. Provide adequate income maintenance support.

The criteria used to analyze these proposals are equity, efficiency, preference satisfaction, right to privacy, avoidance of stigma, and unintended consequences. Two types of equity are considered in this analysis, vertical and horizontal. Vertical equity is unequal treatment of unequals in an effort to make them more equal. Vertical equity suggests that a good policy proposal is one that favors the "have nots" over the "haves" in the distribution of benefits.[27] Horizontal equity seeks to treat equals as equals. Thus, for example, a policy proposal that targets services to all pregnant women residing in the United States satisfies the criterion of horizontal equity. Efficiency is defined as the use of resources to produce the maximum benefit for the smallest expenditure. Preference satisfaction requires that a policy produce the most happiness for the greatest number of people, usually by creating options and allowing individuals to maximize their own preferences. The right to privacy stipulates that a policy does not permit intrusion into the life of the individual. Avoidance of stigma means that individuals will not be labeled as different in a negative way from other citizens not affected by the policy. Unintended consequences are the unanticipated negative side-effects of a policy. Political feasibility means the possibility that the particular policy alternative has a chance of being adopted and implemented.

Evaluation of the alternative policy options is summarized below:

Do Nothing

The do-nothing alternative is listed simply to indicate a baseline against which other policies may be judged. The rations in Table 7.3 show that, on the basis of the criteria selected, the do-nothing policy is clearly unacceptable. This policy would require a continuation in the reductions in funding for programs designed to improve access to health services to pregnant poor and low-income women. The reduction in programs—such as Medicaid, Maternal and Child Block Grants, Women, Infant and Children Food Supplement Programs, and Community and Migrant Health Programs—would intensify the disparity between black and white infants in low birth weight. These federal programs were created by a web of legislation in the 1960s and 1970s to meet the health needs of underserved pregnant, high-risk women.

These programs experienced massive budget reductions, however. As shown in Table 7.4, there has been a significant erosion in the funds for these programs that affect the lives of pregnant women and their children.[28] This means that approximately 750,000 people—many of them women—have lost services that impact on positive pregnancy outcomes.[29] Acceptance of a policy proposal to do nothing would mean an exacerbation of the low-birth-weight problem. Therefore, this option does not merit further consideration, if the reduction of low birth weight is our goal.

Expand Medicaid Coverage

This policy proposal expands the *largest source* of public funding for maternal and child health. The real significance of this alternative is that it has the capacity to reduce low birth weight by reducing financial barriers to care in general and by increasing the proportion of low-income women receiving prenatal care in particular. In addition, its sheer size and ability to support and enhance other maternal and child health programs gives it a central role in policy discussions regarding the reduction of low birth weight.

Medicaid is a grant-in-aid program that creates an entitlement to a set of health services for people who satisfy its eligibility criteria. Although states have discretion in establishing eligibility criteria, there are requirements that all states must meet before qualifying for federal matching funds. At minimum, states must provide Medicaid to Dependent Children (AFDC) and Social Security's Supplemental Income (SSI) beneficiaries. The states are required to match federal contributions for Medicaid-covered services for eligible individuals.

The most available estimate of Medicaid costs is $35.5 billion.[30] This breaks down to $19.3 billion for the federal government and $16.2 billion for states. It is estimated that 2.5 million women of childbearing age live in poverty but receive no Medicaid[31] (see Table 7.5). Unfortunately, blacks are disportionately represented in this group of nonrecipients.

Table 7.3
Decision Matrix for Reducing the Black-White Differential in Infant Mortality Rates

Policy Alternatives

Analysis Criteria	(a) Do Nothing	(b) Expand Medical Coverage	(c) Target Selected Groups for Special Services	(d) Making Prenatal Care Accessible to All Pregnant Women	(e) Provide Income Maintenance Support
A. General					
Horizontal Equity	−	−	−	+	+
Vertical Equity	−	−	+	+	+
Stigma	−	−	−	+	−
Preference Satisfaction	−	−	±	+	+
Unintended Consequences	−	±	−	±	−
Efficiency	−	+	+	+	−
Privacy	−	−	−	+	−
B. Other					
Political Feasibility	−	+	±	−	−

Note: + = satisfies criterion
− = fails to satisfy criterion
± = equivocal or no effect

Table 7.4
Changes in Federal Outlay Between 1982 and 1985*

	$ billions	Percent
Unemployment Insurance	−7.8	− 7
AFDC	−4.8	−13
Food Stamps	−7.0	−13
Medicaid	−3.9	− 5
WIC	+0.2	+ 0.4
Other Health Family Planning Migrant Health Primary Care Maternal and Child Health	−1.4	−22

* Resulting from Legislative Changes between
  1981 and 1983.

Source: Center for Health and Manpower
         Policy Studies, Univ. of Texas
         Health Science Center, Houston

States have tremendous discretion in fashioning Medicaid programs to conform to political and budgetary constraints. Until recently, some states did not provide Medicaid coverage in the early months of pregnancy, when services such as prenatal care are essential. Although enormous gains have been made in ensuring that poor women have access to health services, there is evidence that black women still are twice as likely not to receive prenatal care.[32]

Proposals to expand Medicaid coverage have recently surfaced in congressional debates. The Proposed Child Health Assurance Programs (CHAP) resulted from a fourteen-year effort to pass federal laws to expand coverage to groups of pregnant women and children. Specifically, under CHAP, states will be required to give Medicaid to large numbers of poor women from the date of medical verification of pregnancy. Women affected by this change are: (1) those who are pregnant and the child's father is absent, incapacitated, or dead; and (2) those who are pregnant and living with the child's father who qualifies for Aid to Dependent Children of Unemployment Parents (AFDC-UP). It is esti-

Table 7.5
Medicaid Coverage of Women and Children in Poverty 1980*
(in millions)

	Total No. in poverty	Medicaid No.	%	Non-Medicaid No.	%
Women (age 18-44)	5.1	2.6	51.0	2.5	49.0
Children (age 0-17)	9.4	5.2	55.3	4.2	44.7

* Level of Poverty designated by the U.S. Census Bureau

Source: Infant Mortality Rates: Failure to Close the Black/White Gap. (Materials submitted for the record by Carolyn Davis for hearings before the Subcommittee, health and the Environment of the Committee on Commerce, House of Representatives, 98th Congress, 2nd Sess., March 16, 1984, p. 323.

mated that 200,000 pregnant women will potentially benefit from the expanded eligibility for Medicaid under CHAP.[33] But this is only a fraction of those estimated to be living in poverty.

Since CHAP legislation became effective in 1984, not all states have implemented these changes in Medicaid coverage. In a number of states, legislation is required before the Medicaid Programs can be amended. Even with the passage of CHAP, not all poor pregnant women are covered. For example, those poor pregnant women residing in families that do not meet AFDC or AFDC-UP requirements either because they do not meet technical or unemployment criteria are still not covered. In order to address the gaps in the CHAP legislation, Representatives Henry Waxman (D-Calif.) and Henry Hyde (R-Ill.) proposed AR 1382 which would make it mandatory for states to provide Medicaid coverage for pregnant women living in two-parent families who meet income eligibility requirements regardless of employment status.[34]

Both CHAP and House Bill 1382 would increase but not fully satisfy horizontal and vertical equity. This proposal violates the criteria of stigma, privacy, and preference satisfaction. The criterion of privacy is violated because in order for women to receive services under the program, they must present evidence of incomes that are well within the limits established by states. There is also a violation of the criterion of preference satisfaction with Medicaid in that it does not cover services rendered by nontraditional health care providers unless the providers collaborate with physicians. Preference satisfaction and stigma are also violated because clients who want to receive care from office-based physicians find they are limited by the number who accept Medicaid reimbursement.

The efficiency of Medicaid has been documented, but not in a systematic manner. While it is an accepted maxim that expanding coverage to more poor pregnant women will require additional public expenditures, the exact amount of those expenditures vary from state to state and are not very precise.

Blackwell et al. have provided cautious estimates of increased expenditures. For example, she and her associates estimate that the additional cost of providing prenatal care to *all* Medicaid eligible women is only $62.5 million.[35] If other populations of needy women who are currently ineligible were included, the total costs would be about $187.1 million. Furthermore, it is estimated that the federal government spends approximately $59 million annually to rehospitalize low-birth-weight babies. The cost to the federal government of providing care to these babies is about $638 million.[36] Thus, the increased cost of expanding the eligibility requirements for women is offset by a $509.9 million savings from the initial cost of caring for low-birth-weight babies plus rehospitalization costs.

Similar savings have been estimated at the state level. For example, Florida recently calculated that it could save $27 million in expansions of benefits for women and children.[37] Similarly, Mississippi recently enacted a medically needy program (which covers only pregnant women and children) that will cost the state $4 million in contrast to $10 million the state would spend to cover bad debts of hospitals that provided services to the disadvantaged and uninsured women.[38] North Carolina estimated that extending coverage to low-income children and low-income pregnant women in two-parent families would cost $6.6 million, but that these costs would be offset by a 20 percent savings in Crippled Children's and perinatal care programs.[39]

The assumption that Medicaid contributes to a significant reduction in infant mortality through a reduction in low birth weight has not been demonstrated by empirically sound studies and evaluations. In fact, a study by Gorman and Grossman suggests that Medicaid has minimal impact on the neonatal mortality rate for blacks.[40] This study of the effects of maternal and child health program elements found that the factor which explains most of the reduction in the neonatality rate for blacks was abortion, followed by availability of neonatal intensive care centers and the rise in female schooling. The Medicaid contribution rated fourth for blacks and third for whites. These results should be viewed with caution because of the incomplete implementation of some of the elements of maternal and child programs by state governments.[41] Nevertheless, some studies suggest that participation in Medicaid is associated with improved pregnancy outcomes, especially infant mortality, rather than improved birth-weight distribution. Two recent examinations of women who had received Medicaid reported greater incidence of improved pregnancy outcomes among these women than among their counterparts with no medical coverage.[42]

In sum, despite conflicting evidence of its effectiveness, expanding the eligibility requirements of Medicaid is an incremental approach that seems to have wide acceptance among states. There was state government support for recent CHAP legislation because that eases their burden of providing indigent care to non-Medicaid clients. In addition, important advocacy groups, such as the Children's Defense Fund, have backed proposals to extend coverage to noneligible groups.

Target Selected Groups for Special Services

This policy option directs resources to groups that have been identified to be at highest risk of low birth weight. Two policy proposals that epitomize this policy option are the Infant Mortality Action Plan and Senate Bill (S.505). The Infant Mortality Action Plan, which recently passed the Michigan State Legislature, allocated $1.1 million to the "10 worst counties based on a three year average of infant mortality rates."[43] Senate Bill (S.505), which was introduced by Senator David Durenberger (R-Minn.), allows states to provide a package of prenatal services to selected recipient populations through a waiver of Medicaid requirements.[44]

A policy proposal that would target black communities for a special package of prenatal services would satisfy vertical equity but reduce horizontal equity. Horizontal equity is reduced because targeting services to black women would tend to exclude other women who do not reside in black communities. This policy also violates the criterion of lack of stigma. Singling out black women for prenatal services might lead to labeling the beneficiaries as different in a negative sense. This policy could also have an unintended negative consequence such as racial polarization. That is, providing special services to black women could arouse opposition from other groups who might perceive their needs to be just as great. Preference satisfaction may or may not be violated, depending on whether beneficiaries who refuse the special services would have access to services from other sources. Finally, the policy of targeting services to black women seems to be efficient since the evidence indicates that black women are at higher risk of having low-birth-weight babies than white women.

It is difficult to assess the political feasibility of this policy proposal. For example, a bill such as S.505 might successfully pass Congress because it is consistent with the pervasive philosophy of transferring responsibilities to states.[45] But whether a state decides to target black women for special services depends on the availability of funds in general and for poor minorities in particular. Indeed, states with a more liberal philosophy (and greater wealth) might be more willing to target services. The policy choice for most states will be to use Medicaid resources for one subpopulation at high risk rather than for other sub-populations or for the overall indigent population or for some other public good. The choice will be a function of political constraints, advocacy on behalf of a selected group (or groups), and the state's financial resources.

Provide Access to Comprehensive Prenatal Care for All Pregnant Women

This policy option would make prenatal care accessible to all women by using the private and public insurance mechanisms. The proposal is to make the federal government responsible for the poor families and mandate that employees with tax-deductible insurance plans be covered for prenatal services for the employee or spouse. Making prenatal care available to all without financial constraints is an approach followed by countries such as Canada and Sweden. This policy option, which is favored by many U.S. child health advocates, is designed to address the gaps observed between and within Medicaid and private insurance systems. That is, Medicaid fails to cover all of the poor and the uninsured. As noted above, approximately 49 percent of poor women between 18 and 44 years of age are not covered. In addition, some women have insurance but still lack coverage for prenatal care either because the insurance plan does not cover prenatal services or because the deductible is at a level difficult to meet, thus creating out-of-pocket expenses for the employee. Nationally, one-half of all private insurance plans do not cover prenatal care.[46]

The problem of the underinsured or uninsured is especially acute for individuals employed in marginal and part-time jobs. According to a study of insurance coverage, approximately 25 million Americans are without public or private health insurance.[47] However, as many as 34 million may be uninsured for some part of the year. Among women of childbearing age, 1 in 7 is uninsured.[48] This problem of uninsured and underinsured is especially relevant to low birth weight because minorities are disportionately represented in these groups. In fact, data for the National Center for Health Services Health Interview Survey from 1978 and 1980 show that 18 percent of blacks had no health insurance coverage compared with 9 percent of whites.[49]

The above policy proposal meets the criteria of horizontal and vertical equity because prenatal care will be accessible financially to all pregnant women residing in all states. The lack of stigma criterion is satisfied by the elimination of the financial barrier to prenatal care and the resulting indistinguishability between "nonpaying" and "paying" patients during care. In addition, stigma will not exist if reimbursement policies for Medicaid are comparable to those for private insurance plans. If reimbursement policies are the same, and if the provider is unaware of the source of payment, the incentive to distinguish between "public" and "private" patients is eliminated.

This policy has some unintended consequences which may undermine the accomplishment of the policy goal. First, mandating that employers provide insurance plans including comprehensive prenatal care would increase employers' costs. Employers would most likely pass on these costs to consumers or employees in the form of higher charges for goods or services, or increasing premium charges to employees. In addition, coverage for other services might be eliminated. It is also conceivable that employers might respond by reducing the number of marginal and part-time employees. The employment of these individuals would no longer be a "savings," for employers would have to provide insurance plans with prenatal coverage. Another unintended consequence is the differential burden that would be placed on working poor families, unless deductibles are not permitted. With increased coverage, there will be an increase in premiums or deductibles. These increases would impact differently on poor working families than on nonpoor working families.

In contrast with the unintended effects of this policy, there are some positive consequences. The proposed policy could increase health sector employment and distribution of personnel by spurring an aggregated demand for prenatal services. Although such a demand cannot be estimated here, considering studies of medical care in countries such as Canada following the introduction of universal health insurance, one can guess that there will be an increase in the "consumption" of prenatal care—especially among the poor and near poor. That prenatal care is associated with low birth weight has been demonstrated by a few studies and evaluation.[50] It has also been shown that prenatal care is cost-effective. According to a study conducted by the Harvard School of Public Health, for every dollar spent on prenatal care, three dollars were saved in hospitalization costs.[51] However, in terms of political feasibility, it is doubtful that this policy proposal will gain acceptance among policymakers.

Although this proposal is relatively conservative since it does not change much of the current structure of financing, it is likely to generate considerable opposition from formidable interest groups, such as the insurance industry, Chamber of Commerce, and Business Trade Associations. In the past, these groups have effectively derailed similar efforts. For example, these groups were instrumental in preventing the passage of the Child Health Incentive Reform Plan (CHIRP), a bill mandating the insurance coverage of preventive health services for children.[52] However, this policy is likely to have a great deal of support from the American Hospital Association and state and local governments. These groups will most likely support this proposal because the cost of care for the uninsured poor is assumed by these entities and hospitals. State and local governments support care to the uninsured primarily through grants and appropriations to public hospitals. In 1982 state and local governmental units spent $9.5 billion for hospital care through appropriations and other non-Medicaid programs.[53] Furthermore, private hospitals paid approximately $3.2 billion for indigent care through funds designated as charity care and uncollectible files. Unfortunately, 40 percent of all hospital care for uninsured patients involves obstetrical care which costs approximately $5.08 billion a year.[54]

Provide Adequate Income Maintenance Support

This policy focuses on all women and their families. It assumes that the problem of infant mortality is poverty. Gortmaker examined extensively the relationship between poverty and infant mortality in the United States.[55] Using national data, he estimated the relative impact of biological, social, and economic factors on the risk of infant deaths. The estimates indicated that poverty is associated with relative risks of neonatal and post-neonatal mortality. In fact, the relative risk was 1.5 times greater for infants born in poverty than for infants not born in poverty. That poverty is associated with low birth weight is of special concern because black families are disproportionately poor. Black poor women tend to have low-birth-weight infants, and they are more likely not to receive prenatal care. The United States currently has an income support program in the form of AFDC. However, some critics note that the program provides meager benefits and fails to provide for basic needs. As evidence of the program's failure, they cite the fact that the maximum AFDC benefit for a family of three in January 1985 was less than 75 percent of the poverty level.[56]

By providing adequate income maintenance support, the focus is on providing financial access to services that would improve not only pregnancy outcomes but also the family's overall quality of life. That is, there is evidence that families which lack adequate income support not only have limited access to appropriate health services but experience other difficulties as well, such as stress, drug and alcohol abuse, and family violence.[57]

The possibility of a positive policy impact from income supplement on low birth weight has not been examined extensively. Kehrer and Wolen's study showed that the incidence of low birth weight in a low-income black population provided with adequate income maintenance support was lowered over the period of the study.[58] The authors noted that it was difficult to attribute these improved pregnancy outcomes to specific factors, such as patterns of utilization of health services. Instead, they suggested that increased income enables families to improve their nutritional intake, allows them to take the time (without losing essential wages) to obtain medical services, and enhances their overall quality of life.

The low utilization of health services in the Kehrer-Wolen study is not surprising. It seems unrealistic to expect that an income support program would provide income at a level to enable an individual to "purchase" prenatal care out-of-pocket. This seems highly unlikely when it is estimated that maternity expenses average $3,000. Therefore, mounting an expensive program that would not result in an increase in prenatal care for high-risk women is inefficient. This policy proposal also fails to meet the criterion of lack of stigma since individuals would have to show that their incomes are below an established standard to receive benefits.

This policy has several unintended consequences. First, income support might be a deterrent for entering the labor force. Second, there might be an increase in divorces. That is, with income support, spouses would be more likely to dissolve unstable marriages. Third, there would be an increase in single heads-of-household, which could mean an increase in out-of-wedlock births with an attendant increase in low birth weight.

CONCLUSION

The appropriate policy response to the problem of disparity in black-white infant mortality rates is the subject of numerous debates. These options have been more fully developed through the policy analysis approach of this chapter. By using the decision-making criteria developed by Gallagher and others, we have more clearly delineated the options available to policymakers. More importantly, the chapter presents a rationale for policy decision-making given retrenchment politics, budgetary cutbacks, and the overall concern for deficit spending.

Given the goals of the 1980 Surgeon General's Report, it is doubtful that any policy option will be successful in an era of retrenchment politics. If 55 percent of the states cannot meet their mortality goals by

1990, then the future, under a more conservative government, is bleak indeed. Without long-term federal intervention, it is impossible to implement policies that will reduce mortality rates in all states. In addition, federal intervention can provide a standard by which prenatal care can be measured. Quality standards, controlled patient visitation, and cost control are all important aspects of effective federal intervention.

The most plausible alternative, given Gallagher's decision-making criteria, is to make prenatal care accessible to all pregnant women. This option would require federal government responsibility for the poor and private insurance for others through their employment. The unintended consequences of this policy are quite similar to those of any redistributive policy. However, the positive consequences of increased consumption of prenatal care far outweigh the negative consequences. Unfortunately, the political feasibility of adopting such a policy in the present political climate is formidable.

NOTES

1. National Center for Health Statistics (NCHS), *Advance Report of Final Mortality Statistics, United States, 1982*, U.S. Department of Health and Human Services, Vol. 33, no. 9, supplement, December 20, 1984.

2. *The Nation's Health* 15, no. 4 (1985): 1.

3. Letter from Assistant Secretary of Health Edward Brandt to State Health Officers, December 1984.

4. See NCHS, *Advance Report of Final Mortality Statistics, p. 55*.

5. A. Blackwell, L. Salisbury, and A. Arriola, *Administrative Petition to Reduce the Incidence of Low Birthweight and Resultant Infant Mortality (An Administrative Petition to the United States Department of Health and Human Services* (Washington, D.C.: unpublished document (1983), pp. 21-22.

6. P. Buescher, *The Impact of Low Birthweight on North Carolina Neonatal Mortality*, SCHS Studies (Raleigh: North Carolina State Center for Health Statistics, December 30, 1983).

7. A. Sanders, "The Widening Gap: The Incidence of Infant Mortality and Low Birth Weight in the United States 1978-82" (Washington, D.C.: Food Research and Action Center, 1984): and Blackwell et al., *Administrative Petition*, p. 26.

8. Ibid.; see also M. Wegman, "Annual Summary of Vital Statistics—1983," *Pediatrics* 74 (December 1984): 981-990.

9. See J. Taylor, "Infant Mortality: An Analysis and Recommendation for Action," Testimony presented to the House Commerce Sub-committee on Oversight and Investigators and Healthy and the Environment Hearing, March 16, 1984 (Washington, D.C.: GPO, 1985), pp. 32-87; and M. Poland, *Unemployment, Stress and Infant Mortality in Detroit* (Chapel Hill: University of North Carolina, 1984).

10. See J. Klieman, "The Recent Decline in Infant Mortality," *Health, United States*, DDHS publication no. (PHS) 81-1232 (Washington, D.C.: National Center

for Health Statistics, 1980); M. Kovar, "Pregnancy and Childbirth," *Better Health for Our Children: A National Strategy*, Vol. 3., Report of the Select Panel for the Promotion of Child Health, DHHS publication no. (PHS) 79-55071 (Washington, D.C.: GPO, 1981); and K. Lee, P. Paneth, L. Gartner, M. Pearlman, and L. Gruss, "Neonatal Mortality: An Analysis of Recent Improvement in the United States," *American Journal of Public Health* 70 (January 1984): 15-21.

11. Department of Health and Human Services, *Promoting Health/Preventing Disease: Objectives for the Nation*, DHHS (PHS) publication no. (OM) 81-0007 (Washington, D.C.: GPO, 1980), p. 17.

12. Ibid.

13. See Children's Defense Fund, "Overview and Major Findings," in *America's Children in Poverty* (Washington, D.C.: 1984).

14. R. Haskins and J. J. Gallagher, eds., *Analysis of Social Policy: An Introduction* (Norwood, N.J.: Ablex, 1981).

15. See, for example, "Survival of the Fittest: Infant Mortality and the Poor," *Harvard Science Report*, January/February 1983, p. 3; and Institute of Medicine, *Preventing Low Birthweight* (Washington, D.C.: National Academy Press, Division of Health Promotion and Disease Prevention, 1985).

16. See N. Binken, R. Williams, C. Hogue, and P.Chen, "Reducing Black Neonatal Mortality: Will Improvement in Birth Weight Be Enough?" *Journal of American Medical Association* 3 (January 18, 1978): 372-375; E. Hemminki and B. Starfield, "Prevention of Low Birthweight and Pre-Term Birth," *Milbank Memorial Fund Quarterly* 3 (1978): 339-361; S. Shapiro, "New Reductions in Infant Mortality: The Challenge of Low Birthweight," *American Journal of Public Health* 4 (1981): 365-366; and M. McCormick, "The Contribution of Low Birth Weight to Infant Mortality and Childhood Morbidity," *New England Journal of Medicine* 312, no. 2 (January 10, 1085): 82-90.

17. See McCormick, "Contribution of Low Birth Weight to Infant Mortality and Childhood Morbidity" and Institute of Medicine, *Preventing Low Birthweight*, p. 52.

18. See S. Taffel, "Factors Associated with Low Birth Weight: United States, 1976," DHEW Publication No. (PHS) 80-1915 (Washington, D.C.: National Center for Health Statistics, 1981).

19. Institute of Medicine, *Preventing Low Birthweight*, p. 53.

20. See C. A. Miller, "Infant Deaths as a Social Indicator" (University of North Carolina, Department of Public Health, Maternal and Child Health, 1984), p. 17.

21. Ibid.

22. Ibid.

23. See Institute of Medicine, *Preventing Low Birthweight*, p. 55.

24. See S. Gortmaker, "The Effects of Prenatal Care Upon the Health of the Newborn," *American Journal of Public Health* 7 (1979): 653-660.

25. S. Chao, S. Imaizume, S. Gorman, and R. Lowenstein, "Reasons for Absence of Prenatal Care and Its Consequences" (Harlem Hospital, New York, Department of Obstetrics and Gynecology, 1984).

26. See L. Berger, "Public/Private Cooperation in Rural Maternal Child Health Efforts: The Lea County, New Mexico Perinatal Program" (unpublished paper, 1983).

27. See J. Klotch, C. Osslre, and D. Howze, "A Policy Analysis of the Repro-

ductive Health of Women in the Workplace," *Journal of Public Health Policy* 15 (June 1984): 213-227.

28. "Survival of the Fittest," *Harvard Science Report*, p. 3.

29. Ibid., p. 4.

30. Ibid., p. 4.

31. See C. Berquist, "Current Perspectives on Prenatal Care," A University Associates Report, March 1984, p. 30.

32. *Infant Mortality Rates: Failure to Close the Black-White Gap*, Materials Submitted for the Record by Carolyn Davis for Hearings Before the House Subcommittee on Oversight and Investigations and the Subcommittee on Health and the Environment of the Committee on Commerce, 98th Cong., 2nd Sess., March 16, 1984 (Washington, D.C.: GPO, 1985), p. 323.

33. Blackwell et al., *Administrative Petition*, p. 23.

34. Children's Defense Fund, "The Deficit Reduction Act of 1984," p. 4.

35. Blackwell et al., *Administrative Petition*, p. 25.

36. *The Nation's Health* 15, no. 4 (April 1985): 5.

37. See F. Norris and R. Williams, "Perinatal Outcomes Among Medicaid Recipients in California," *American Journal of Public Health* 74 (1984): 1112-1117.

38. Ibid.

39. See J. Johnson and G. Adams, *Maternal and Child Health in North Carolina: Options for Medicaid Expansion*, Prepared for the Office of Policy and Planning (Raleigh: North Carolina Department of Administration, May 1984), p. 30.

40. See H. Gorman and M. Grossman, "Determinants of Neonatal Mortality Rates in the United States: A Reduced Form Model," NBER Working Paper No. 1387 (June 1984); and C. Miller, E. Counter, E. Schorr, A. Fine, and S. Adams-Taylor, "The World Economic Crisis and the Children: United States Case Study, *International Journal of Health Services* 15, no. 1 (1985): 115.

41. McManus, "The Role of Medicaid in Delivering Prenatal Care to Low Income Women," p. 47.

42. R. Schwartz and P. Poppen, *Measuring the Impact of CHCS on Pregnancy Outcomes: Final Report* (Cambridge, Mass.: ABT Associates, 1982).

43. Poland, "Unemployment, Stress and Infant Mortality in Detroit," p. 6.

44. Ibid.

45. See S. Butler, M. Sanera, and B. Weinrod, *Mandate for Leadership: Continuing the Conservative Revolution* (Washington, D.C.: Heritage Foundation, 1984).

46. See Johnson and Adams, *Maternal and Child Health in North Carolina*, p. 54.

47. Ibid.

48. See Institute of Medicine, *Preventing Low Birthweight*, p. 154.

49. S. Rosenbaum, *Providing Effective Prenatal Care to Pregnant Teenagers*, Children's Defense Fund's Adolescent Pregnancy/Prevention Prenatal Campaign (Washington, D.C.: 1985).

50. See Institute of Medicine, *Preventing Low Birthweight*, p. 154; "Infant Death: An Analysis by Maternal Risk and Health Care," *Contrasts in Health Status*, Vol. 1, D. M. Kessner, ed. (Washington, D.C.: Maternal Academy of

Science, 1973); and V. Eisner, J. Brozce, M. Pratt, and A. Hexter, "The Risk of Low Birthweight," *American Journal of Public Health* 69 (1979): 887-893.

51. See S. Taffel, "Prenatal Care: United States, 1969-1975," *Vital and Health Statistics*, ser. 21, no. 33, DHEW No. (PHS) 78-911, Public Health Services (Washington, D.C.: GPO, September 1978).

52. See S. Rosenbaum, Testimony of the Children's Defense Fund Before the Subcommittee on Health and the Government, Committee on Energy and Commerce, U.S. House, Hearing, July 15, 1983 (Washington, D.C.: GPO, 1984).

53. See J. Feder, J. Hadley, and R. Mullner, "Falling Through the Cracks: Poverty, Insurance Coverage, and Hospital Care for the Poor, 1980 and 1982," *Milbank Memorial Fund Quarterly, Health and Society* 62 (1984): 544-566.

54. Children's Defense Fund, *A Children's Defense Budget: An Analysis of the President's FY 1986 Budget and Children, 1985* (Washington, D.C.: 1985), p. 85.

55. See S. Gortmaker, "Poverty and Infant Mortality in the United States, *American Sociological Review* 44 (April 1979): 280-297.

56. Children's Defense Fund, *Children's Defense Budget*, pp. 99-114.

57. See Poland, "Unemployment, Stress and Infant Mortality in Detroit," p. 37.

58. See B. Kehrer and C. Wolen, "Impact of Income Maintenance on Low Birthweight Evidence from Gary Experiment," *Journal of Human Resources* 14 (1979): 434-462.

PART III

Issues in the Delivery of Health Services

8. Substance Abuse in the Black Community

Patrick R. Clifford

Differential affinity to chemical substances of common abuse has persisted for many centuries among various ethnic groups.[1] Substance abuse, including alcohol, is the number one health and social problem among black Americans.[2] The correlation between substance abuse and a multiplicity of other problems (e.g., marital discord, unemployment, underemployment, disease, crime) serves to intensify the overall negative impact of substance abuse in the black community.[3] Yet, the development and implementation of prevention strategies, including treatment, designed to accommodate the sociocultural needs of the majority of blacks have not proliferated.

Medical and social epidemiological data demonstrate the increased risk of premature mortality and morbidity (e.g., heart disease, pancreatic cancer, esophageal and mouth cancers, liver disease, homicide, accidents) associated with substance abuse.[4] For example, approximately 10 percent of all deaths within the United States are alcohol-related. Furthermore, an estimated 80 percent of all cirrhosis and pancreatitis deaths have been associated with alcoholism. Chemical dependency is involved in approximately 50 percent of all violent deaths; much higher rates (i.e., 70 percent to 80 percent) have been reported for specific forms of violent death such as homicide.

This chapter (1) describes the epidemiology of substance abuse within the black community; (2) discusses problems related to epidemiological measures utilized for ascertaining prevalence and incidence rates which pertain to substance abuse within specific populations; (3) identifies sociocultural factors that contribute to the maintenance and escalation of substance abuse and mitigate the efficacy of various prevention efforts, and (4) recommends alternatives to present approaches to prevention in an effort to enhance the amelioration of substance abuse problems in the black community.

Reported prevalence rates of alcohol and other types of drug abuse vary considerably. For example, according to Westermeyer, 3 to 8 percent of the adult U.S. population is chemically dependent.[5] The Office of Technology Assessment (OTA) has reported that an estimated 9 percent of the adult population within the United States are problem drinkers.[6] Nevertheless, it is critical to note that even the more conservative estimates indicate a major public health problem. Two factors that contribute to the difficulties of accurately ascertaining prevalence rates pertaining to substance abusers are: (1) problems of definition (i.e., specifically defining a case); and (2) the stigma associated with the abuse of alcohol and other type drugs. Consequently, the actual prevalence of various types of substance abuse has probably been underestimated. Furthermore, when attempting to discern the epidemiology of substance abuse within a specific community sampling biases and changing temporal trends, with respect to different age cohorts, present additional problems. This is particularly troublesome given the fact that a majority of the studies conducted are of a cross-sectional nature.[7]

EPIDEMIOLOGY OF SUBSTANCE ABUSE

The changing epidemiological patterns of substance abuse within various subgroups of the U.S. population lend support to these contentions. For example, within the United States prior to the early 1900s the use and abuse of opiates was limited mostly to white females; at that time approximately two-thirds of the users were female. By the 1960s the sex ratio changed, and male opiate users outnumbered females by five or more to one.[8] During the 1950s the trend changed, and the abuse of opiates, as well as other narcotics, increased significantly in the black community. This trend apparently shifted again during the 1960s and 1970s as evidenced by the increased number of whites arrested for narcotic drugs.[9] Currently, heroin addiction is the most serious drug problem, with the exception of alcohol, in the United States.[10]

Numerous studies have indicated that a disproportionate amount of opiate abuse is practiced within the black community.[11] Espada notes that more than 60 percent of all heroin abusers come from minority communities.[12] On the other hand, a number of studies indicate that the prevalence of polydrug abuse, excluding heroin, in the black community is not dissimilar to that of the white community.[13] Chambers and Inciardi report that the regular use pattern of marijuana and hashish is similar among blacks and whites.[14] Moreover, some studies demonstrate that the prevalence of nonopiate abuse (e.g., amphetamines, barbiturates and nonbarbiturate sedative hypnotics) is more prevalent in the white community.[15] Furthermore, according to O'Donnell et al., racial differences among heroin abusers are diminishing.[16] Although prevalence estimates concerning specific substances of abuse may differ among blacks and white, it is imperative to recognize that substance abuse is a significant problem in both populations. Unfortunately, given the disproportionate amounts of poverty and unemployment in the black community, the negative impact of substance abuse is experienced as much more severe.[17]

PATTERNS OF ALCOHOL ABUSE

Alcohol is the major drug of choice in both the black and white communities. The National Institute of Alcohol Abuse and Alcoholism (NIAAA) has estimated that alcohol abuse costs the American economy more than $25 billion per year.[18] A more recent estimate of its annual cost has been reported by OTA to be as high as $120 billion dollars.[19] The cost of drug abuse, excluding alcohol, has been estimated at $10 billion annually.[20] The fact that various types of substance abuse are so highly correlated with other types of problems (e.g., marital, legal, financial, medical) adds considerably to the overall costs of these maladies to the economy.[21]

Disposable income has been positively correlated with the amount of alcohol consumed.[22] For example, among members of the upper socioeconomic strata there is a higher rate of light or social drinkers as well as a lower rate of abstainers. Noble reports that the drinking patterns of blacks and whites are dissimilar.[23] In his report to the U.S. Congress on Alcohol and Health, Noble reported that 51 percent and 38 percent of black females and males were abstainers as compared to 39 percent and 31 percent of their white counterparts, respectively. This report also indicated that 22 percent and 4 percent of white males and females were heavy drinkers as compared to 19 percent and 11 percent of their black counterparts, respectively. Thus, it appears that although black females comprise the largest group of abstainers, they also have almost three times the risk of white females for developing alcohol problems.

Drinking among blacks tends to lead either to abuse or abstention. That is, blacks are more likely to be either abstainers or heavy drinkers as opposed to moderate drinkers.[24] In addition, it appears that blacks are more status-oriented with respect to their drinking as evidenced by the high proportion of scotch consumed.[25] For example, one survey revealed that 34 percent of black middle-class men drank scotch as compared with 21 percent of the white male population.[26] As Bourne and Light point out, this suggests the importance of the relationship between alcohol and status among a highly status-conscious group.[27]

The greatest resource of any people is their young; yet, the most debilitating aspects of substance abuse (e.g., its negative impact on employment, education, self-esteem, familial life) may be experienced by black youth. Viamontes and Powell observe that, on the average, black males begin drinking approximately three or four years earlier than their white counterparts.[28] Furthermore, drinking at an earlier age has been correlated with subsequent heavier drinking. The occurrence of heavier drinking (i.e., consumption of at least four drinks daily or one seven-drink occasion per week) was more than twice as frequent among a sample of black male youths as compared to a similar study of whites. Moreover, the rate of medical or social problems resulting from drinking was 3.5 times greater among blacks.[29]

PROBLEMS OF MEASUREMENT

Although it has been estimated that the prevalence of alcoholism and problem drinking is approximately 9 percent of the adult U.S. population, this rate may be as high as 26 percent among the lower socioeconomic groups.[30] Given the disproportionate number of poor within the black community, one would expect alcohol problems to be significantly more prevalent among them than among the white community. Unfortunately, empirical data necessary to confirm the actual prevalence of substance abuse within the black community are lacking. This point is exemplified by Harper and Dawkins' assertion that of the 16,000 alcohol-related studies appearing in the scientific literature during the 30 years prior to their publication only 77 concerned blacks. Of these 77 articles, 27 were classified under "drinking patterns and behavior."[31] This lack of empirical data is further illustrated by the fact that the U.S. Department of Health and Human Services publication entitled *Health: United States, 1983*, which presents statistical data concerning trends in health care, generally classified according to age, sex, and race, reports statistical data concerning the consumption of alcohol without providing a breakdown for race or age.[32]

Other data available to discern the prevalence of substance abuse in the black community include medical and police records. However, caution must be used whenever attempts are made to interpret such data because these records may be more a reflection of our society's discriminatory attitude than a true indicator of the extent of the problem. For example, police records provide information concerning only that portion of the substance-abusing community that gets arrested and, thus, do not provide a representative sample of all abusers. Waldorf addresses this issue directly when he points out that blacks are more likely to serve sentences after arrest than whites, and generally they spend a greater amount of time in jail.[33] In addition, it is not unlikely that blacks are at greater risk of drawing police attention than whites as a result of inequities in our system of law enforcement.

Medical records regarding the treatment of substance abusers are also not representative of the total drug-abusing population. This point is exemplified by the fact that over 85 percent of all individuals experiencing alcohol problems do not receive treatment for their problem.[34] Furthermore, given the stigma associated with various types of substance abuse and the fact that until recently many types of insurance policies did not cover the treatment of substance abuse, it is not improbable that many treatment providers would indicate some other problem as the primary disorder (e.g., liver disease, depression). Consequently, substance-abusing individuals from the lower socioeconomic strata receiving treatment from government-funded providers are at greater risk of having some type of chemical abuse problem recorded as their primary disorder. Given the disproportionate number of poor within the black community, it is reasonable to assume that they may be overrepresented in government-supported treatment programs. Nevertheless, such data can be of value when attempting to ascertain prevalence rates, as long as the limitations of the data sets are recognized and interpretations concerning the data are made cautiously and conservatively.

Police and prison records indicate that various forms of substance abuse exact an extremely heavy toll from the black community. For example, the proportion of minorities arrested for heroin charges is greater than that in treatment programs. Furthermore, of those individuals found on the Drug Enforcement Administration's active users of narcotics list 55 percent are black.[35] Thus, it becomes apparent that there are substantial drug-related problems in the black community and, furthermore, that repressive drug laws have been implemented as a mechanism for dealing with these maladies. A consequence of these actions has been the exacerbation of drug-related problems in the black community.

UTILIZATION OF TREATMENT SERVICES

Racial differentiation is also reflected in various treatment programs. For example, in a national followup study of admissions to drug abuse treatment programs, in the Drug Abuse Reporting Program (DARP) Joe et al. reported that of the 36 and 50 agencies reviewed during the periods June 1, 1971, through May 31, 1972, and June 1, 1972, through

May 31, 1973, respectively, more than half of the methadone maintenance programs were comprised of a predominantly black clientele (i.e.,
greater than 75% black).[36] A Johns Hopkins University study reported
that minorities comprise less than 50 percent of clients receiving treatment for narcotic abuse, with the exception of methadone maintenance
programs where they comprise 66 percent of the population. Halikas et
al. reported that 85 percent, 70 percent, and 85 percent of the treatment
populations of the Missouri Department of Mental Health Methadone
Clinic, Archway House (an in-resident therapeutic community), and Narcotics Service Council (NASCO) (an out-resident therapeutic community) were black, respectively.[37] St. Louis, Missouri, the city which provided the setting for this investigation, had a metropolitan area population of approximately 2.4 million people of which an estimated 16 percent were black.

The OTA has asserted that 17.4 percent of the clients receiving treatment from programs funded by the National Institute of Alcohol Abuse
and Alcoholism (NIAAA) were black.[38] Given that blacks comprise 11.7
percent of the general population, they are overrepresented in treatment programs funded by NIAAA. These figures are particularly dis-
concerting inasmuch as programs designed to meet the sociocultural
needs of various subgroups of the black community have not proliferated, despite the overrepresentation of blacks in specific types of treatment modalities. Furthermore, OTA has indicated that sociocultural
factors prohibit the vast majority of alcohol-abusing blacks from
receiving treatment and that more research on blacks and alcoholism is
required.[39]

SOCIOCULTURAL FACTORS IN TREATMENT
AND PREVENTION

The importance of sociocultural factors in understanding the etiology of
substance abuse, as well as the design and implementation of successful
prevention strategies, including treatment, cannot be overemphasized.
Substance abuse is not a unidimensional condition comprised of a simple
cause-and-effect relationship. Rather, it is an extremely complex phenomenon comprised of a multiplicity of sociocultural, psychological, and
physiological variables. However, of these variables sociocultural factors
are primary.[40]

Whether or not a specific drug is abused within a given culture is
determined, at least in part, by that culture's tolerance for such
behavior. Mendelson and Mello assert that individuals are likely to
internalize the beliefs and attitudes of their culture with respect to drug
(i.e., alcohol) usage.[41] If a culture condones excessive drug use, then the

individual is likely to internalize that attitude; conversely, if the culture demands moderate use of a drug, then there is an increased probability that the individual will engage in controlled usage. However, an interesting paradox is that the goal of prevention (i.e., concerning alcohol abuse) is moderate use. Ironically, increased drug usage occurs when controls are directed toward abstinence rather than responsible use.[42]

SOCIOCULTURAL DETERMINANTS

Sociocultural factors have contributed substantially to the all or none type drinking pattern demonstrated by many blacks, not to mention their significance in prohibiting blacks access to appropriate treatment. For example, during slavery blacks were prohibited from drinking alcohol except on special occasions (e.g., holidays and harvest) when it was made available in large quantities. On these occasions intoxication was not only condoned but expected.[43] Harper points out that the present pattern of heavy drinking on weekends and paydays among contemporary blacks is tied to the drinking practices established during slavery.[44] Bourne and Light note that, although these factors contributed to the present drinking practices of many blacks, their influence has been steadily diminishing. They contend that current excessive weekend drinking among the black urban poor is a practice employed to alleviate stress and thus is not viewed as deviant.[45]

Drug abuse affords the individual, at least temporarily, with a psychological time-out period. For example, the pharmacolgical effects of many of the drugs of common abuse are euphoria, reduced anxiety, disinhibition, and relief from physical discomfort. Escapism has repeatedly been implicated as a major factor in the etiology of substance abuse among black Americans. Unfortunately, the relief provided by the drug is short-lived, and so the individual must repeat the process; in the long run, the drug tends to produce many more negative than positive effects. Consequently, drug abuse in the black community is both the result and cause of a plethora of other problems.

On the other hand, moral condemnation of alcohol, viewing even small amounts as sinful, encourages many to be abstinent. Thus, it appears that a middle ground where moderate drinking practices can be learned and accepted is lacking. In addition, it has proven extremely difficult to involve ministers in the treatment of alcoholics because of their strict adherence to a moralistic perspective denoting the alcoholic a sinner. With this background, it should not be surprising that the black community displays a high tolerance for excessive drinking behavior and thus does not incorporate the social controls necessary to prevent pathological drinking.

TREATMENT OUTCOMES

Numerous scientific investigations have focused on attempting to discern the relationship between outcome and race/ethnicity,[46] and the results have been equivocal mainly because of methodological and definitional inconsistencies across studies.[47] Methodological problems associated with across-study comparisons are highlighted in Emrick's review of alcoholism treatment. Of 384 studies reviewed, only 72 were considered methodologically appropriate.[48] Definitional difficulties associated with various treatment outcome measures are also problematic. For example, defining treatment efficacy in clinical terms requires an understanding of how a particular disorder naturally progresses. If an intervention yields results that are void of client improvement, this does not necessarily mean that the treatment approach lacked efficacy. The ability of a particular treatment intervention to alter the otherwise natural course of a health problem in a favorable direction may be considered extremely efficacious in many situations.[49] Unfortunately, thorough understanding of the natural progression of vairous forms of substance abuse is lacking. Clearly, the term "efficacy," as used in the clinical sense, is a relative term related to "expectation."

The overwhelming majority of studies comparing whites and nonwhites indicate more positive treatment outcomes for whites.[50] However, differences owing to race/ethnicity may be spurious given the greater proportion of minorities that are poor relative to nonminorities. Cahalan and Room as well as Goodwin et al. have demonstrated that social stability factors (e.g., higher education level, steady employment) are correlated with whites.[51] Furthermore, social stability has been consistently implicated as a positive prognostic variable in treatment outcomes.[52] Kissin has indicated that when social stability factors are controlled for black and white treatment, outcome differences dissipate.[53] Supporting Kissin's assertion is Mindlin's study, conducted in a workhouse setting, which demonstrates better treatment outcomes for blacks.[54] Royce postulates that black alcoholics admitted to treatment programs show a higher level of motivation, complain less, and are more cooperative than their white counterparts.[55] Cronkite and Moos have demonstrated, via path analysis, that differential treatment outcomes are not direcdtly attributable to various demographic, occupational, or social variables. Their analysis indicates that various sociodemographic variables indirectly influence choice of available treatment programs, thereby affecting differential treatment outcomes.[56] Thus, it becomes apparent that sociocultural factors influence not only patterns of substance use but treatment accessibility and outcomes as well; consequently, these factors are of paramount importance in understanding the etiology of substance abuse and positively impacting prevention efforts in the black community.

APPLICABLE PREVENTION STRATEGIES

Few concepts in public health occupy a more pivotal position than that of prevention. Various public health models emphasize the importance of the design, implementation, and evaluation of programs and strategies developed to positively affect the health status of populations. Substance abuse is a complex, multifaceted problem that can be impacted at different levels, based on problem severity.

From a public health perspective, substance abuse, or any other health problem for that matter, can be addressed within the conceptual framework of any, or all, of three prevention strategies:

1. Tertiary prevention, which consists of those procedures implemented to treat or rehabilitate individuals presently manifesting symptomatology associated with the disorder under consideration.
2. Secondary prevention, which includes those practices geared toward identifying asymptomatic cases (i.e., early identification of health disorders).
3. Primary prevention, which incorporates those approaches aimed at precluding the onset of a particular disorder.

Unfortunately, treatment outcome measures concerning tertiary prevention have not been very impressive. Although such approaches have experienced great success in initiating behavioral change, they have been much less fortunate with respect to maintaining such change.

Problems associated with tertiary prevention strategies, with respect to substance abuse, include high dropout and recidivism rates. For example, the Rand report stated that only 28 percent and 7 percent of the people treated for alcohol abuse had remained abstinent for six months and four years, respectively.[57] However, the report did indicate that an additional 18 percent were drinking nonproblematically at the end of the four-year period. Costello et al. summarized 80 studies concerning treatment outcome, each of which had incorporated at least a twelve-month followup period, and reported an average success rate (i.e., abstinent + improved cases) of 26 percent.[58]

Investigations that have focused on measuring the efficacy of Alcoholics Anonymous (AA), perceived by many to be the most efficacious treatment available for the abatement of alcohol abuse, have yielded results that are no more optimistic. Miller has reported that uncontrolled studies of AA indicate that dropout rates are as high as 80 to 90 percent, while controlled investigations have failed to demonstrate significant differences between AA participation and untreated controls.[59] Nevertheless, it appears that AA may achieve abstinence rates of approximately 50 percent among regular participants. Within the black community AA is often perceived as a treatment organization for white, middle-class alcoholics.[60]

The lack of demonstrated effectiveness on the part of tertiary substance abuse programs in conjunction with the fact that state-of-the-art treatment is often extremely expensive leads one to the conclusion that further investments of time, energy, and money to enhance the proliferation of such programs would not result in fruitful gains. Rather, a restructuring of existing programs to maximize the sociocultural fit between client and agency may prove more useful. Furthermore, if such programs are to enhance their treatment efficacy, it is imperative that their reorganization efforts include procedures and techniques designed to mitigate dropout and relapse rates and enhance client access (e.g., culturally oriented programs located in ethnic neighborhoods that provide long-term aftercare and followup).

A redistribution of resources in an attempt to enhance the earlier identification of substance abusers (i.e., secondary prevention strategies) would be beneficial. This is not to imply that there is no place for tertiary prevention efforts; rather, it is suggested that the limited resources available to impact such problems positively would be better invested if a significant portion were directed toward secondary and primary prevention strategies. Common sense and simple humanitarianism dictate that tertiary treatment should be made available to those now suffering this malady.

Secondary prevention strategies offer the opportunity to increase the efficacy of substance abuse treatment outcomes. Earlier identification provides the opportunity for earlier intervention; thus, treatment can be made available when treating cases that are less severe (e.g., outpatient versus inpatient versus residential care, controlled usage versus abstinence-oriented outcomes). This approach would be especially valuable within the black community, given the fact that blacks tend to enter treatment in the later stages of their problematic drug usage, if they enter at all. The notion that the sooner the intervention the better the prognosis would seem to apply here. Although this concept intuitively makes sense, empirical data necessary to confirm such a hypothesis are lacking. Nevertheless, the potential of secondary prevention strategies to positively impact the problem of substance abuse in the black community warrants their implementation, at least on an experimental basis.

Examples of prevention approaches embedded in a secondary prevention model which hold promise for significantly abating the problem include efforts aimed at implementing programs in schools (e.g., student assistance programs designed to detect students displaying deteriorated academic performance and providing them with services to discern and alleviate the underlying cause(s) of their poor performance). In addition, a secondary prevention model could be effective in community settings, such as the local "Y" and various churches, where programs designed to help the family of a substance-abusing individual conduct a successful intervention could be offered at relatively little cost by training community volunteers. Although secondary prevention approaches to the treatment of substance abuse hold greater promise than tertiary prevention programs, it is those strategies designed within the conceptual framework of primary prevention that are likely to produce the greatest results.

A Public Health axiom posits that no major health problem has ever been controlled or cured by focusing attention solely on the victims of a disorder. Substance abuse in the black community, or in any other community for that matter, will be no exception. Consequently, it is recommended that a disproportionate amount of the resources available for substance-abuse programming be allocated for primary prevention programs that are socioculturally tailored to meet the needs of blacks. It is further recommended that these programs not be limited to attempts at increasing awareness or modifying attitudes and practices concerning drug use and abuse, although this type of programming would be beneficial. Rather, programming geared toward enhancing self-esteem, job skill training, academic skill building, and so on will yield the most benefits and have the greatest impact. It is precisely those programs that are aimed at alleviating many of the problems associated with the initiation and, more important, the continuance of substance abuse (e.g., unemployment, underemployment, poor education, poverty) in the black community that will be the most efficacious in mitigating the problem. Furthermore, it is the young who hold the key to the future of any people; thus, if programs in the black community are to influence the blacks' health status and standard of living positively, it is imperative that efforts be targeted for black youth. Again, schools, churches, and other community agencies could provide adequate settings for such programming.

The evaluation of these primary prevention efforts will undoubtedly prove to be the most difficult of the prevention strategies discussed. The extent of the substance-abuse problem in the black community warrants extensive consideration of prevention programs. Any program that significantly impacts the substance-abuse problems will have evaluation problems that will prevent long-range changes in the black community.

CONCLUSIONS

In any investigation of the health status of black Americans, it soon becomes obvious that the overall poorer health status of black Americans is directly tied to racism. For example, the disproportionate amounts of unemployment, underemployment, crime, and poverty in the black community are, at least in part, the result of discriminatory policies and practices of the white majority, and they are also highly correlated with substance abuse—which is highly correlated with many of the leading causes of death among black Americans. Furthermore, the response of the white community, with respect to substance abuse, particularly among minorities, has been the implementation of repressive drug laws applied in a discriminatory fashion. This point is exemplified in the following excerpt form John Helmer, cited in Espada:

Return to class we must, where public policy is the strategem of class conflict and law enforcement the weapon, as sharp as the exclusion campaigns against Chinese and Mexicans, or the repression of ghetto blacks. . . . Not science but mythology potentiates this history and the social forces whose movements it records. If the monkey on the man's back were only the drug, he would still be a free man.[61]

Thus, if the problem of substance abuse as well as other health problems in the black community are to be significantly reduced, so must the racist and discriminatory practices of our larger society. All the treatment in the world will be of little consequence if the individual must return to function in a society in which he or she is viewed and treated as less than equal.

NOTES

1. See Joseph Westermeyer, *Primer on Chemical Dependency: A Clinical Guide to Alcohol and Drug Problems* (Baltimore, Md.: Williams and Wilkins, 1976).

2. See Peter G. Bourne and Enid Light, "Alcohol Problems in Blacks and Women," in Jack H. Mendelson and Nancy K. Mello, eds., *The Diagnosis and Treatment of Alcoholism* (New York: McGraw-Hill, 1979), ch. 5.

3. F. D. Harper, *Alcohol Abuse and Black America* (Alexandria, Va., Douglas, 1976).

4. U.S. Department of Health and Human Services, *Health and Prevention Profile: United States, 1982* ((Hyattsville, Md.: GPO, December 1983).

5. Westermeyer, *Primer on Chemical Dependency*, ch. 5.

6. Leonard Saxe, Denise Dougherty, Katharine Esty, and Michelle Fine, *Health Technology Case Study 22: The Effectiveness and Costs of Alcoholism Treatment* (Washington, D.C.: Congress of the United States, Office of Technology Assessment, March 1983).

7. For a discussion on these points, see Lee N. Robins, "Surveys of Target

Populations," in the National Institute of Drug Abuse Research Monograph, ser. 10, *The Epidemiology of Drug Abuse Current Issues* (Washington, D.C.: GPO, March 1977), pp. 39-48.

8. See Edward M. Brecher and the Editors of Consumer Reports, *Licit and Illicit Drugs* (Boston: Little, Brown, 1972).

9. See Bruce D. Johnson, National Institute on Drug Abuse Research Issues 21, *Drugs and Minorities* (Washington, D.C.: GPO, December 1977).

10. See *Healthy People: The Surgeon's Report on Health Promotion and Disease Prevention* (Washington, D.C.: GPO, 1979), ch. 10.

11. See, for example, Joanna Tyler and John R. Sherican, "Patterns of Primary Drug Abuse," *The International Journal of the Addictions* 15 (August 1980): 1169-1178.

12. Frank Espada, "The Drug Abuse Industry and the Minority Communities: Time for Change," in Robert L. DuPont, Avram Goldstein, John O'Donnell, and Barry Brown, eds., *Handbook on Drug Abuse* (Rockville, Md.: National Institute of Drug Abuse, 1979), ch. 28.

13. See, for example, John P. Callan and Carroll D. Patterson, "Patterns of Drug Abuse Among Military Inductees," *American Journal of Psychiatry* 130 (March 1973): 260-264.

14. Carl D. Chambers and James A. Inciardi, *An Assessment of Drug Use in the General Population* (New York: Narcotic Addiction Control Commission, 1972), Special Report Number 2.

15. See, for example, Dwayne D. Simpson, Bill Curtis, and Mark C. Butler, "Description of Drug Users in Treatment: 1971-1972 DARP Admissions," *American Journal of Drug and Alcohol Abuse* 2 (January 1975): 15-28.

16. John A. O'Donnell, Harwin Voss, Richard Clayton, Gerald Slatin, and Robin Room, *Men and Drugs—A Nationwide Survey*, NIDA Research Monograph Vol. 5 (Rockville, Md.: National Institute on Drug Abuse, February 1976).

17. On this point, see Peter G. Bourne and Enid Light, "Alcohol Problems in Blacks and Women," in Mendelson and Mello, eds., *The Diagnosis and Treatment of Alcoholism*, ch. 4.

18. See Joseph F. Follman, *Alcoholics and Business Problems, Costs, and Solutions* (New York: Amacom, 1976).

19. See Saxe et al., *Health Technology Case Study 22*, p. 3.

20. See B. L. Rufener, J. V. Rachal, and A. M. Cruze, *Management Effectiveness Measures for NIDA Drug Abuse Treatment Programs*, Vol. 2 (Washington, D.C.: National Institute on Drug Abuse, May 1976), p. 22.

21. See C. Ryan, P. Zagaria, C. DeCoster, S. Mamoureaux, and G. Rivera, *Battered Women, the Hidden Problem* (St. Paul, Minn.: Community Planning Organization, 1976), p. 44.

22. See George R. Jacobson and Diane Lindsay, "Screening for Alcohol Problems Among the Unemployed," in Marc Galanter, ed., *Currents in Alcoholism Volume VII: Recent Advances in Research and Treatment* (New York: Grune & Stratton, 1980), pp. 357-371.

23. Ernest P. Noble, ed., "Alcohol Use and Abuse Among Black Americans," in *Third Special Report to the U.S. Congress on Alcohol and Health from the Secretary of Health, Education, and Welfare* (Rockville, Md.: National Institute on Alcohol Abuse and Alcoholism, June 1976), pp. 31-33.

24. See F. D. Harper and M. P. Dawkins, "Alcohol and Blacks: Survey of the Periodical Literature," *British Journal of Addiction* 71 (1976): 327-334.

25. On this point see P. G. Bourne, "Alcoholism in the Urban Negro Population," in P. G. Bourne and R. Fox, eds., *Alcoholism: Progress in Research and Treatment* (New York: Academic Press, 1973), pp. 211-226.

26. See Bourne and Light, "Alcohol Problems in Blacks and Women," in Mendelson and Mello, eds., *The Diagnosis and Treatment of Alcoholism*, ch. 4.

27. Ibid.

28. J. A. Viamontes and B. J. Powell, "Demographic Characteristics of Black and White Male Alcoholics," *The International Journal of the Addictions* 9 (1974): 489-494.

29. On these points, see Geoffrey P. Kane, *Inner-City Alcoholism* (New York: Human Sciences Press, 1981).

30. See George R. Jacobson and Diane Lindsay, "Screening for Alcohol Problems Among the Unemployed," in Galanter, ed., *Currents in Alcoholism Volume VII*, p. 358.

31. Harper and Dawkins, "Alcohol and Blacks," p. 328.

32. U.S. Department of Health and Human Services, *Health and Prevention Profile: United States, 1983.*

33. Dan Waldorf, *Careers in Dope* (Englewood Cliffs, N.J.: Prentice-Hall, 1973), ch. 3.

34. See Saxe et al., *Health Technology Case Study 22*, p. 4.

35. See Espada, "The Drug Abuse Industry and the Minority Communities," p. 294.

36. G. W. Joe, B. K. Singh, D. Finklea, R. Hudiberg, and S. B. Sells, "Community Factors, Racial Composition of Treatment Programs and Outcomes," *National Institute on Drug Abuse Services Research Report* (Rockville, Md.: National Institute on Drug Abuse, 1977), ch. 1.

37. James A. Halikas, Harriet S. Darvish, and John D. Rimmer, "The Black Addict: 1. Methodology, Chronology of Addiction, and an Overview of the Population," *American Journal of Drug and Alcohol Abuse* 3 (1976): 529-543.

38. See Saxe et al., *Health Techology Case Study 22*, p. 15.

39. Ibid.

40. See David W. Martin, "Socio-cultural Factors in Alcoholism," in William L. Godeon, ed., *Alcoholism Counseling*, Vol. 1 (Matteson, Ill.: Good & Golden, 1976), ch. 2.

41. Mendelson and Mello, eds., *The Diagnosis and Treatment of Medicine*, pp. 362-374.

42. See N. E. Zinberg, R. C. Jacobson, and W. M. Harding, "Social Sanctions and Rituals as a Basis for Drug Abuse Prevention," *American Journal of Drug and Alcohol Abuse* 2 (1975): 165-181.

43. See James E. Royce, *Alcohol Problems and Alcoholism: A Comprehensive Survey* (New York: Free Press, 1981), p. 44.

44. Harper, *Alcohol Abuse and Black America*, ch. 3.

45. Bourne and Light, "Alcohol Problems in Blacks and Women," p. 85.

46. See Todd C. Flynn, P. Balch, P. Lewis, B. Susan, and B. Katz, "Predicting Client Improvement from and Satisfaction with Community Mental Health Center Services," *American Journal of Community Psychology* 9 (March 1981):

339-346; L. Michelson, "Psychotherapeutic Outcome for Children in a Community Mental Health Center: Psychological, Demographic, and Treatment Predictors," *Psychological Reports* 48 (1981): 323-326; L. Luborsky, J. Mintz, and P. Christopher, "Are Psychotherapeutic Changes Predictable? Comparing of a Chicago Counseling Center Project with a Penn Psychotherapy Project," *Journal of Consulting and Clinical Psychology* 47 (March 1979): 469-473; R. Moos and F. Bliss, "Difficulty of Follow-up and Outcome of Alcoholism Treatment," *Journal of Studies on Alcohol* 39 (March 1979): 473-490; Reginald G. Smart, "Characteristics of Alcoholics Who Drink Socially After Treatment," *Alcoholism: Clinical and Experimental Research* 2 (January 1978): 49-52; and Joseph Westermeyer and P. G. Bourne, "Treatment Outcome and the Role of the Community in Narcotic Addiction," *The Journal of Nervous and Mental Disorders* 166 (January 1978): 51-58.

47. See Susan D. Solomon, *Tailoring Alcoholism Therapy to Client Needs* (Rockville, Md.: National Institute on Alcohol Abuse and Alcoholism, 1981), p. 7.

48. Chad D. Emrick, "A Review of Psychologically Oriented Treatment of Alcoholism: The Relative Effectiveness of Different Treatment Approaches and the Effectiveness of Treatment Vs. No Treatment," *Journal of Studies on Alcohol* 36 (January 1975): 88-108.

49. See Stanley I. Greenspan and Steven S. Sharfstein, "Efficacy of Psychotherapy Asking the Right Questions," *Archives of General Psychiatry* 38 (November 1981): 1213-1219.

50. See, for example, S. Y. Choi, "Dreams as a Prognostic Factor in Alcoholism," *American Journal of Psychiatry* 130 (1973): 699-702 and P. Edwards, C. Harvey, and P. C. Whitehead, "Wives of Alcoholics: A Critical Review and Analysis," *Quarterly Journal of Studies on Alcohol* 34 (1973): 112-132.

51. D. Cahalan and R. Room, *Problem Drinking Among American Men* (New Brunswick, N.J.: Rutgers Center on Alcohol Studies, 1974); and D. W. Goodwin, J. B. Crane, and S. B. Guze, "Felons Who Drink: An Eight Year Follow-up," *Quarterly Journal of Studies on Alcohol* 32 (1971): 136-147.

52. J. M. Polich, D. J. Armor, and H. B. Braiker, *The Course of Alcoholism: Four Years After Treatment* (Rockville, Md.: Rand Corporation, National Institute on Alcohol Abuse and Alcoholism, 1980), p. 88.

53. B. Kissin, "Patient Characteristics and Treatment Specificity in Alcoholism," in C. M. Idestrom, ed., *Recent Advances in the Study of Alcoholism: Proceedings of the First International Magnus Huss Symposium* (Amsterdam-Oxford: Excerpta Medica, 1977).

54. C. Mindlin, "Evaluation of Therapy for Alcoholics in a Workhouse Setting," *Quarterly Journal of Studies on Alcohol* 21 (1960): 90-112.

55. Royce, *Alcohol Problems and Alcoholism*, p. 63.

56. R. C. Cronkite and R. H. Moos, "Evaluating Alcohol Treatment Programs: An Integrated Approach," *Journal of Consulting and Clinical Psychology* 46 (May 1978): 1105-1119.

57. J. M. Polich, D. J. Armor, and H. B. Braiker, *The Course of Alcoholism: Four Years After Treatment* (New York: John Wiley, 1981), ch. 2.

58. R. M. Costello, P. Biever, and J. G. Baillargeon, "Alcoholism Treatment Programming: Historical Trends and Modern Approaches," *Alcoholism: Clinical and Experimental Research* 1 (1977): 311-318.

59. William R. Miller, "Controlled Drinking: A History and Critical Review," *Journal of Studies on Alcohol* 44 (January 1983): 68-83.

60. Connie Smith-Peterson, "Substance Abuse Treatment and Cultural Diversity," in Gerald Bennett, Christine Vourakis, and Donna S. Woolf, eds., *Substance Abuse: Pharmacologic, Developmental, and Clinical Perspectives* (New York: John Wiley, 1983).

61. Espada, "The Drug Abuse Industry and the Minority Communities," p. 294.

9. Promoting Mental Health: The Potential for Reform

Woodrow Jones, Jr., and Mitchell F. Rice

In recent years a substantive change has occurred in public health policy. Realizing that advances in medical science do not deter the development of mental disorders, health professionals have displayed "excessive zeal" in pursuing the prevention of mental disorders and the promotion of mental health. The old aphorism that "an ounce of prevention is worth a pound of cure" has become the new slogan of the community mental health movement in the United States.

A substantial number of articles, conferences, and books have been directed at the prevention and promotion of mental health.[1] In examining the relationship between health prevention and the black community, however, we find a paucity of research efforts.[2] Despite the disproportionate impact of various types of mental disorders on minority populations, only general references are made in the literature to prevention efforts for the black population.[3] Furthermore, the problems of implementing and administering a prevention and promotion strategy for blacks have not been discussed. In fact, the field of mental health prevention is presently struggling with several critical problems as to the dimension of conceptualization, organization, and implementation of strategies aimed at preventing mental illness and promoting mental health.

This chapter focuses on the concept and techniques of prevention. Prevention is broadly defined as actions taken to avoid the occurrence of a mental disorder. Although the broadness of this definition leads to some doubts about what a definable prevention activity is, it does suggest an endless variety of preventive behaviors. Using this definition, this chapter examines a conceptual framework for implementing health prevention activities for the black population. Using this framework as a guide, we will examine critically the administrative problems of implementing a mental health prevention program.

BLACK MENTAL HEALTH STATUS

The increasing urbanization and industrialization of American society has produced both alienation and stress within minority communities. For blacks these broad changes in the social fabric have resulted in poverty, unemployment and underemployment, and inadequate housing. These living conditions are conducive neither to a healthy lifestyle nor to good mental health. They often result in mental and health disorders that relate to the stressful conditions of urban black America.

Mental health concerns have not been a high priority for either blacks or whites. Cultural biases explain most of the fears Americans express when discussing the possibility of a mental disorder. For blacks deep-seated spiritual symbols are attached to feelings about mental health. In addition, mental health services involve social costs. Often these services are the most underfunded and underused of all the components within the health care system. Thus, the lack of availability and accessibility of mental health services is compounded by a lack of understanding of the value of these services.

The rates for inpatient admissions to county mental hospitals can be used to show the prevalence of black mental health problems. In Table 9.1, we find a difference in the admission rates of black and white males in the 45 to 64 age group. The age-adjusted admission rate for black males is twice that of white males and four times that of white females.

The overall age-adjusted rate of admission for blacks is twice the rate for whites of both sexes. The critical period for black males is between the ages of 25 and 44, and for black females, the period between the ages of 45 and 64. In all age groups there is a difference in admission rates when examining the racial characteristics of the patient.

The diagnoses of patients admitted to mental health facilities also demonstrate racial differences for the same disorder. Alcoholism and schizophrenia are the leading causes of white male admissions; black males are admitted for the same disorders at nearly three times the rate of whites. Black women are admitted for the same disorders and at the same rate as black males (see Table 9.2).

Table 9.1

Percent Distribution, Age-Specific and Age-Adjusted Rates of Inpatient Admissions to State and County Mental Health Hospitals, by Race, Sex, and Age, 1975 (per 100,000 population)

	Both Sexes	White		Both Sexes	Black	
		Male	Female		Male	Female
Total admissions	296,151	190,788	105,363	83,367	53,646	29,721
			Percent Distribution			
All ages	100.0%	100.0%	100.0%	100.0%	100.0%	100.0%
Under 18	5.9	5.8	6.1	8.9	9.2	8.3
18-24	18.0	20.0	14.3	21.0	24.7	14.3
25-44	42.1	41.4	43.4	46.6	48.9	42.5
45-64	28.1	27.1	30.0	19.8	14.2	29.9
65 plus	5.9	5.7	6.2	3.7	3.0	5.0
Median age	35.2	34.2	37.3	32.1	30.0	38.0
Age-adjusted rates	157.6	213.3	109.9	367.3	509.4	248.5
All ages	161.1	214.2	111.2	344.2	469.5	232.2
Under 18	31.6	39.3	23.6	77.8	103.1	52.2
18-24	234.0	343.9	129.4	539.6	892.1	241.3
25-44	270.2	349.3	194.2	688.3	1032.7	406.3
45-64	213.4	276.0	155.7	414.1	414.2	413.9
65 plus	66.0	130.9	54.0	171.9	210.8	143.7

Source: Based on data from U.S. Department of Health and Human Services, Public Health Service, Health of the Disadvantaged, Chart Book II (Washington, D.C., September 1980), p. 81, Table 65, Chart 65.

Table 9.2
**Major Leading Diagnoses for Admissions to State
and County Hospitals, by Race and Sex, 1975
(rates per 100,000 population)**

White Male		Black Male	
Alcohol disorders	79.5	Schizophrenia	197.1
Schizophrenia	56.3	Alcohol disorders	122.0
Depressive disorders	21.7	Personality disorders	35.6
Drug disorders	10.0	Adjustment reaction and	
		behavior disorders of children	22.6

White Female		Black Female	
Schizophrenia	42.8	Schizophrenia	118.2
Depressive disorders	23.1	Alcohol disorders	50.1
Alcohol disorders	12.4	Organic brain syndrome	17.3
Organic brain syndrome	7.8	Depressive disorders	10.2
Personality disorders	6.6	Adjustment reaction, adult	9.8

Source: Based on unpublished data from the National Institute of Mental
Health, Division of Biometry and Epidemiology.

   Outpatient care and followup care are important elements in integrating patients into the community. However, blacks as a group are more reluctant to admit that a relative may have mental problems, and they are just as reluctant to admit the nature of the disorder.[4] When blacks do seek outpatient mental care, they are often subjected to discrimination. Gross and Herbert, in a survey of psychiatric emergency rooms, has found that blacks are systematically treated and discharged with little followup.[5] This finding lends support to an earlier study by Brill and Storrow who found that blacks were less often treated by senior staff members and, in many instances, were often rejected for treatment.[6] When treatment is initiated, blacks will often terminate some treatment sessions until their symptoms become acute.[7] Table 9.3 provides some support for the assertion that blacks do not have the same outpatient services as whites. The number of visits before termination is less for blacks than for whites. In summary, display of acute symptoms and failure to respond to outpatient treatment discourage blacks from effectively utilizing mental health services.

APPROACHES TO PREVENTION
IN THE BLACK COMMUNITY

The problems of mental illness prevention in the black community stem from lack of an adequate conceptualization of a public health strategy.

Table 9.3
Median Number of Visits for Outpatient Psychiatric
Services by Race/Ethnicity and Termination Status, 1975

Termination Status	White	Black
Total	3.8	2.8
Terminated	2.6	2.2
Not terminated	6.9	6.6

Source: Based on unpublished data from the
National Institute of Mental Health,
Division of Biometry and
Epidemiology.

The traditional public health approach distinguishes among three levels of prevention activities.[8] *Primary prevention* is directed at people who are at risk of exposure to a particular disorder. At this level, prevention programs seek to delineate the population at risk and provide information that will help avoid the occurrence of the disorder. *Secondary prevention* programs are designed to reduce the severity of a particular disorder's effects on the population at risk. *Tertiary prevention* efforts involve surveillance and rehabilitation directed at controlling the incidence of the disorder in the population. Each level of prevention suggests implicitly that governmental intervention can be an effective method of preventing mental illness and promoting mental health.

In the case of specific disorders, the public health approach seems plausible and gives a rationale for governmental intervention. Unfortunately, many blacks experience several disorders simultaneously from multiple causes. For example, blacks are more likely than whites to experience the cumulative effects of stressful life events, such as abject poverty, unemployment, divorce, and sexual abuse.[9] An individual might be exposed to several different levels of prevention activities. Furthermore, the interaction of these prevention activities and various social problems may produce conflicting results.

The levels of prevention in the public health approach are merely indicators of where our efforts should be directed and the probable effects; they do not suggest approaches to intervention. Two approaches to mental health intervention dominate the literature—the proactive and the reactive. The proactive emphasizes the avoidance of stressors that may cause the onset of a disorder.[10] In contrast, the reactive approach attempts to prepare the individual to react to the stressor in a nondetrimental way.[11] Each approach involves a number of techniques that can be used to accomplish the prevention goal. The contrast between these approaches can be best illustrated by a stressful life event such as family death. The reactive approach would use techniques that encourage coping and adapting to the event, whereas the proactive approach would enhance other life events and encourage the avoidance of the painful experiences associated with death. Obviously, most of the effort in the community mental health movement is directed at reactive techniques at every phase of prevention and promotion activity.

The proactive strategy suggests changing the environment or the preconceptions of the individual within that environment. These types of changes are beyond the conceptual focus of primary prevention efforts. They also suggest that the administrator of any local program may not have the capabilities to implement the desired changes. For example, economic causative factors are difficult to manipulate to the advantage of the black population. Governmental intervention to manipulate basic structural arrangement has a history of inconsistent results. Thus, mental health administrators have not attempted to implement a proactive strategy that involves a rearrangement of power.

These different approaches to prevention suggest different governmental responses. The reactive strategy requires a slow incremental effort to change the causative factors that affect minority mental health. On the other hand, the proactive approach stresses the link between mental health and the total environment of the individual. Despite different conceptual viewpoints, each approach shares the same basic problems in implementation in the black population.

PROBLEMS IN PREVENTION STRATEGIES FOR MINORITIES

Choice of Goals or Targets

The key to implementing a prevention strategy is definition of goals.[12] Goals should be operational and relevant for the target population. Goal attainment and program success in any prevention effort are linked to the demonstration that prevention has occurred.[13] However, in practice, several problems are likely to create difficulties in the setting of realistic goals and targets for the mental health administrator.

First, goals are difficult to specify when data are not available on the prevalence and incidence of mental disorders in the black community. Because the black population in some areas is small and is not concentrated in any one site, a large prevalence survey is not an adequate measurement technique. On the other hand, small surveys on specific populations may not provide the data to justify large-scale intervention. At present, most of the data on black mental disorders are a result of behavioral outcomes from other institutions.[14] Although this information is useful from an epidemiological viewpoint, it is of little value for the baseline data for establishing a mental illness prevention program. Scientifically obtained patient information and situational context reflect the actual needs of the black population. Without an adequate data base for setting prevention and promotion goals, the outcomes may be inappropriate or inadequate.

Second, the lack of information is further compounded by lack of research on black mental health problems. Because they do not have a strong research base, programs have been implemented without clear causal linkages to a known prevention strategy. Without these linkages, prevention efforts lack direction, clarity, and a demonstrable behavioral outcome.[15] Furthermore, in the absence of research, assumptions about the independent effects of the prevention effort can misguide any policy evaluation. For instance, we assume that a plan geared to eliminate the attitudes, practices, and conditions that affect blacks adversely will make a significant difference without other types of governmental intervention. Thus, efforts to target the black population for prevention efforts without knowledge of the sociogenic cause of mental disorders cannot be efficient.

Third, the criterion of choice of goals becomes dubious when programs lack goals and causality. The prevention effort is based on the selection of objectives that are manageable given a specific goal. Many of our preventive programs for blacks and other minorities have no defensible criteria for the selection of program goals. Why is the majority of the prevention dollar directed toward children? Why are so few programs directed toward alcoholism in the nonworking environment? Each question begs recognition of the implied assertion that black and white participants agree on the criteria by which goals are chosen. However, this is not the case in other policy areas and is not likely to be the case in mental health policy.

Boundaries of Prevention Activities

Despite the various prevention strategies, the questions of boundaries of prevention activities is critical for a successful program.[16] These boundaries are important not only in a geopolitical sense, but also in terms of the limits of activities and intervention. Each boundary presents a formidable barrier to the intervention efforts and raises some issues of ideological choice. Presently, the boundaries of intervention activities can be divided into two levels, micro and macro.[17] Micro-level intervention places primary responsibility on the individual. Each individual is seen as the source of change within the community. Moreover, being responsible for your own mental health necessarily requires the internalization of the norms of the majority.[18] Therefore, reactive strategies are preferred to proactive strategies of prevention because of the threat to authorities.

At the micro level, a reactive strategy for black mental health stresses adaptation and coping. Adaptation and coping are symbolic codes for the socialization of individuals to certain role choices, behavioral therapies, and cognitive restructuring. Each of these techniques stresses the individual's ability to acquiesce to life events in order to ameliorate some of their impact.[19] In essence, at the micro level, prevention can be equated with compliance through the patient's ability to recognize, learn, and implement the correct pattern of behavior.

In comparison, macro-level changes focus on normative changes in the society rather than on the individual. This intervention level suggests that mental health is a normative condition requiring operationalization in a particular environment. The environmental content provides many of the stressful events that affect black mental health. However, normative changes in the environment would require responses beyond the boundaries of the mental health administrator. An appropriate response would require changes in large social and economic organizations which are stressors on the individual. Or it may suggest the unavoidable reality of removing stressors in the environment altogether, which is congruent with the protest philosophy of earlier periods.

A prevention strategy at the macro level necessarily involves a proactive strategy of prevention. Such a strategy could only be possible in a society undergoing rapid transformation in the normative order. However, the micro-level strategy fits more closely present realities of a fragmented mental health delivery system.

Ideological Biases

The present set of ideological biases that dominate primary prevention presents a formidable barrier. These barriers center around a set of political and social factors within the liberal political tradition. This tradition places an emphasis on the individual actor within the context of a pluralistic political system. Blacks, in particular, become one among many interest groups competing for scarce resources. Invariably, the problems of liberalism affect the ability of either a reactive or proactive strategy in several ways.

First, liberalism prevents the planning of an adequate mental health system. Planning, like other forms of intervention, requires the ability to coerce through legitimate authority. Authority within the present system of administration is fragmented, asymmetric, and incapable of control. Conflicts of authority often arise over treatment modality, standards of treatment, and personnel. Such questions are far removed from the general thrust of psychotherapy-oriented clinics. Because of the lack of legitimate authority, many efforts to organize an effective community mental health system have been unsuccessful.[20]

Second, the pluralistic nature of democratic governments is manifest in the pluralistic approach to problem-solving. Instead of a comprehensive approach to mental health service delivery, we find pluralistic policies that are often conflicting. Housing quality is not linked to mental health policy, nor is welfare reform, both of which could have a direct impact on the mental status of blacks. Studies have linked mental health status with several causative agents that have not been integrated in any comprehensive mental health movement. The resulting pragmatic approach to problem-solving has resulted in a patchwork of programs, policies, and federal guidelines, all of which serve to emphasize the lack of effective planning and control.

Finally, the ideological bias of pluralism prevents the addressing of racism as a primary stressor for blacks. The impact of racial prejudice has been well documented as a stressor in the black community. Because reactive strategies dominate most of our prevention efforts, racism is conceptualized as a matter of individual perception which can be changed only through individual awareness and social adaptation. Advocacy is not seen as effective in changing the milieu of blacks because of pluralistic assertions that incrementalism as practiced by the present structure is the only feasible way of bringing about change. Programs and proposals that threaten the basic distribution of power within the pluralist universe are viewed as being outside the professions' social mandate to perform specialized tasks. Such prescriptions will not allow the kind of proactive prevention that will improve the black population's overall mental health.

Political Impediments

Federal policy on prevention in the mental health field has a twenty-year history. Only recently has there been a renewed effort to make prevention an important element in the delivery of health services. The impact of presidential commissions, surgeon generals' reports, and academic literature has been to increase interest in the field as a means of reducing the ever-escalating cost of treatment. The President's Commission on Mental Health was important in including within its recommendations a chapter entitled "Strategies for Prevention."[21] Despite the grandiose nature of these recommendations, federal efforts have not had an impact on the black community.

Although prevention has generally been accepted in principle, the actual allocation of resources to prevention activities has been meager. Instead, most medical and mental health resources are directed toward institutional and other treatment programs. Despite contradictory evidence of the effectiveness of treatment service, large-scale prevention efforts have not been evaluated as cost-effective. For blacks, these findings suggest that prevention efforts may not deter the onset of mental disorders. Because treatment is stigmatized in the black community and fewer treatment services are available, there is little chance that prevention and promotion strategies will have the desired outcome. The delayed effect of lack of treatment is increased institutionalization of blacks, thus increasing mental health care cost and defeating the goal of prevention.

In addition to lack of resources, there is also a general lack of coordination of mental health implementation strategies. Although the federal government has assumed the burden of research efforts, it has not assumed effective control of the administrative process necessary for successful implementation of a prevention program. Implementing any prevention strategy is still the responsibility of state governments. The dismal record of state governments in implementing federal policy leaves little doubt of their inability to allocate resources to minorities in any effective manner. Rather than promoting equity in the distribution process, states have been noted as the source of much inequity faced by blacks (e.g., Medicare, SSI, AFDC). Whereas on the national level the recommendations of the Conference on Minority Group Alcohol, Drug Abuse and Mental Health Issues included concern about the design of prevention materials in the local "dialect," state mental health departments have not had the money or resources to perform such an onerous task. Thus, before prevention can be a policy option, efforts must be made to alleviate the mixture of coordination problems that tend to undermine prevention policies.

Implementation Barriers

Since the beginning of the Community Mental Health Movement, there have been many barriers to the delivery of mental health services. These barriers are similar to those facing policy implementation in other arenas. The pitfalls most likely to be faced by community mental health directors are produced by agency characteristics, personnel, organizational conflict, and local commitment. Each of these internal factors can have a detrimental effect on successful implementation. Thus, any health promotion or prevention activity that is nationally mandated must solve these problems before it can have any effect on its target population.

First, a number of agency characteristics may hinder the development of an effective program. The centrality of power in an agency directly affects its ability to design an effective program. Decentralized agencies have difficulty coordinating implementation. In addition, the organization of the agency may also determine effectiveness. Poorly organized agencies do not adapt quickly to the problems of implementing new programs. Furthermore, poor organizations tend not to be able to deliver adequate mental health services.

Another important factor is the cost to the agency for delivery of program services. Tangible costs as well as intangible costs decrease the effectiveness of program delivery. Tangible costs are those for personnel, administration, and various field costs, whereas intangible are those incurred in resistance to the program plan, behavioral changes, and administrative conflict. As these costs accumulate, fewer resources are applied to implementation, and the effectiveness of prevention efforts declines.

Second, other resources important to program effectiveness include adequate funding, equipment, and support. Underfunding is a tradition in certain policy arenas of public health. Lack of resources undermines any attempt to design effective programs. In addition, underfunding affects the availability of adequate personnel with the expertise required to implement programs. Unfortunately, many programs are headed by inexperienced workers who are hired because they are affordable. Thus, personnel and resources interact in a direct manner in providing the foundation for effective implementation.

Third, at the local level the most important variable is the commitment of mental health agencies to the development of national programs. Programs require the total commitment of resources, personnel, and leadership in order to be effective. Besides the commitment of the agency, there has to be the commitment and support of the target population. Efforts must be made to develop lines of communication so that feedback can help in augmenting the program.

Finally, a most damaging obstacle to the implementation process is conflict within the implementing authority. Conflict over resources, personnel, and authority is bound to occur in an environment dominated by scarcity. Disparate goals within a community health agency are only compounded by funding inadequate for acquiring personnel capable of completing the implementation process. Finally, competition between public and private agencies for control of the mental health marketplace further undermines effective long-range preventive policies.

CONCLUSION

As prevention strategies become more dominant in the mental health field, the effects on black mental health concerns become critical. Programs for preventing drug abuse, alcohol abuse, and mental illness among blacks must receive the kind of funding which will eliminate or at least reduce sources of stress. Top priority for program development, training, and research in primary prevention should be directed toward infants and young children and their environments including, particularly, efforts to increase competence and coping skills in the young. Thus far, emphasis has not been on primary prevention but on secondary and tertiary prevention. If primary prevention is to be a major priority for blacks, a strategy for implementing a prevention program must meet the needs and conditions of the communities in which they are based.

Within a local or regional mental health program several organizations might be configured to aid in the development of mental health promotion activities.[22] First, prevention and promotion activities should focus on existing black organizations. Several organizations, such as the NAACP, the Urban League, and other minority coalitions, are a source of legitimacy for health promotion efforts. For example, local efforts in promoting hypertension detection and treatment have been successfully implemented by local schools, clubs, and social organizations. These organizations can supplement health department services through the use of their resources and personnel.

A second organization that could be useful in mental health promotion efforts is the place of employment. In sites of concentrated black employment, efforts could be directed at promoting mental health awareness. These efforts should be part of a general occupational health promotion plan. Presently, black and other minority males have been targeted for prevention efforts in the areas of substance abuse through Employee Assistance Programs (EAP). There is a need to expand EAPs into all sectors of the labor market in order for prevention efforts to be more effective. Thus, by working with black employees in a positive environment, we can develop prevention strategies that are tied to tangible rewards which will induce behavioral change.

A final organization that might be utilized in promoting black mental health is the black church. Black churches provide a variety of services to black communities. At present, the American church has evolved into an organization that rivals local service providers. In addition to traditional social services, the church provides a network of other social support. Many churches have developed a system of peer counseling and crisis management that duplicates local agency services. Rather than instigating new health promotion efforts, it might be more effective to configure a network of churches as the center of a mental health promotion plan. By using the religious community as an agent of change, promotion and prevention efforts can function within a context of community support.

Even if we are able to achieve this voluntary organizational configuration, there is no certainty that success can be attributed to promotion and prevention activities. Some mental disorders will not be affected by promotion and prevention activities. Furthermore, changes in factors external to promotion and prevention efforts might be more effective (employment, housing, etc.). However, lack of data on the status of black mental health presents a formidable barrier for effective prevention programming. In addition, evaluative measures of any prevention programs must reflect the social, psychological, and physical milieu in which the individuals function. Finally, the ideological biases implicit in planning and administering a prevention program for minorities often allows the denial of the importance of political factors in creating an environment conducive for mental disorder. Consequently, an ultimate proactive prevention strategy would be to increase the power of blacks in society.

NOTES

1. See B. L. Bloom, "Prevention of Mental Disorders: Recent Advances in Theory and Practice," *Community Mental Health Journal* 15, no. 3 (August 1979): 179-191.

2. See C. R. Payton, "Substance Abuse and Mental Health: Special Prevention Strategies Needed for Ethnics of Color," *Public Health Reports* 96, no. 1 (February 1981): 20-25.

3. See S. Sue, "Ethnic Minority Research: Trends and Directions," Paper presented at the National Conference on Minority Group Alcohol, Drug Abuse and Mental Health Issues (Denver: May 1978).

4. See W. Nobles, "Black People in White Insanity: An Issue for Black Community Mental Health," *Journal of Afro-American Issues* 4 (Winter 1976): 21-27.

5. See Herbert S. Gross et al., "The Effect of Race and Sex on the Variation of Diagnosis and Disposition in a Psychiatric Emergency Room," *Journal of Nervous Mental Disease* 148 (June 1969): 638-642.

6. See Norman Q. Brill and Hugh Storrow, "Social Class and Psychiatric Treatment," *Archives of General Psychiatry* 3 (October 1960): 340-344.

7. Anna M. Jackson et al., "Race as a Variable Affecting the Treatment Involvement of Children," *Journal of the American Academy of Child Psychiatry* 13 (January 1974): 20-31.

8. See B. L. Bloom and D. P. Buck, eds., *Preventive Services in Mental Health Programs* (Boulder, Colo.: Wiche, 1967).

9. See T. S. Langer et al., "Children of the City: Affluence, Poverty and Mental Health," in V. L. Allen, ed., *Psychological Factors in Poverty* (New York: Academic Press, 1970).

10. See P. C. McCulloch, "The Ecological Model: A Framework for Operationalizing Prevention," *Journal of Prevention* 11, no. 1 (Fall 1980): 30-45.

11. See S. Schwartz and E. A. Bodanke, "Environmental Strategies for Primary Drug Abuse Prevention Programs," *Journal of Prevention* 1, no. 3 (Spring 1981): 188-198.

12. See J. R. Lamb and J. Zusman, "Primary Prevention in Perspective," *American Journal of Psychiatry* 136, no. 1 (Fall 1979): 12-17.

13. See C. A. Maher, "An Evaluation System for School-Community Prevention Programs," *Journal of Primary Prevention* 2, no. 2 (Winter 1981): 101-113.

14. See W. B. Kramer and B. Brown, eds., *Racism and Mental Health* (Pittsburgh: University of Pittsburgh Press, 1973), p. 14.

15. See S. E. Goldston, "Overview of Primary Prevention Programming in Primary Prevention: An Idea Whose Time Has Come," edited by D. C. Klein and S. E. Goldston, DHEW Publications No. (ADM) 77-447 (Rockville, Md.: National Institute of Mental Health, 1977, pp. 23-41.

16. See C. T. Adam, "A Descriptive Definition of Primary Prevention," *Journal of Primary Prevention* 2, no. 2 (Winter 1981): 67-80.

17. See T. F. Babor and Steven Berglas, "Toward a Systems-Ecological Approach to the Prevention of Adolescent Alcohol Abuse," *Journal of Prevention* 2, no. 1 (Fall 1981): 25-39.

18. See G. W. Albee, "The Fourth Mental Health Revolution," *Journal of Prevention* 1, no. 2 (Winter 1980): 67-70.

19. G. Spivack and M. D. Shure, *Social Adjustment of Young Children: A Cognitive Approach to Solving Real Life Problems* (San Francisco: Jossey-Bass, 1974).

20. For a general discussion of these points as they relate to health planning, see Woodrow Jones and Mitchell Rice, "Liberalism, Politics and Health Planning," *Journal of Health and Human Resources* 3, no. 1 (August 1980): 56-66.

21. President's Commission on Mental Health, *Task Panel Report* (Washington, D.C.: GPO, 1978).

22. B. L. Bloom, "Prevention/Promotion with Minorities," *Journal of Primary Prevention* 3 (Summer 1983): 224-234.

10. Long-Term Care and the Black Elderly

Verna M. Keith

By 1970 the U.S. population had begun to age as an increasing proportion of its citizens became 65 years and older. The elderly's representation in the total population increased from 4 percent at the turn of the century to 11.2 percent in 1980.[1] The proportional increase of persons 65 years and older has also been experienced in minority populations. During the next twenty years, the number of black elderly is projected to increase at a faster rate than the number of white elderly.[2] Current projections indicate that the elderly, both majority and minority, will continue to increase relative to the remainder of the population at least two decades into the next century. This trend will be accompanied by increases in the absolute number of elderly.

Those 75 years of age and older, often referred to as the "old old" or the "frail elderly," will be the fastest growing segment within the population 65 and over. Individuals who have survived to reach advanced ages are likely to have one or several chronic illnesses that may impair their ability to care for themselves on a daily basis. Functional disability, usually defined as the inability to fulfill social roles, is a threat to the elderly because it may mean becoming dependent on family members or requiring intervention from public or private agencies. Loss of the ability to do for one's self requires that the frail elderly have a network of supportive services to assist them with activities of daily living—bathing, dressing, housekeeping, food preparation, management of medical regimes, and other needs. This system of support is usually referred to as long-term care.

Long-term care as defined by Kane and Kane is a "range of services that address the health, personal care, and social capacity for self-care."[3] The goals of long-term care are to maximize functional independence, to rehabilitate and restore individuals to a previous level of functioning, to utilize the least restrictive environment in rendering care, to provide humane care for those who are permanently dependent, and to ensure death with dignity.[4] Because one of the goals of long-term care is to promote independent living, coordination of numerous services is required.

This chapter examines the long-term care system as it relates to the needs of black Americans surviving to advanced ages. The objectives will be to document the long-term care needs of the black elderly including the social, economic, and health care needs—all of which contribute to the ability to maintain independent functioning. In addition, the responsiveness of various institutions to the needs of the black elderly are also reviewed as are policy changes in the 1980s.

Although the present inefficiencies in U.S. policy regarding the long-term care of the aged weigh heavily on the lives of all older Americans, the black elderly are particularly vulnerable. Their disproportional representation among the impoverished elderly via life-long discrimination, their greater reliance on the public sector for financial viability, and the fact that they are increasing at a faster rate than the majority population indicate their importance in any policy decisions regarding long-term care.

LONG-TERM CARE NEEDS

In order to maximize effective functioning and independence, long-term care must address the social as well as physical needs of the elderly. Some indication of the potential number of elderly at risk is also required. In evaluating the long-term care needs of the black elderly, the following issues will be explored: number at risk, economic status, health status, health care service needs, informal support and institutional services.

Number at Risk for Long-Term Care

Ideally, the elderly should come to the end of their lives having experienced full economic independence, little or no disability resulting from chronic conditions, and a relatively short period of illness before death, at the end of the maximum life span possible for the human body.[5] Most elderly, however, will not attain the ideal and will vary in how closely they approxmate it. For some a relatively long time will elapse between loss of capacity for self-care and death, whereas for others this will be a relatively short period.

Manuel and Reid have examined minority/majority aging trends since the beginning of the twentieth century and have noted some black/white differences.[6] Relative to the white population, for example, the number of black elderly increased at substantially lower rates prior to 1940. After 1940, however, the relative rates of growth were reversed, possibly because of high black fertility levels following the Civil War. This trend continued in the last decade and is projected to continue into the next century. Table 10.1 shows the number, race, and distribution for all ages and 65 years and over in the United States for every ten years from 1970 to the year 2000. It should be noted that the 1980 figures for the category "other" are severely distorted owing to changes in the classification of Hispanic-origin persons.[7]

In 1980 the number of elderly 75 years and older was approximately 9.9 million out of 25 million total individuals aged 65 and over. By 1990 the frail elderly will number 13 million, and by 2000 16 million. The number of black elderly 75 years and older will have tripled from 515,000 in 1970 to 1.2 million in 2000, and the number of white elderly in these ages will have doubled from 7 million to 14.7 million in this 30-year time period.

Calculations of percentage change from decade to decade show that the number of black elderly 75 and over will increase 45, 44.5, and 20.1 percent from 1970-80, 1980-90, and 1990-2000, respectively. Similar changes for the white elderly will be 28, 34.6, and 21 percent, respectively, for the same years. The increase in absolute numbers is attributed to the birth of large cohorts around the turn of the century and to the effects of declining mortality from infectious disease.[8] This combination of factors has resulted in a larger number of individuals than ever before surviving infancy and childhood when infectious diseases have their greatest impact.

Not only has the number of elderly increased dramatically in this century, but their proportion of the total population has also grown. This has resulted in aging of the population and is attributed to declining fertility levels.[9] In 1970 the elderly accounted for just under 10 percent of the population. The proportion who were 75 years and older was 3.8 percent, almost the same proportion as those 65 years and older in 1940—4 percent. In 1980, 7.9 and 11.3 percent of the black and white population, respectively, were elderly. Just under 3 percent (2.8 percent) of the black population was 75 years and older in 1980, compared to 4.8 percent of the white population. By the end of the century, these figures are projected to be 3.8 percent and 6.4 percent for the black and white elderly, respectively.

Table 10.1
Number and Distribution for All Ages and 65 Years and Over,
by Race: United States, 1970-2000

	1970 Number (1000s)	1970 %	1980 Number (1000s)	1980 %	1990 Number (1000s)	1990 %	2000 Number (1000s)	2000 %
Total Population	203,212	100%	226,546	100%	245,753	100%	256,098	100%
White	177,749	87.5	188,371	83.1	207,799	84.5	213,498	83.4
Black	22,580	11.1	26,495	11.7	31,352	12.7	33,957	13.2
Other	2,883	1.3	11,680	5.5	6,606	2.6	8,643	3.4
Total								
65 and over	20,066	9.8	25,549	11.3	31,352	12.8	33,621	13.1
75 and over	7,630	3.8	9,969	4.4	13,428	5.5	16,331	6.4
Black								
65 and over	1,558	6.9	2,086	7.9	2,537	8.2	2,833	8.3
75 and over	515	2.3	747	2.8	1,080	3.5	1,297	3.8
White								
65 and over	18,331	10.3	22,948	12.2	28,312	12.8	30,032	14.7
75 and over	7,050	4.0	9,040	4.8	12,170	5.5	14,747	6.9
Other[1]								
65 and over	177	1.0	515	2.0	503	1.6	756	2.2
75 and over	165	0.9	182	1.8	178	1.3	287	1.8

[1] Increase in population classified as Other between 1970 and 1980 and subsequent decrease is due in large part to changes in classification of the Hispanic population. See text note 7 for further explanation.

Source: U.S. Bureau of the Census, 1980 Census of the Population: United States Summary, General Population Characteristics, PC 80-1-B1. Washington, D.C.: USGPO, 1981. Current Population Reports, Series P-25, No. 952. Projections of the Population of the United States by Age, Sex and Race, 1983-2080. Washington, D.C.: USGPO, 1984.

Table 10.2 permits an examination of the age distribution and sex composition of the black and white elderly populations from 1970 to 2000. Particularly noteworthy is the declining proportion of the elderly population in the youngest age category, 65-69, and the increasing proportion in the oldest age category, 85 years and older. This occurs in all race and sex groups except black males, 1970-80. The proportion 85 years and older is slightly smaller for blacks than for whites. However, by 1990 a higher proportion of elderly black males than elderly white males will be 85 years and older, 7.7 and 7.0 percent, respectively.

In 1980 there were 68 black males for every 100 black females 65 years and older and approximately 72 white males for every 100 elderly white females. Racial differences reflect sex differences in mortality experience within each group. Black males experience higher mortality throughout their lives, and fewer survive to old age. Sex differences in mortality are greater among blacks than among whites. Sex ratios decline with advancing age for both racial groups. In 1980 the sex ratio at age 85 and older was 50 for blacks and 42.9 for whites. Thus, the population at risk will be increasingly dominated by females.

Economic Status

Estimates of the impact of retirement on the economic status of the elderly indicate that personal income is reduced by one-third to one-half after age 65, the age when the majority of older persons leave the labor force.[10] A declining standard of living seriously affects the frail elderly's ability to purchase assistance with personal care and to continue to maintain independent living arrangements. Many are not eligible for means-tested programs such as Medicaid which provide some in-home services. A great many fall into the gap of having too much income to qualify for assistance from public programs but too little to be able to afford to purchase services in the marketplace.

Present cohorts of black elderly face greater economic hardship than white elders. Income distribution and median income for 1981 are presented in Table 10.3. The open-ended category of $7,000 and over is used because of the small number of black females with incomes above that level. The table indicates that the black elderly are concentrated in the lower income categories, although this varies by sex. Black males, for example, are less likely than white females to have incomes lower than $3,000—13.6 and 20.4 percent, respectively. White males continue their race-sex advantage into old age. Over 60 percent have incomes of $7,000 or more compared to 31.2 percent for white females, 26.6 percent for black males, and 8.5 percent for black females. The advantage for white males would be even greater had more income categories been used since black males would have been concentrated in those categories within a few thousand dollars of the $7,000 cut-off.

Table 10.2
Percent Distribution by Sex and Sex Ratio of Population,
65 Years and Over for Blacks and Whites, 1970-2000

Age and Year	Black			White		
	Male	Female	Sex Ratio	Male	Female	Sex Ratio[1]
1970						
Total 65 and over	100%	100%	76.6	100%	100%	71.6
65-69	41.0	39.6	79.1	36.7	32.7	80.4
70-74	27.2	26.3	79.3	27.6	26.9	73.3
75-79	16.3	16.4	75.8	18.8	19.8	68.0
80-84	8.7	9.6	69.4	10.5	12.2	61.3
85 and over	6.8	8.0	64.8	6.3	8.3	54.7
1980						
Total 65 and over	100%	100%	68.3	100%	100%	67.2
65-69	39.2	35.9	74.6	37.7	31.5	80.4
70-74	27.6	26.5	71.1	27.7	25.8	72.3
75-79	18.1	19.0	65.1	17.9	19.4	62.0
80-84	8.8	10.1	60.0	10.0	12.8	52.0
85 and over	6.3	8.5	50.0	6.7	10.4	42.9
1990[2]						
Total 65 and over	100%	100%	60.6	100%	100%	66.7
65-69	35.4	30.6	70.0	35.4	29.0	81.0
70-74	26.0	24.4	64.6	27.1	24.2	74.1
75-79	19.5	20.6	57.4	19.3	20.1	64.0
80-84	11.4	13.4	51.7	11.2	14.1	53.0
85 and over	7.7	11.0	42.5	7.0	12.5	37.9

TABLE 10.2 (continued)

Age and Year	Black			White		
	Male	Female	Sex Ratio	Male	Female	Sex Ratio
2000[2]						
Total 65 and over	100%	100%	54.9	100%	100%	66.1
65-69	32.6	27.2	65.5	29.9	23.5	84.1
70-74	26.4	24.5	58.9	26.9	23.5	75.0
75-79	19.7	19.8	54.4	21.0	21.4	65.2
80-84	11.9	13.7	47.4	12.9	15.6	54.7
85 and over	9.9	14.7	36.8	9.2	16.1	38.1

[1] Sex ratio is number of males per 100 females.

[2] Projections based on Census Bureau's lower series.

Source: U.S. Bureau of the Census, 1980 Census of the Population: United States Summary, General Population Characteristics, PC 80-1-B1. Washington, D.C.: USGPO, 1983. Current Population Reports, Series P-25, No. 952. Projections of the Population of the United States by Age, Sex and Race, 1983-2080. Washington, D.C.: USGPO, 1984.

The impact of racial discrimination appears to be clearly illustrated by a comparison of black males and white females. In 1981 black males had a median income of $4,875 and white females a comparable median of $4,934. These amounts are similar, even though in 1979, 21 percent of black males 65 and over were in the labor force compared to 7.9 percent of white females. It can be postulated that these differences reflect the effects of discrimination on black males throughout their working lives. Furthermore, black females do worse economically than any race-sex group, with nearly 80 percent having had incomes of less than $5,000 in 1981.

Poverty rates are perhaps a better indicator of economic need because they indicate the proportion of persons below the level of income needed to maintain a minimum acceptable standard of living. In 1983 poverty levels for the population 65 and over were set at $4,775 for those living alone and $6,023 for an elderly couple.[11] Blacks, however, are still more likely to have incomes below the poverty level than are whites. Table 10.4 shows poverty rates for the elderly covering a thirteen-year period by race and sex. An examination of the data for 1983 indicates that black poverty rates were generally two to three times that of whites. Black females, who had a poverty rate of 41.7 percent overall and a rate of 63 percent for those who did not live in a family setting, were the most economically disadvantaged. Black males 65 years and older had a poverty rate of 28.3 percent. Among whites, poverty rates for males and females were 8.2 and 14.7 percent, respectively. Sex differences were generally smaller for those living in families but substantially wider for the elderly not in families. Black elderly females living with nonfamily members appear to have greater need for long-term care intervention in lieu of their greater inability to purchase services.

Racial disparities in economic status occur for a number of reasons. Blacks receive lower Social Security benefits, are less likely to have income from private pensions, and have fewer assets.[12] Williams reports that, in 1977, about 51 percent of all elderly living in family settings derived half or more of their total income from Social Security.[13] Comparable figures for the elderly in nonfamily settings were 80 percent for blacks and 69 percent for whites. Disparities in Social Security benefits are therefore an important consideration in the racial income gap. Snyder examines potential reasons for the lower Social Security benefits for black males and points out that lower pension levels reflect differences in earnings and work history which are the basis of current Social Security benefit formulas.[14] Labor force attachment is a critical determinant of lifetime earnings. Frequent spells of unemployment during teen and young adult years are related to frequency of employment in the middle and later years, resulting in lower earnings on which benefits are calculated. Added to this are the striking differences in types of jobs

Table 10.3
Total Money Income and Median Income for Persons 65 Years and Older, by Race and Sex: United States, 1981

| Income | Black | | White | |
	Male	Female	Male	Female
	100%	100%	100%	100%
		Percent[1]		
$1-2,999 or less	13.6	33.2	5.6	20.4
$3,000-4,999	38.9	45.6	15.6	31.4
$5,000-6,999	20.7	12.5	17.8	17.2
$7,000 and over	26.6	8.5	61.0	31.2
Median Income	$4,875	$3,528	$8,586	$4,934

1 Percent may not sum to 100 due to rounding.

Source: U.S. Bureau of the Census, Current Population Reports, Series P-60. No. 137, "Money Income of Households, Families, and Persons in the United States: 1981," Washington, D.C.: USGPO, 1983.

Table 10.4
Percent Below Poverty Level for Blacks and Whites,
Aged 65 Years and Over by Race, Sex, and Family
Relationship: United States, 1970, 1980, and 1983

Year and Family Relationship	Black		White	
	Male	Female	Male	Female
1970				
Total	41.2	52.5	17.1	26.5
In Families	36.9	37.1	13.2	12.6
Unrelated individuals	58.5	78.2	36.1	47.5
1980				
Total	31.4	42.6	9.0	16.8
In Families	25.6	26.6	6.8	7.1
Unrelated individuals	45.1	66.5	21.1	29.3
1983				
Total	28.3	41.7	8.2	14.7
In Families	21.9	26.4	6.1	7.1
Unrelated individuals	45.9	63.4	18.4	24.5

Source: U.S. Bureau of the Census, Current Population Reports, Series P-60, No. 147, "Characteristics of the Population Below the Poverty Level: 1983," Washington, D.C.: USGPO, 1985.

which the present cohort of elderly males was able to secure over their lifetimes, with many being substantially underemployed.[15]

For the very poor elderly, Supplemental Security Income (SSI) provides an income minimum. This program, established in 1972 as Title XVI of the Social Security Act, federalized all previous state programs providing income maintenance to the elderly and disabled. This program is important to long-term care because recipients automatically qualify for Medicaid in most states and Medicaid is the primary source of public funding for long-term care. Unlike Social Security, it is means-tested and carries the stigma of welfare. In 1983 maximum monthly payment for a single person was $304.30 and $456.40 for a married couple—benefits that are well below the poverty level.[16] In 1977, 49.4 percent of aged families depending on both SSI and Social Security were below the poverty line. States have the option of supplementing these payments further, and about half of all 50 states provide such supplementation to persons living independently.[17]

In 1981, 1.7 million elderly were SSI recipients.[18] The black elderly are disproportionately represented among recipients and are therefore at the mercy of state agencies.[19] Estes has noted that programs designed for the poor are not as well funded, for beneficiaries are generally individuals who have been poor all their lives and are viewed as undeserving.[20] The combination of erratic labor force participation resulting in lower Social Security benefits and greater dependence on public assistance programs is translated into less economic security for the black elderly.

Health Status: Mortality and Morbidity

Incapacity from the impact of chronic disease is a direct determinant of long-term care needs. Entrance into formal long-term care services is usually precipitated by an illness event and diagnosis of incapacity. A number of methods may be used in assessing the health status of the elderly population. Although physiological examinations may be more accurate than typical indicators, such as mortality and self-reported morbidity, this type of data is seldom available on a nationally represented sample of elderly. In this section, mortality, morbidity, and functional ability are examined as indicators of health status.

All age groups have benefited from the decline in mortality that accompanied industrialization in the United States. Declining mortality was most beneficial to the young during the first half of the century.[21] Since 1950, the elderly have also shown marked benefits. Between 1950 and 1979, mortality among those 65 and older declined by 17 percent, although the level was not the same in all race-sex groups.[22] Declining mortality has also been reflected in increasing life expectancy at age 65.

In 1950 average years of life remaining were 12.8 for males and 15 for females. In 1980 life expectancy at 65 was 14.1 and 18.3 for males and females, respectively.[23]

Older blacks also benefited from declining mortality.[24] In 1960, for example, the death rates for black males and females aged 64 to 74 were 5,978 and 4,064 per 100,000 population, respectively (Table 10.5). By 1980 these figures were 5,131 and 3,057 per 100,000. Mortality declined

Table 10.5
Death Rates for Aged Blacks and Whites, by Race, Sex, and Age: United States, 1960, 1970, 1980

Race, Sex and Age	1960[1]	Year 1970	1980
Black Males			
65-74	5,978.7	5,803.2	5,131.1
75-84	8,605.1	9,454.9	9,231.6
85 years and over	14,844.8	14,415.4	16,098.8
White Males			
65-74	4,848.4	4,810.1	4,035.7
75-84	10,299.6	10,098.8	8,829.8
85 years and over	21,750.0	20,392.6	19,097.3
Black Females			
65-74	4,064.2	3,860.9	3,057.4
75-84	6,730.0	6,691.5	6,212.1
85 years and over	13,052.6	12,131.7	12,367.2
White Females			
65-74	2,779.3	2,470.7	2,066.6
75-84	7,696.6	6,698.7	5,401.7
85 years and over	19,477.7	16,729.5	14,979.6

[1] Includes deaths of non-residents of the United States

Source: U.S. Department of Health and Human Services, Health-United States, 1983. DHHS Publication No. (PHS) 84-1232. Washington, D.C.:   USGPO, 1983.

in all age groups except for black males 75 to 84 between 1960 and 1970. This is probably due to a fluctuation for that year. Averages over several years are generally used to present a more accurate picture of trends but were not immediately available.

Although both blacks and whites have experienced improvements in mortality, blacks still have higher death rates than whites in age groups under 75. At age 75, racial differences in death rates reverse for both males and females (Table 10.5). The "crossover" phenomenon is still a mystery to researchers, given the higher death rates for blacks at younger ages. The leading explanation is that the higher mortality of blacks at younger ages selects out those who are most susceptible to disease, leaving a relatively healthier black population in the old age categories.[25] The "survival of the fittest" hypothesis suggests that the elderly black is indeed in better physical condition than the elderly white. However, survival does not necessarily mean good health. The lower mortality levels of blacks in advanced age may be interpreted as a signal that their need for long-term care is greater because they may be functionally incapacitated.

Cause of death statistics provide some insight into the nature of illness present prior to death. Jackson has presented an excellent analysis of racial differences in cause of death and in changes over the last twenty years.[26] In general, diseases of the heart, malignant neoplasms, and cerebrovascular disease account for the vast majority of deaths at advanced old age for both blacks and whites. However, there are some interesting differences. In 1977, for example, the death rate for all heart disease was higher for black males than for white males aged 75 to 79. Within that category, white males had higher death rates for ischemic heart disease.[27]

Morbidity data, particularly those that are self-reported, may be a better indicator of need because the elderly's own definitions of health will precipitate help-seeking behavior. Self-reported health status by the elderly is considered fairly reliable, for it has been found to be highly congruent with physicians' ratings of health[28] and related to level of functioning.[29]

Information from the National Health Interview Survey indicates that a greater proportion of blacks than whites in all age groups report poor health.[30] Among those aged 65 and over, 41.5 percent of blacks and 30 percent of whites reported poor health in the 1978 interviews.[31] Socioeconomic status and other factors affecting self-ratings were not controlled for. In a comparative study of white, black, and Cuban elderly, Linn, Hunter, and Linn found that blacks as well as Cubans were more likely to rate their health less favorably.[32] Blacks were also found to have significantly more hypertension and reported more pain.

Restricted activity days and days spent in bed are behavioral indicators of responses to illness. A day of restricted activity "is one on which a person cuts down on his or her usual activities for the whole of that day because of an illness or injury."[33] Restricted activity days increase with age (Table 10.6) for both blacks and whites. However, in both middle and old age, blacks have more restricted activity days, and, within each racial group, females tend to restrict their activities more than males. Among blacks 65 and over, males reported 54.3 days of restricted activity per person and females 58.7. Similar figures for whites were 34.1 for males and 41.8 for females. It may be noted that these are aggregate measures and do not indicate the behavior of each individual. When perceived health status and income were controlled, racial differences remained. The black elderly with poor health reported 91.3 days of restricted activity per person compared to 83.7 for whites. For those with incomes of less than $10,000, blacks 65 and over reported 62.5 days per person and whites 45.4 days.

Bed disability days are those days on which more than half the daylight hours are spent in bed.[34] As with restricted activity days, blacks in both middle age and old age were more likely to report a higher number of days spent in bed (Table 10.6). Among those 65 and over, black males reported 24.8 bed days of disability per person and black females 21.5 days. White elders spent less time in bed, with males reporting 11.4 days and females 13.9 days. As in the case of restricted activity days, perceived health status and income did not account for the racial differences.

Because acute, transitory illness may restrict activity or confine one to bed, disability from chronic illness may be a closer approximation of long-term health care needs. Limitation of activity from a chronic condition means being limited in an activity other than the usual activity.[35] For example, a housewife may be able to carry out her usual housework activities but may be unable to attend church or engage in other activities. Limitation in a major activity means not being able to fulfill one's ordinary activities.[36]

Table 10.7 presents limitation of activity and limitation in major activity by sex, perceived health status, and family income for blacks and whites in middle and old age. On both indicators, limitation increases with age. Among those 65 and over, the data indicate that a greater proportion of black males and females reported limitation than did whites. Among blacks, 60.7 percent of males and 54.6 percent of females reported limitation in some activity. Similar figures for whites were 47.6 percent for males and 41.9 percent for females. Blacks were also more likely to be limited in their major activity; 56.5 percent for black males, followed by black females (46.5%), white males (42.5%), and white females (34.2%). There were almost no racial differences among those with fair or poor health, indicating that self-rated health may account for much of the difference between the black and white elderly. Racial differences could not be attributed to disparities in family income.

Functional status, the capacity to meet the needs of family living—

Table 10.6
Restricted Activity and Bed Disability Days per Person per Year, for Blacks and Whites, Aged 45 and Over, by Sex, Perceived Health Status, and Family Income: United States, 1978-80

Sex, Health Status and Family Income	Restricted Activity Days		Bed Disability Days	
	Black[1]	White[1]	Black[1]	White[1]
Sex				
Male				
45-64	33.9	22.8	12.2	6.7
65 and over	54.3	34.1	24.8	11.4
Female				
45-64	42.1	26.3	15.5	8.7
65 and over	58.7	41.8	21.5	13.9
Health Status				
Excellent or Good				
45-64	14.7	12.0	5.2	3.5
65 and over	27.6	19.6	10.1	5.6
Fair or Poor				
45-64	76.1	75.8	27.8	24.8
65 and over	91.3	83.7	37.9	30.2
Family Income				
Under $10,000				
45-64	53.6	47.8	19.3	15.3
65 and over	62.5	45.4	24.2	14.1
$10,000 and over				
45-64	23.5	19.0	9.1	5.9
65 and over	40.5	28.9	15.9	10.3

1 Excludes persons of Hispanic origin.

Source: National Center for Health Statistics. F. M. Trevino and A. J. Moss. "Health Indicators for Hispanic, Black and White Americans." Vital and Health Statistics, Series 10, No. 148. DHHS No. (PHS) 84-1576. Washington, D.C.: USGPO, 1984.

Table 10.7
Percent of Persons with Limitation of Activity and Limitation in Major Activity Due to Chronic Conditions for Blacks and Whites, Aged 45 and Over, by Sex, Perceived Health Status, and Family Income: United States, 1978–80

Sex, Health Status and Family Income	Limitations of Activity Black[1]	Limitations of Activity White[1]	Limited in Major Activity Black[1]	Limited in Major Activity White[1]
Sex				
Male				
45–64	31.7	24.5	27.9	19.3
65 and over	60.7	47.6	56.5	42.5
Female				
45–64	21.8	32.6	26.9	16.4
65 and over	54.6	41.9	46.5	34.2
Health Status				
Excellent or Good				
45–64	14.2	12.9	10.8	8.2
65 and over	40.9	30.4	34.3	23.8
Fair or Poor				
45–64	61.3	64.5	54.2	56.7
65 and over	76.1	77.3	69.8	70.7
Family Income				
Under $10,000				
45–64	47.2	42.6	41.2	36.8
65 and over	61.0	49.0	54.2	41.8
$10,000 and over				
45–64	18.8	18.5	14.9	13.1
65 and over	42.9	38.7	36.0	32.6

1 Excludes persons of Hispanic origin.

Source: National Center for Health Statistics. F. M. Trevino and A. J. Moss. "Health Indicators for Hispanic, Black and White Americans." Vital and Health Statistics, Series 10, No. 148. DHHS No. (PHS) 84-1576. Washington, D.C.: USGPO, 1984.

such as eating, bathing, dressing, and meal preparation—is a sensitive indicator of the need for long-term care. Shanas, in a national study, found that about 12 percent of the elderly reported major limitation on the Activity of Daily Living Scale (ADL).[37] Major limitation was defined as a score of 3 or higher. Functional incapacity was twice as high for blacks as for whites, 21 percent and 11 percent, respectively, with a score of 3 or more. Differences by socioeconomic status were not reported. Black women were the most incapacitated group. As age increased, functional disability increased, but racial differences tended to narrow.

In summary, the black elderly have higher mortality rates than whites until age 75 when death rates reverse. Blacks 65 and over are more likely to report fair or poor health status, more restricted activity days, and more limitation in major activities.

Health Care Services

The higher rates of morbidity observed among the black elderly relative to the white elderly should result in greater utilization of health care services. Table 10.8 shows the number of physician visits averaged over all persons middle-aged and older by selected characteristics. The data do not reflect that some individuals will be high utilizers of services and that others will use no services at all.[38] Physician visits usually increase with age. However, for both blacks and whites, health status and family income appear to influence this relationship. Middle-aged persons with fair or poor self-assessed health had more physician visits than the elderly. Visits by elderly black males and females were 6.3 and 7.0 visits per person, respectively, according to the 1978-80 Health Interview Survey data. For the elderly reporting excellent or good health status, racial differences were negligible. For those reporting fair or poor health status, the black elderly had 8.9 visits, whereas the white elderly had 9.6 visits. Among those with incomes under $10,000, blacks had more physician visits (7.2) than whites (6.2).

Equity in access has been studied in numerous research investigations and is commonly defined as having attained a situation whereby utilization is based on health status or need rather than economic or racial characteristics.[39] Data from the 1960s generally indicated significant racial and income disparity for the elderly seeking health care here.[40] More recently, Wolinsky et al. used a multivariate model to test the influence of need for health care, race, income, and other factors on several measures of utilization.[41] Health status was the primary determinant, suggesting that race and poverty do not seriously hamper the elderly from seeking care when other determining factors are adjusted for. Regular source of care was a significant contributing factor, and

Table 10.8
Physician Visits per Person per Year, for Blacks and Whites,
Aged 45 and Over, by Sex, Perceived Health Status,
and Family Income: United States, 1978-80

Sex, Health Status and Family Income	Black[1]	White[1]
Sex		
Male		
45-64	5.0	4.6
65 and over	6.3	5.7
Female		
45-64	6.6	5.6
65 and over	7.0	6.6
Health Status		
Excellent or Good		
45-64	3.5	3.8
65 and over	4.8	4.9
Fair or Poor		
45-64	9.7	10.2
65 and over	8.9	9.6
Family Income		
Under $10,000		
45-64	6.9	6.3
65 and over	7.2	6.2
$10,000 and over		
45-64	4.9	4.9
65 and over	5.4	6.6

[1] Excludes persons of Hispanic origin.

Source: National Center for Health
         Statistics. F. M. Trevino and A. J.
         Moss. "Health Indicators for
         Hispanic, Black and White Americans."
         Vital and Health Statistics, SEries
         10, No. 148. DHHS No. (PHS) 84-1576.
         Washington, D.C.: USGPO, 1984.

there may be differences by race and income status in this predictor. Wolinsky and colleagues did note an inverse relationship between a regular source of dental care and income.[42]

Improved access to health care services for the elderly and declining racial and income disparities have been attributed in part to the impact of Medicare and Medicaid.[43] Medicare is a federal program available to all elderly regardless of income. Part A provides hospitalization insurance (HI) for all elderly eligible for Social Security and other federal pension programs at no cost for premiums and the opportunity to purchase coverage for others. Part B provides supplemental medical insurance (SMI) for a premium that covers physician visits and other services. Both require recipients to pay deductibles and coinsurance amounts and, consequently, only supplement the health care costs of the elderly. Medicare HI also supplements, on a limited basis, the cost for the elderly discharged to skilled nursing facilities and pays for some in-home health care.[44]

Medicare does not absorb all the costs associated with health care. Deductibles and coinsurance place a great burden on the elderly. In 1978 only 44 percent of the elderly's medical bills were paid for by the Medicare program, although the poor elderly on Medicaid may have done better. Out-of-pocket cost increased by 64 percent between 1978 and 1982, owing in part to the failure of reimbursement for "reasonable" costs to keep pace with rising physician fees, failure to cover long-term care, and failure to provide other services such as prescription drugs.[45]

In 1977 the black elderly had higher out-of-pocket expenses than the white elderly, $563 and $438, respectively.[46] Even if personal expenditures had been the same, the lower income status of the black elderly means that they were burdened by medical care costs to a greater extent. Deductibles and coinsurance payments are not based on ability to pay. Increasingly, all elderly individuals need private insurance coverage to offset these costs.

Link, Long, and Settle found that, among the elderly with no additional insurance, Medicare Part A deductibles acted as a barrier to hospitalization and Part B deductibles acted as a barrier to use of ambulatory services for those with no chronic illness.[47] In 1976 approximately 29 percent of Medicare enrollees had no such additional insurance. These authors noted no differential effects on low-income and nonwhite elderly, which is difficult to accept given the cost of such premiums. Premiums under SMI continue to inhibit participation— 460,000 elderly in 1978, a disproportionate number of whom are poor, black, rural, and reside in the South.[48]

Estimates indicate that the elderly use mental health facilities at about half the rate of the general population—7 versus 16 admissions per 1,000 population.[49] Part of the low utilization rates of institutional facilities is accounted for by the movement since the 1960s to shift mental health care to the community setting.[50] Deinstitutionalization resulted in many elderly being transferred to nursing homes. Although treatment in community health centers and other outpatient facilities has increased, the elderly make up only about 5 percent of case loads in these alternative treatment sites.[51] Medicare provisions for mental health services are much more restrictive than for physical disorders, and Medicaid benefits are strongly biased against outpatient services.[52] The structure of the Medicaid program encourages institutionalization of the mentally impaired elderly.

Informal Support

The informal support system includes family, friends, and neighbors who assist the disabled elderly in their daily activities. Although only 5 percent of the elderly are institutionalized, evidence indicates that a much larger proportion of the noninstitutionalized are in need of help with functional activities. Shanas, in a national survey of the community residing elderly, found that about 3 percent were bedfast and about 7 percent were homebound.[53] Adding to this figure those who have some difficulty moving about yielded a ratio of 3 elderly in the community needing long-term care services to every 1 institutionalized.[54]

The primary role of the informal support system in long-term care has raised a number of issues that should be reviewed, including the composition of the informal support system, the kinds of assistance given, the impact of providing services on caregivers, and the likelihood that such support will continue.[55] In view of the greater likelihood of being institutionalized when an elder is without family support, family composition clearly provides information on the nature of the informal support system.[56] Marital status and living arrangements, as indicators of family composition, provide a general view of potential kin resources. Much of this research has not given consideration to racial differences, and many areas remain unexplored for the black elderly and their families.

Spouses are the primary source of assistance for the married elderly.[57] The probability of being married declines with increasing age as mortality takes its toll and varies by both race and sex. Blacks 75 years and older are less likely to be married than whites in this age group, and, within both racial groups, females have significantly lower probabilities of being married than males. Women's longer life expectancy places them at risk of being without spouses for a considerable number of years. Current Population Survey data show that, in 1980, 53 percent of black males and 17.5 percent black females 75 and over were married and living with their spouse. Similar figures for whites were 72.3 percent and 24.5 percent for males and females, respectively.[58] Based on the availability of a spouse, white males had the greatest advantage and black females the greatest disadvantage.

Although the presence of a spouse can be an advantage, other family members may assist that spouse or act as substitutes when no spouse is available. Examination of living arrangements indicates the potential availability of kin from the wider family network. Living arrangements for the elderly aged 65 to 74 and 75 and over are presented in Table 10.9.

Table 10.9
Living Arrangements of Persons 65 Years and Older,
by Race, Sex, and Age: United States, 1980

Age	Black		White	
	Male	Female	Male	Female
65-74				
Number	595	776	5874	7699
Percent	100%	100%	100%	100%
Householder	84.7	56.3	92.3	45.4
Head of family household	78.2	39.4	87.2	19.2
Head of nonfamily household	2.4	3.2	0.9	1.5
Living alone	19.4	57.4	13.8	79.3
Not a Household	15.3	42.3	7.7	54.6
Relative of Head	72.5	96.7	82.6	98.1
Nonrelative of Head	27.5	3.3	17.4	1.9
75 and over				
Number	252	407	2929	4944
Percent	100%	100%	100%	100%
Householder	80.2	65.6	90.5	61.9
Head of family household	64.3	34.8	75.8	16.6
Head of nonfamily household	2.5	4.1	0.8	2.1
Living alone	33.2	61.0	22.5	81.3
Not a Household	19.8	34.2	10.4	38.1
Relative of Head	90.0	95.0	86.8	96.9
Nonrelative of Head	10.0	5.0	13.2	3.1

Source: U.S. Bureau of the Census, Current Population Reports, Series P-20, No. 365, Marital Status and Living
Arrangements: March, 1980. Washington, D.C.: USGPO, 1981.

Among those 65 to 74 years of age, the majority of elders were house-holders (headed their own households) in 1980; 84.7 percent of black males, 56.3 percent of black females, and 92.3 percent of white males. The only exception were white females: only 45.4 percent headed their own household.

Males of both racial groups were more likely to be householders than were females. Females were more likely to head single-person house-holds. Among all household heads, 57.4 percent of black females and 79.3 percent of white females headed households in which they were the only member. The overrepresentation of white females living alone is consistent with their predominance in the nursing home population.[59] Other differences included the greater likelihood of black females (39.4% of all householders) than white females (19.2% of all householders) being heads of family households. This reflects the greater tendency for older black females to have children under eighteen residing in the home.[60]

Among those 75 years and older in 1980, females of both racial groups were more likely to be householders than were those in the younger group. This probably resulted from the experience of widowhood. In contrast, the proportion heading a family household was significantly less likely for this older group, indicating that many do not have family available in the same living quarters. Among all persons in this age group heading a household in 1980, white females were more likely to live alone (81.3%), followed by black females (61%), black males (33.2%), and white males (22.5%). Over a third of both black and white females were nonhouseholders. Of these, 95 and 96.9 percent of black and white females, respectively, resided with relatives. Just under 20 percent of black males and 10 percent of white males were not household heads. Of this group, white males were more likely to reside in the households of nonrelatives (13.2%) than were black males (10%).

Living arrangements for the frail elderly suggest that a substantial number head single-person households and may not have the support needed when they become incapacitated. This information tells us noth-ing about the informal support available from kin, friends, and neighbors not residing in the household. Shanas found that the potential for support is high. About 80 percent of all persons 65 and over had living children at the time of the 1975 survey, and a significant proportion lived within ten minutes of at least one child. Moreover, 77 percent had seen one of their children within the week before the survey, with 50 percent of these having seen a child the day of the survey.[61] Unfortunately, the quality of the visiting patterns was not determined.

Siblings also represent potential sources of help for the elderly. Shanas found that 70 percent of the elderly 75 years and over had surviv-ing siblings, and a third had seen at least one during the week of the survey. Among those who had never married, three-fourths had seen a sibling during the previous week. It would also appear that other relatives figure prominently in the informal support system, for 30 percent of the elderly reported seeing more distant kin.[62] This area needs to be explored more closely for the black elderly because higher mortality levels in younger ages may reduce the pool of children and siblings available to those at advanced ages. It is conceivable that younger, more distant kin might play a proportionately greater role in providing assistance within black families.

An issue that has a direct bearing on long-term care is the extent to which the informal system renders care to the sick and disabled elderly. The findings that twice as many infirm elderly reside in the community and are cared for mostly by family members suggest that the informal support system provides more services than merely visiting the sick.[63] Watson, in a sample of black elderly residing in the South, also found that assistance in times of illness was more likely to come from family members.[64] Within the informal care system, the spouse generally takes the greatest responsibility in giving care to the ill and disabled.[65] Among nonspouse caregivers, it is usually a woman who takes the primary role, with daughters being the most likely source.[66]

Sangl discusses the type of assistance given to disabled elderly. Informal caregivers provide assistance with basic activities of living (walking, bathing, dressing, eating, and grooming) and with instrumental activities (housekeeping, transportation, food preparation, grocery shopping, and personal business affairs).[67] Emotional support is also provided, especially by friends and neighbors.[68]

Caring for a disabled older relative or spouse may eventually take its toll, resulting in financial, social, and emotional strain on the caregiver. Financial strain has been reported among spouse caregivers with few economic resources.[69] It is generally agreed, however, that the social and emotional problems are more acute than the financial. They include feelings of worry, being burdened, and being socially isolated.[70] Women, who make up the majority of caregivers, must often balance competing demands from work, spouses, and their own housework.[71] The issue of role conflict between work and caregiving is particularly salient to black families, where a working wife is perhaps more critical to family survival and whose income cannot be foregone to care for an elderly relative.

Johnson and Catalano have found that the stress of caregiving may also influence the relationship between the older person and family members, becoming characterized by conflict as time passes. They have also found that caregivers employ a number of coping mechanisms, including psychological distancing and enlarging the family network to include other members. Some caregivers become totally consumed by the caring role, making it a full-time responsibility and defining it as psychologically rewarding.[72]

Institutional Services

Until recently, long-term care was synonymous with nursing home care in the United States, reflecting a historical emphasis on institutional care for the elderly unable to meet the requirements of daily living. The emphasis on institutional care was of little concern until escalating public expenditures and a growing population at risk forced the recognition that the long-term care system was not adequate to meet rising demand. According to Fox and Clauser, 1.3 million persons 65 years of age and older were in nursing homes in 1977; this figure is expected to reach 2.8 million by 2000.[73] They also report that public payments for nursing home care increased from $3 billion in 1973 to $10 billion in 1979.

Medicaid is the predominant source of public financing for nursing home care. In 1979 the program accounted for 49.3 percent of all nursing home expenditures.[74] Given that the black elderly are more likely to be eligible for Medicaid owing to their disproportional representation among SSI recipients, one would expect equal, if not greater, access to nursing homes.

Table 10.10 presents information on the elderly residing in personal care and nursing homes from 1963 to 1977.[75] In each period nonwhite elderly were substantially less likely to be institutionalized in these types of facilities than were the white elderly. In 1963, prior to passage of Medicaid legislation, the nonwhite elderly were institutionalized at a rate of 10.3 compared to a rate of 26.6 for elderly whites. By 1977, over a decade after enactment of Medicaid, the rates were 30.4 for the nonwhite elderly and 49.7 for the white elderly. Differences were greater for the frail elderly, those 75 to 84 and 85 years and older. Disparities declined between 1963 and 1977, and, interestingly, rates were higher for nonwhites aged 65 to 74 in 1977.

Explanations for the lower utilization of nursing home services by the black elderly range from family preferences for retaining elderly members in the home to discrimination on the part of operators. Part of the explanation may be that older blacks are still more likely to be placed in mental institutions.[76] *Health Care in a Context of Civil Rights*, a report from the Institute of Medicine of the National Academy of Science, made the following points concerning racial differences:

(1) Racial differences in life expectancy do not account for lower use by Blacks because the disparities in use of nursing homes exist above 75 where survivorship by Blacks is high, (2) superior health status of Blacks does not account for lower use since elderly Blacks have more disabilities than elderly whites, (3) it is possible that Blacks living as part of the extended family is a result rather than a reason for less use of nursing homes, (4) some persons believe that Blacks reside proportionately higher in unlicensed boarding facilities, (5) nursing homes dis-

Table 10.10
Nursing Home and Personal Care Home Residents 65 Years
and Older per 1,000 Population, by Race: United States,
1963, 1969, 1973–74, and 1977

Year and Age	Nonwhite	White
1963		
65 and over	10.3	26.6
65–74	5.9	8.1
75–84	13.8	41.7
85 years and over	41.8	157.7
1969		
65 and over	17.6	38.5
65–74	9.6	11.7
75–84	22.9	54.1
85 years and over	52.4	221.9
1973–1974[1]		
65 and over	21.9	47.3
65–74	10.6	12.5
75–84	30.1	61.9
85 years and over	91.4	269.0
1977[2]		
65 and over	30.4	49.7
65–74	16.8	14.2
75–84	38.6	70.6
85 years and over	102.0	229.0

[1] Excludes residents in personal care or
domiciliary care homes.

[2] Includes residents in domiciliary care
homes.

NOTE: Hispanic origin not designated for
years 1963 and 1969 and may be included in
either racial category. Hispanics included in
white category for years 1973–1974 and 1977.

Source: U.S. Department of Health and Human
Services, Health-United States, 1983. DHHS
Pub. No. (PHS) 84-1232. Washington, D.C.:
USGPO, 1983.

criminate against Medicaid patients, a disproportionate number of whom are
Black.[77]

With regard to discrimination against Medicaid patients, the report
went on to note that in some Southern states, such as Mississippi, Alabama, and South Carolina, white Medicaid recipients reside in nursing
homes in excess of their representation among the state's elderly poor.[78]

Schafft suggests that discrimination may operate in the placement of individuals in institutional care owing to the "ambiguity of the guidelines directing the implementation of Title VI" of the Civil Rights Act.[79] Nursing homes receiving federal funds must use referral sources in such a way as to preclude discrimination in "relationship to the population of the service area or potential service area.[80] Yet, as Schafft points out, definitions of the service area are often not specified in compliance investigations. Furthermore, Title VI guidelines do not apply to other referral agents in the community and may, therefore, be a source of discrimination in placement.

Researchers in this area have also noted that institutionalization often results when the family has exhausted its resources and stamina and question whether family support can continue at its present level.[81] Some studies have shown that willingness to care erodes over time.[82] Several suggestions have been made for shoring up the informal system, including public provision of more homemaker and companion services and a variety of economic incentives.[83] Policy has not moved in this direction and probably will not unless it can be shown that such support will reduce institutionalization, thereby reducing costs.

FEDERAL AND STATE POLICY IN THE 1980S

The need for long-term care is expanding at a time when the country is experiencing economic uncertainty. A fiscal crisis was declared at both the federal and state levels early in the decade, resulting in a number of austerity measures.[84] Austerity measures instituted at the federal level included dismantling social programs, altering Social Security and Medicare, and shifting increased fiscal and managerial responsibility to the states in jointly funded programs.[85] The Omnibus Budget Reconciliation Act of 1981, for example, reduced the federal Medicaid and Title XX contribution to states in exchange for greater flexibility in program administration. States responded by changing eligibility and services and shifting more responsibility to recipients.[86] The shift to more administrative control by states means that the states will have more discretion in programs that provide long-term care services. The black elderly who live in poverty and who receive state assistance will depend on state generosity and fiscal ability to meet their long-term care needs. Changes in major programs instituted by the Reagan administration will be reviewed in this section. Policy changes discussed here will have implications for the black elderly and long-term care because they affect the ability to attain an adequate standard of living, decent health care, and social services.

Income Maintenance

Social Security, threatened by a short-term funding problem in 1980, became a central policy issue. A number of changes have been implemented, including gradually raising the age for full benefits to 67 between the years 2000 and 2027, eliminating minimum benefits for future beneficiaries, increasing the payroll tax on employees, and gradually ending benefits for dependents aged eighteen to twenty-two enrolled in school.[87]

Some changes will affect only future elderly cohorts, whereas others are having an immediate effect on their families. Black families will be particularly affected by increases in the already regressive payroll tax because a greater proportion have incomes below the level where taxation ends. Families provide care for impaired elderly, and their financial viability will affect their ability to continue such support. Eliminating minimum payments will reduce the incomes of many black elderly whose benefits are lower. Because racial discrimination does not appear to be lessening in the 1980s, future cohorts of blacks may face problems similar to those of their parents and grandparents. Raising the retirement age may mean that even fewer blacks will live long enough to draw benefits. McFadden notes that for the elderly working in manual occupations, where minorities are concentrated, two more years of employment imposes a burden.[88] In addition, eligibility for the Social Security Disability program, which has benefited middle-aged blacks, was tightened during the 1980s.

SSI provides a guaranteed minimum to the aged and disabled, and states have the option of supplementing these payments. SSI recipients are automatically eligible for Medicaid in most states, so the program is important not only as an income maintenance strategy but also because of Medicaid's relationship to the financing of long-term care. Black elderly are overrepresented in this program.

Few changes were proposed in the SSI program during the 1980s. Benefit amounts were increased slightly.[89] On the other hand, the program has problems that continue to affect long-term care. Because the program reduces benefits to the elderly living with relatives by one-third, families are discouraged from taking the frail elderly into their homes, and those who do are penalized. Full benefits are given to nursing home residents. It is more advantageous for poor families to place their elderly kin in nursing homes where they can receive room, board, and other services at no cost to the family.

States have full discretion in determining eligibility for their supplemental SSI payments, and sixteen states have opted to make their Medicaid eligibility more restrictive than eligibility requirements under

SSI. Consequently, there is substantial inequality in benefits. In many states, individuals below poverty do not qualify for Medicaid.[90] In response to fiscal problems, state supplemental payments have not kept pace with inflation, and many new applicants cannot qualify because income eligibility standards have not been adjusted for inflation.[91]

Health Care

Medicare expenditures increased by 104 percent between 1978 and 1982.[92] As a result, cost containment in the Medicare program has been pursued with vigor in the 1980s. The new regulations are aimed at reducing eligibility and benefits and changing the reimbursement structure.[93] Under the Omnibus Budget Reconciliation Act of 1981, Part A Medicare deductibles were increased. The Part B premium was set at a constant percentage of program costs by the Tax Equity and Fiscal Responsibility Act of 1982.[94] These changes mean greater financial burdens for the black elderly and may result in reduced access. These changes also mean less money for purchasing private insurance.

Prospective payments were implemented to restructure Medicare hospital reimbursements, the most costly part of the program. Medicare now reimburses hospitals on the basis of diagnostic related groups (DRGs). The DRG reimbursement plan has raised a number of issues, including whether patients will be discharged too soon and whether it will result in hospitals admitting the most inexpensive cases.[95] It also raises questions concerning the disposition of the elderly after hospitalization, such as whether placement in nursing homes will increase and whether more home health services with be forthcoming.[96] The DRG reimbursement plan could have both positive and negative effects on the black elderly. On the one hand, it could reduce their length of stay and thereby reduce out-of-pocket costs. On the other, they may be released to home care before it is suitable. This problem becomes even more salient when the low utilization of skilled nursing facilities by blacks is taken into consideration.[97]

Medicaid, the health program for the poor, has become one of the most expensive items in state budgets. State Medicaid expenditures increased by 91 percent between 1978 and 1982.[98] As a result, the states have sought to cut costs during the 1980s. Federal policy changes reduced funding to states but gave them greater flexibility in determining eligibility and in structuring programs. States have responded to the combination of less federal money, declining state revenues, and greater discretion in a number of ways. Some states have reduced their Medicaid rolls by failing to raise income standards for public assistance payments.[99] As fewer become eligible for means-tested programs, fewer qualify for Medicaid. States have also instituted restrictions on utilization, such as limiting days of hospitalization, frequency of service use, and pre-authorization screening for hospital, physician, skilled nursing home care, and home health care.[100] States can also require copayments for a number of services.[101] Medicaid cuts have disproportionately affected the young by affecting eligibility standards under the AFDC program. On the other hand, between 1978 and 1982 the number of aged Medicaid recipients declined by 4 percent.[102]

Social Services

Many long-term care programs, such as chore and homemaker services, are funded through the social welfare system. Social services have never been adequately funded, and retrenchment has characterized the 1980s. Expenditures for the food stamp program were reduced by eliminating inflation adjustments to income in 1982 and by postponing later adjustments.[103] Housing assistance programs have increased tenants' share of rental payments from 25 to 30 percent, and funding for low-income energy assistance has been reduced.[104]

Federal funding under Title XX, absorbed by the Social Services Block Grant, was reduced by 20 percent.[105] States now have greater control over these monies, and federal reporting requirements have been reduced. State control raises some issues of equitable distribution in light of apparent retrenchment on civil rights issues and the historical relationship between states' rights and black freedom. States have responded to the federal reduction by restricting eligibility for optional groups, such as the medically needy, requiring cost sharing, reducing hours of and number of services, prioritizing services, and supplementing social services with funds from other programs.[106]

CONCLUSIONS: ALTERNATIVES TO THE PRESENT SYSTEM

Long-term care of the elderly, as repeatedly stressed throughout this chapter, requires both medical and social support services. Long-term care has traditionally been biased toward the provision of health services. Within the medical approach, institutionalization has received the bulk of public funding. Medicare, the most expensive in-kind program for the elderly, is oriented toward hospital care. The limited amount of home care permitted is biased in favor of medical services, such as nursing care, physical therapy, and home health aid.[107] Medicaid expenditures overwhelmingly support services offered by nursing homes. Home health receives lower priority, and even nonmedical services must be prescribed by a physician.

States, given greater flexibility by the federal government in packaging services, are now experimenting with various alternatives to institutionalization. Alternatives include home health care, day health care, day care, and other in-home services. The black elderly may benefit from such programs in the long run because they are less likely to reside in nursing homes. However, the development of alternative arrangements is still in its infancy and is characterized by conflicting goals and opinions concerning appropriate target groups for various types of alternatives.

The arguments for alternatives include the extensive unmet need and the heavy economic burden on families in caring for functionally disabled elderly. Many have argued that a number of elderly are inappropriately placed in nursing homes owing to lack of alternatives.[108] Kane and Kane have commented on the quality of care problems found in institutions, including the overuse of medication and the often negative impact of institutional living on the elderly.[109] Increasing costs, the fragmentation of long-term care across social and health care programs, and inequality across states and consumer groups round out the arguments for changing the present system.[110] These are contradictory guides for policy, because some suggest expansion of services (to eliminate unmet need) and others suggest restrictions (the need to control costs).

The contradictions stemming from varying arguments for alternatives are reflected in conflicting definitions of alternatives. Should alternatives be substitutes or complements to institutional care? The differences in orientation are really questions concerning the appropriate target population. Should change be aimed at all persons presently institutionalized, those at risk of institutionalization, or those who are inappropriately living in nursing homes? If the noninstitutionalized are the target, which subgroups should have priority?[111]

Several demonstration projects have been undertaken or are in progress. Most have focused on comparing cost and quality outcomes for noninstitutionalized and institutionalized persons. A number of methodological problems have been encountered. Some projects have failed to include all costs associated with providing care in the home, such as room and board, and the opportunity cost foregone by the caregiver.[112] Some findings have been contradictory. For example, some studies have found that community-based care is less expensive, while others have found that it is more expensive. Palmer cites a study by Pollack showing that, at some level of impairment, home care becomes more expensive than nursing home care.[113] Some studies have also shown better outcomes for community-based studies at higher costs.[114] Research that evaluates differences between community-based alternatives has been lacking.

The debate over long-term care alternatives is likely to go on for some time. Any significant change in policy will require changes in all the programs that create the long-term care system. For example, changes in Medicaid policy would have to remove or modify spend-down provisions so that the elderly would truly have the alternative of returning to the community. Another issue that will have to be addressed is cost containment in community-based care, for it will be difficult to regulate.[115] Wood and Estes have observed that the service delivery system is increasingly characterized by a decline in nonprofit organizations providing multiple services and an increase in proprietary organizations contracting to provide discrete services.[116] Community-based care may not be the answer to nursing home care in terms of costs or quality. Proprietary providers may have the same bias against minorities and the poor as proprietary nursing homes seem to.

Policy changes and budget cuts implemented in the 1980s pose serious threats to the black elderly's access to long-term care services. Recognizing that the black elderly need protection in this area, the National Caucus and Center on Black Aged (NCBA) formed the Committee on Long Term Care and the Black Aged in 1983. Public hearings were subsequently held during NCBA's 1984 annual meeting, and a list of recommendations was made.

Although general issues were addressed in the policy statement, specific recommendations were made for the minority elderly. Minority-specific suggestions include: (1) documentation of service denial, (2) enforcement of affirmative action in nursing homes, (3) increased emphasis on community-based care and provision of fiscal and technical assistance to minority vendors, (4) development of institutional care for minority neighborhoods, (5) low-income loans to minority institutions for improvements, and (6) greater emphasis on outreach and referrals.[117] However, the chances for implementing these recommendations are remote. Instead, further fragmentation, underfunding, and under-utilization of services will continue as new legislation is forced into old frameworks.

NOTES

1. Beth Soldo, "America's Elderly in the 1980s," *Population Bulletin* 35 (1980): 3-47.

2. Ron Manuel and John Reid, "A Comparative Demographic Profile of the Minority and Nonminority Aged," in Ron Manuel, ed., *Minority Aging: Sociological and Social Psychological Issues* (Westport, Conn.: Greenwood Press, 1982), pp. 31-52.

3. Robert L. Kane and Rosalie A. Kane, "Long-term Care: A Field in Search of Values," in their *Values and Long Term Care* (Lexington, Mass.: D. C. Heath, 1982), p. 4.

4. James Callahan, Jr., and Stanley S. Wallack, "Major Reforms in Long-Term Care," in their *Reforming the Long-Term Care System* (Lexington, Mass.: D. C. Heath, 1981), pp. 3-10.

5. James Fries, "Aging, Natural Death and the Compression of Mortality," *New England Journal of Medicine* 303 (1980): 130-135.

6. See Manuel and Reid, "A Comparative Demographic Profile of the Minority and Nonminority Aged," p. 32.

7. The sharp increase in the Other 1970-80 category and subsequent decrease are due in large part to changes in the classification of the Hispanic population. In 1970 those who identified their ethnic origin as Other but who also indicated Spanish ancestry were classified as white. In 1980 these persons were left in the Other category. Furthermore, within the Other category black and white Hispanics cannot be distinguished in the published data for purposes of assigning them to the black and white racial categories.

8. Abdel Omran, "Epidemiologic Transition in the U.S.: The Health Factor in Population Change," *Population Bulletin* 32 (1977), pp. 3-41.

9. Soldo, "America's Elderly in the 1980s," p. 15.

10. Ibid.

11. U.S. Bureau of the Census, *Current Population Reports*, ser. P.60, no. 147, "Characteristics of the Population Below the Poverty Level: 1983" (Washington, D.C.: GPO, 1985).

12. Donald Snyder, "Social Policy and Economic Status: Reducing Income Differences Between Elderly Whites and Nonwhites," in Manuel, ed., *Minority Aging*, pp. 151-157.

13. Blanche Williams, *Characteristics of the Black Elderly, 1980* (Washington, D.C.: U.S. Department of Health and Human Services, 1980).

14. Snyder, "Social Policy and Econmic Status," p. 55.

15. Manuel and Reid, "A Comparative Demographic Profile of the Minority and Nonminority Aged," p. 33.

16. James Schulz, *Economics of Aging* (Belmont, Calif.: Wadsworth, 1985), p. 146.

17. Williams, *Characteristics of the Black Elderly, 1980*, p.56.

18. Charlene Harrington, "Social Security and Medicare: Policy Shifts in the 1980s," in Carroll Estes, Robert Newcomer, et al., eds., *Fiscal Austerity and Aging: Shifting Government Responsibility for the Elderly* (Beverly Hills, Calif.: Sage, 1983), pp. 83-111.

19. Williams, *Characteristics of the Black Elderly, 1980*, p. 57.

20. Carroll Estes, "Fiscal Austerity and Aging," in Estes, Newcomer, et al., eds., *Fiscal Austerity and Aging*, pp. 17-40.

21. Omran, "Epidemiologic Transition in the U.S.," p. 21.

22. Dorothy Rice, "Health Care Needs of the Elderly," in Charlene Harrington, Robert Newcomer, Carroll Estes, et al., eds., *Long Term Care of the Elderly: Public Policy Issues* (Beverly Hills, Calif.: Sage, 1985), pp. 41-66.

23. Ibid.

24. Jacquelyne J. Jackson, "Death Rates of Aged Blacks and Whites, United States, 1964-1978," *The Black Scholar* 13 (January-February 1982): 36-48; and Jacquelyne J. Jackson, *Minority Aging* (Belmont, Calif.: Wadsworth, 1980), pp. 61-81.

25. Kenneth Manton, "Differential Life Expectancy: Possible Explanations During the Later Aging," in Manuel, ed., *Minority Aging*, pp. 63-68; and Kenneth Manton, Sharon Poss, and Steve Wing, "The Black/White Mortality

Crossover: Investigation from the Perspective of the Components of Aging," *The Gerontologist* 19, no. 3 (June 1979): 291-299.

26. Jackson, "Death Rates of Aged Blacks and Whites, United States, 1964-1978," pp. 36-48; and Jackson, *Minority Aging*, pp. 61-81.

27. Ibid.

28. George Maddox, "Self-Assessment of Health Status," *Journal of Chronic Disease* 17 (1964): 449-460; and George Maddox and Eleanor Douglas, "Self-Assessment of Elderly Subjects," *Journal of Health and Social Behavior* 14 (1973): 87-93.

29. Margaret Linn, Kathleen Hunter, and Bernard Linn, "Self-Assessed Health, Impairment and Disability in Anglo, Black, and Cuban Elderly," *Medical Care* 18, no. 3 (March 1980): 282-288.

30. P. M. Ries, "Americans Assess Their Health: United States, 1978," *Vital and Health Statistics* 10, no. 142 (Washington, D.C.: NCHS-Public Health Service, no. 83-1570, 1983).

31. Ibid.

32. Linn, Hunter, and Linn, "Self-Assessed Health," p. 283.

33. F. M. Trevino and A. J. Moss, "Health Indicators for Hispanic, Black and White Americans," *Vital and Health Statistics* 10, no. 148 (Washington, D.C.: NCHS-Public Health Service, No. 84-1576, 1984).

34. Ibid.

35. Ibid.

36. Ibid.

37. Ethel Shanas, "Self-Assessment of Physical Function: White and Black Elderly of the United States," in Susanne Haynes and Manning Feinlab, eds., *Epidemiology of Aging*, NIH Publication No. 80-969 (Washington, D.C.: Department of Health and Human Services, 1980), pp. 269-281.

38. Karen Davis and Cathy Schoen, *Health and the War on Poverty: A Ten Year Appraisal* (Washington, D.C.: Brookings Institution, 1978), p. 102.

39. Lu Ann Aday and Ronald Andersen, *Access to Medical Care* (Ann Arbor, Mich.: Health Administration Press, 1975); and Lu Ann Aday and Ronald Andersen, "A Framework for the Study of Access to Medical Care," *Health Services Research* 9 (1974): 108-220.

40. Davis and Schoen, *Health and the War on Poverty*, p. 103; and Karen Davis, "Equal Treatment and Unequal Benefits: The Medicare Program," *Milbank Memorial Fund Quarterly* 53 (1975): 449-488.

41. Fredrick Wolinsky et al., "Health Services Utilization Among the Non-institutionalized Elderly," *Journal of Health and Social Behavior* 24 (1983): 325-337.

42. Ibid.

43. Davis and Schoen, *Health and the War on Poverty*, p. 113; and Martin Ruther and Allen Dobson, "Equal Treatment and Unequal Benefits: A Re-Examination of the Use of_Medicare Services by Race, 1967-1976," *Health Care Financing Review* 2 (Winter 1981): 55-83.

44. Susan Lloyd and Nancy T. Greenspan, "Nursing Homes, Home Health Services and Adult Day Care," in Ronald Vogel and Hans C. Palmer, eds. *Long-Term Care: Perspectives from Research and Demonstrations* (Washington, D.C.: Health Care Financing Administration, 1983), pp. 133-166.

45. Carroll Estes and Philip Lee, "Social, Political and Economic Background of Long-Term Care Policy," in Harrington et al., eds., *Long-Term Care of the Elderly*, pp. 17-39.

46. Manuel and Reid, "A Comparative Demographic Profile of the Minority and Nonminority Aged," in Manuel, ed., *Minority Aging*, pp. 31-52.

47. Charles Link, Stephen Long, and Russell Settle, "Cost Sharing, Supplementary Insurance, and Health Services Utilization Among the Medicare Elderly," *Health Care Financing Review* 2 (Fall 1980): 25-31.

48. Davis and Schoen, *Health and the War on Poverty*, p. 105.

49. U.S. Department of Health and Human Services, *The Need for Long-Term Care: Information and Issues* (Washington, D.C.: DHHS Pub. No. 81-20704, 1981), pp. 32-33.

50. Marni Hall, "Mental Illness and the Elderly," in Vogel and Palmer, eds., *Long-Term Care*, pp. 483-505.

51. U.S. Department of Health and Human Services, *Need for Long-Term Care*, pp. 32-33.

52. Hall, "Mental Illness and the Elderly," p. 484.

53. Ethel Shanas, "Social Myth as Hypothesis: The Case of Family Relations of Old People," *The Gerontologist* 19 (1979): 3-9.

54. Judith Sangl, "The Family Support System of the Elderly," in Vogel and Palmer, eds., *Long-Term Care*, pp. 307-336.

55. Ibid.

56. Soldo, "America's Elderly in the 1980s," p. 27.

57. Ethel Shanas, "The Family as a Support System in Old Age," *The Gerontologist* 19 (1979): 169-174; and Eleanor Stoller, "Self-Assessment of Health by the Elderly: The Impact of Informal Assistance," *Journal of Health and Social Behavior* 25 (1984): 260-270.

58. U.S. Bureau of the Census, *Current Population Reports*, ser. P-20, no. 365, "Marital Status and Living Arrangements: 1980" (Washington, D.C.: GPO, 1981).

59. Cary Kart, Eileen Metress, and James F. Metress, *Aging and Health: Biologic and Social Perspectives* (Menlo Park, Calif.: Addison-Wesley, 1978), p. 203.

60. Robert Hill, "A Demographic Profile of the Black Elderly," *Aging* 287-288 (September-October 1978): 2-9.

61. Shanas, "Social Myth as Hypothesis," p. 309.

62. Ibid.

63. Sangl, "The Family Support System of the Elderly," p. 308.

64. Wilbur Watson, *Aging and Social Behavior: An Introduction to Social Gerontology* (Monterey, Calif.: Wadsworth, 1982), pp. 146-147.

65. Shanas, "The Family as a Support System in Old Age," p. 170; and Eleanor Stoller and Lorna L. Earl, "Help with Activities of Everyday Life: Sources of Support for the Noninstitutionalized Elderly," *The Gerontologist* 23 (1983): 64-70.

66. Sangl, "The Family Support System of the Elderly," p. 327.

67. Ibid.

68. Wayne Seelback and William Sauer, "Familiar Responsibility Expecta-

tions and Morale Among Aged Parents," *The Gerontologist* 17 (1977): 492-499.

69. Marjorie Cantor, "Strain Among Caregivers: A Study of Experience in the United States," *The Gerontologist* 26 (1983): 597-604.

70. Alfred Fengler and Nancy Goodrich, "Wives of Elderly Disabled Men: The Hidden Patients," *The Gerontologist* 19 (1979): 175-183.

71. Sangl, "The Family Support System of the Elderly," p. 330.

72. Colleen Johnson and Donald Catalano, "A Longitudinal Study of Family Supports to Impaired Elderly," *The Gerontologist* 23 (1983): 612-618.

73. Peter Fox and Steven B. Clauser, "Trends in Nursing Home Expenditures: Implications for Aging Policy," *Health Care Financing Review* 2 (Fall 1980): 2.

74. Ibid.

75. See Robyn Stone and Robert J. Newcomer, "The State Role in Board and Care Homes," in Harrington et al., ed., *Long-Term Care of the Elderly*, pp. 177-195. The editors classify personal care homes as one type of board and care home and define that type as "the provision by a nonrelative of food, shelter, and some degrees of protective oversight and/or personal care that is generally nonmedical in nature."

76. Cary Kart and Barry Beckham, "Black-White Differentials in the Institutionalization of the Elderly: A Temporal Analysis," *Social Forces* 54 (1976): 901-909.

77. George Sherman, "Medical Care and Civil Rights," *Quarterly Contact* 4 (1981): 2.

78. Ibid.

79. Gretchen Schafft, "The Civil Rights Act and Nursing Home Integration," *Quarterly Contact* 4 (1981): 1-2.

80. Ibid.

81. Watson, *Aging and Social Behavior*, p. 320.

82. Sangl, "The Family Support System of the Elderly," p. 330.

83. Ibid.; and Marvin Sussman, "The Family Life of Old People," in Robert Binstock and Ethel Shanas, eds. *Handbook of Aging and the Social Sciences* (New York: Van Nostrand, 1976), pp. 118-243.

84. Estes, "Fiscal Austerity and Aging," pp. 17-40.

85. Ibid.

86. Charlene Harrington et al., "State Policies on Long-Term Care," in Harrington et al., *Long-Term Care of the Elderly*, pp. 67-88.

87. Harrington, "Social Security and Medicare," in Estes and Newcomer, eds., *Fiscal Austerity and Aging*, pp. 83-112; and Patricia Ruggles and Marilyn Moon, "The Impact of Recent Legislative Changes in Benefit Programs for the Elderly," *The Gerontologist* 25 (1985): 153-160.

88. Martha McFadden, "The Impact of Increasing the National Age at Retirement on the Minority Elderly," in E. Percil Stanford and Shirley A. Lockery, eds., *Trends and Status of Minority Aging* (San Diego, Calif.: University Center on Aging, San Diego State University, 1982), pp. 123-131.

89. Ruggles and Moon, "The Impact of Recent Legislative Changes in Benefit Programs for the Elderly," p. 154.

90. Harrington, "Social Security and Medicare," p. 84.

91. Harrington et al., "State Policies on Long-Term Care," p. 70.

92. Estes and Lee, "Social, Political and Economic Background of Long-Term Care Policy," p. 25.

93. Harrington, "Social Security and Medicare," p. 89.

94. Ibid.

95. Ibid.

96. Harrington, Newcomer, Estes, et al., eds., "Preface," in their *Long-Term Care of the Elderly: Public Policy Issues*, pp. 11-12.

97. Ruther and Dobson, "Equal Treatment and Unequal Benefits," p. 57.

98. Estes and Lee, "Social, Political and Economic Background of Long-Term Care Policy," p. 21.

99. Robert Newcomer and Charlene Harrington, "State Medicaid Expenditures: Trends and Program Policy Changes," in Estes, Newcomer, et al., eds., *Fiscal Austerity and Aging*, pp. 157-186.

100. Newcomer and Harrington, "State Medicaid Expenditures, Trends and Program Policy Changes," and Robert Newcomer and Marjorie Bogaert-Tullis, "Medicaid Cost Containment Trials and Innovations," in Harrington, Newcomer, Estes, et al., eds., *Long-Term Care of the Elderly*, pp. 105-124.

101. Ruggles and Moon, "The Impact of Recent Legislative Changes in Benefit Programs for the Elderly," p. 154.

102. Harrington et al., "State Policies on Long-Term Care," p. 70.

103. Ruggles and Moon, "The Impact of Recent Legislative Changes in Benefit Programs for the Elderly," p. 155.

104. Ibid.

105. David Lindeman and Alan Pardini, "Social Services: The Impact of Fiscal Austerity," in Estes, Newcomer, et al., eds., *Fiscal Austerity and Aging*, pp. 133-156.

106. Ibid.

107. Hans C. Palmer, "The Alternative Questions," in Vogel and Palmer, eds., *Long-Term Care: Perspective from Research and Demonstrations*, pp. 255-306.

108. Robert Morris and Paul Youket, "Long-Term Care Issues: Identifying the Problems and Potential Solutions," in James Callahan, Jr., and Stanley Wallack, eds., *Reforming the Long-Term Care System* (Lexington, Mass.: D. C. Heath, 1981), pp. 11-28.

109. Robert Kane and Rosalie Kane, "Long-Term Care: Can Our Society Meet the Needs of Its Elderly?" *Annual Review of Public Health* 1 (1980): 227-253.

110. Morris and Youket, "Long-Term Care Issues," p. 15.

111. Robert Kane and Rosalie Kane, "Alternatives to Institutional Care of the Elderly: Beyond the Dichotomy," *The Gerontologist* 20 (1980): 249-259.

112. Palmer, "The Alternative Questions," p. 256.

113. See William Pollak, *Costs of Alternative Care Settings for the Elderly* (Washington, D.C.: Urban Institute, Working Paper 963-11, 1973).

114. Kane and Kane, "Alternatives to Institutional Care of the Elderly," p. 251.

115. A. E. Benjamin, Jr., "Community-Based Long-Term Care," in Harrington, Newcomer, Estes, et al., eds., *Long-Term Care of the Elderly*, pp. 197-211.

116. Juanita Wood and Carroll Estes, "The Private Nonprofit Sector and

Aging Services," in Estes, Newcomer, et al., eds., *Fiscal Austerity and Aging*, pp. 227-248.

117. Personal Communication from the National Caucus and Center on Black Aged, Washington, D.C.

11. Health Care of Blacks in American Inner Cities

Marianne Foley and Glen R. Johnson

The year 1965 was a landmark for federal health care legislation. Legislation addressed long-standing social and political concerns about equitable resource allocation to all segments of society. These enactments and subsequent funding were intended to alleviate health care system problems centered around access to care and provision of care to various deprived populations, among which inner-city blacks were predominant. By 1980 two decades of more equitable resource allocation by the federal government had significantly alleviated these two major problems of inner-city health care. The next set of priorities appeared to involve refinement of health care delivery so that quality care could be widely assured and distribution improved.

Quality of care and improved distribution, however, have been dislodged as priorities in the turmoil caused by fundamental changes in social and political policy affecting health care delivery since 1980. These policy changes were sudden and sweeping in their impact and signaled negative consequences affecting the health status of low-income black populations in American inner cities.

New alternative strategies must be developed rapidly by the health care sector to maintain the equity acquired over twenty years and to prevent further erosion of care. These strategies will consist initially of short-term adaptations to public policy. Long-term direction and policy are, as yet, undefined because the present is filled with reaction. The policy change causing the turmoil is the questioning and near cessation of health care as a right of citizenship, and its return to the realm of privilege as a result of the federal governments escalating abandonment in promoting and financing the general welfare. The philosophy behind the change is that marketplace realities should prevail. Massive federal budget deficits, a real and grave problem, operate as philosophic fuel and justification for abandonment of the general welfare.

It is not known exactly what will occur within each city's health care delivery system or to different black populations. It is only known that an unpleasant cascade of events has already begun to occur at the clinical and public levels. This cascade will directly affect the health status of individuals, families, communities, and populations. Solutions to problems appear to be localized and uneven.

The health status of individuals and populations is affected by complex combinations of clinical, genetic, behavioral, cultural, financial, and environmental variables. Years of experience and numerous studies define, with certainty, that good health is related primarily to higher socioeconomic status, of which income is the most common measure. Amount of education and type of employment are less commonly used but are not necessarily less important than income as enabling factors in securing personal health. We also know, with certainty, that more than any other factor poor health in individuals and populations is correlated directly with poverty. Because blacks as a group continue to have incomes lower than those of whites, they continue to have poorer health status. Poor health is particularly pronounced in American inner cities, where the consolidation of poverty results in a generally harsh and aggravating environment that is increasingly difficult to survive.

This chapter examines the current health care of blacks in American inner cities in a period of dynamic change. Emphasis is placed on three crucial areas of public policy: human consequences, health care delivery, and financing.

HUMAN CONSEQUENCES

Human consequences can be viewed at the level of the individual, selected populations, or larger populations to determine the health status of black urban dwellers. At an individual level, necessity dictates that needs be prioritized into hierarchies. Thus, an otherwise healthy woman may not seek prenatal care until late into her pregnancy because of lack of money. The patient with a chronic cough may not feel "sick enough" to seek expensive medical care. A caring and attentive parent may not be knowledgeable enough about the seriousness of symptoms in a child, and then may delay seeking treatment because of scant financial resources. An essential medication may not be purchased. Dosages may be manipulated to meet with fiscal weakness. Necessities compete viciously for scant resources, and one's actions in seeking medical care and paying for it are closely linked to one's ability to pay. While single, uncomplicated illnesses do occur, low-income blacks usually have a multitude of medical problems stemming from long-term chronic illness and more advanced disease when care is finally sought.

Child health is tied closely to family income. Children of poor parents are more likely to become ill, to experience unfortunate effects of illness, and to die than children of parents at higher socioeconomic levels. Children become casualties of poor health care, nutrition, and education, all of which result in long-run higher economic and social costs due to truncated working years.[1]

Clinical problems resulting directly from terminating a specific population from Medicaid coverage in California have already been documented. These problems are excruciating—clinically meaningful deterioration in health status, including uncontrolled disease, increase in risk of death, and death. These deteriorations occurred because terminated Medicaid recipients were not able to find another source of medical care, had no other form of health insurance to buffer the costs, and no income to purchase services, medications, or hospitalization. The racial and gender characteristics of this population were not delineated, but since they were from inner-city Los Angeles and the deterioration principally involved hypertensives it is certain that some, if not most, of these persons were black. In the absence of payment, the teaching hospital involved in these patients' care attempted a well-thought-out but compromised form of care. The clinical results of compromised care bear witness to the importance of income and insurance.[2]

It will be neither convenient nor moral to side-step the human problems caused by fundamental change in public health policy. The health care literature of the past several years has been quite attentive to the human as well as the structural and functional problems arising from fundamental changes in policy. Much of this attention has been focused on black urban-dwelling populations who are welfare-poor, working-poor, or "near poor" according to federal poverty guidelines.

Blacks began to fill these poor roles as they migrated from the rural South to the urban North after the Civil War. World War II and the postwar era brought the largest shift in black populations to cities where overall economic gains were possible in employment, education, and safety-net public benefits. Blacks who found unskilled work began to share the urban inheritance of the white working-class poor, while those who were unable to work inherited welfare status. These roles and statuses are a historical continuation of the English welfare system with its poor laws, workhouses, and relief. Similarly, today's American urban teaching hospital, with its commitment to care for the medically indigent, developed from the English separation of the ill poor into infirmaries which became teaching sources with the rise of scientific medicine.

"Trickle-down" benefits of economic growth have rarely reached the inner city, or have reached there last. In a society with growing numbers of persons in poverty, frozen or curtailed federal support becomes even less suitably distributed. In 1981, 31.8 million Americans lived in poverty, an increase from the previous year of 2.2 million, or 14 percent of the entire U.S. population.[3] In 1979 before the economic revolution, 57.8 percent of black families remained below the medium income of $15,000 compared to 33.1 percent of whites.[4]

Inner-city black populations are increasingly viewed as a permanent American underclass with chronically threatened, already spare resources. Poverty is related to ignorance, unemployment and under-employment, social withdrawal, and certainly to greater health-hazard exposure levels. In addition, all dense population aggregations run a higher risk of disease, and in our time these populations are disproportionately black inner-city dwellers. They are further hampered by low wages and high unemployment, inferior education systems, unstable sources of health care, substandard housing, violence, high transportation and food costs, and they are increasingly burdened with the rising financial costs of city operations. All these conditions shorten life. Gains can be rapidly undone and deterioration can occur with exponential speed.

Although life expectancy has increased dramatically for all Americans in this century, life remains shorter for blacks than for whites. In 1982 life expectancy was 69.3 years for blacks, 74.6 years for whites. Even with violence factored out, the mortality differential is substantial. Newborn deaths have decreased substantially for all races but remain nearly twice as high for black as for whites. As noted in Chapter 2, death rates in 1980 remained higher for blacks than for whites. Black males continue to have the highest death rates.[5]

The outcry, dismay, and strong feelings articulated by physicians with a tradition of caring for the poor inform us that equal care is no longer achievable and that equal access is rapidly deteriorating in many cities.[6] These conditions will worsen as a large segment of the population ages and becomes more ill; and if poverty continues to increase, so will the number of persons at risk. At the health care delivery level, that is, the ill person seeking help from a provider, medical care ceases to be abstraction, rhetoric or theory, and becomes reality, a human interaction. Here finances, behavior, culture, and political philosophy all play out their roles in the health care of the individual and group populations.

According to probability in the Geller tables developed by the Centers for Disease Control from morbidity data, black males aged 50 to 54 have 8,143 more chances (per 100,000 population) of dying in the next ten years than do their white male counterparts. The four leading causes of death for black and white males aged 50 to 54 are heart attacks, lung cancer, strokes, and cirrhosis. Because black males average more deaths from these causes, they have a higher probability of death. The fifth-ranking probability in the 50 to 54 age cohort for black men is homicide, which ceases to be a significant probability for white males after 49 years of age.[7] Hypertension, sickle cell anemia, and cancer are prominent medical problems in inner cities. Blacks continue to suffer higher incidence and mortality through lung, colon/rectal, prostate, esophagus, and breast cancer than do whites.

Both white and black women live longer than their male counterparts, but white women live longer than black women. Women, in general, trade off longer lives for life-long poverty as the feminization of poverty increases with the increase of female-headed families. In 1981 the poverty rate for families headed by single women (widowed, divorced, unmarried) was 30.1 percent compared to 10.1 percent for all families. The black female subset statistics are more dire. Approximately one-half of black inner-city families have one parent, and most of these are women. Women and children are widely acknowledged as the chief losers since 1980 as they have borne greater cuts in health and social programs (Medicare/Medicaid, food stamps, family planning, nutrition, and Aid to Families with Dependent Children.[8]

HEALTH CARE DELIVERY

The inner-city health care delivery system has several main components, none of which is coordinated with another for delivery of care. These components are: private practitioners, hospitals, and public health clinics. Prepaid health care organizations also merit comment. Nursing homes tend not to be a significant component of care for inner-city blacks. This may be due to the shortened lives of blacks, and their continued inclusion in family life as a result of the culturally strong position of elderly persons. Community health centers never quite got off the ground because funding for development was inadequate and short-term. However, it is estimated that the loss of federal funding for community health centers will terminate services for hundreds of thousands of poor persons.

As these components are examined, mutual access to care (patient and provider) and continuity of care remain important in the determination of whether care is successful in its delivery and effective in its purpose. The essential event in all delivery is the physician-patient encounter at whatever location that occurs.

Private Practitioners

The dominant health care model in the United States is fee-for-service care obtained from private practitioners. Not a great deal is known about private practice in inner cities, possibly because too few doctors ever attempt it, remain with it, or are too engrossed with it to describe it. It is known that inner-city practice requires the private practitioner to possess an intrepid spirit because the practice environment is usually unattractive and beset by problems not encountered by other physicians. It is understood that black physicians experience the same gratification from caring for their patients as do other physicians. There are, however, still not enough black physicians. (They constituted 2.1 percent of all physicians, and 5.9 percent of medical school classes in 1980, while blacks constitute 27 percent of inner-city populations).[9] It should come as no surprise that a special cultural understanding is required to be an effective inner-city physician.[10] We know that those who do practice in inner cities do not receive the recognition they deserve for their contribution. Consequently, and alarmingly, it appears that the instability of financial suport for health care has an impact on inner-city physicians as well as on their patients.

The number of physicians in private practice is as important to the functioning of delivery as is the ability of the patient to purchase services in whatever form. Black inner-city residents may prefer private physician care just as other Americans do but are less likely to get that care. The usual source of care for 22.1 percent of the nonwhite elderly, for example, is obtained from institutions and not private practitioners, because physicians may be unavailable.[11] Unstable financial support for health care for inner-city black populations appears to be based on current political/social policy and fashionable economic theory rather than on defined needs. This instabilty greatly reduces the incentive for physicians to practice in inner cities. At best, one's patients are crushed between rising costs of care and curtailed fiscal outlays, physicians do not get paid for their services, and urban hospitals wind up in debt. At worst, patients cannot seek care, are rejected for care, or are given poor medical care.

The insufficiency of black inner-city practitioners, increased unemployment among blacks, decreased Medicaid eligibility, frozen and fixed-cost Medicare reimbursements, curtailment of health-related social programs (e.g., food stamps), and lack of health insurance present a daunting array of barriers to any physician contemplating whether he or she can offer quality medical care—let alone equal care—to patients with a multitude of medical problems. The conservative nature of private practitioners and the competitive, entrepreneurial quality of private practice tend to operate against meaningful private or voluntary solutions for care of inner-city populations on a large scale. The rallying cry is, "If the government won't do it, why should I?" Inner-city practice was never easy and has become more difficult as the delivery system reinstitutionalizes multi-tiered standards of care, and as facilities and services become even more rationed for inner-city black populations.

Hospitals

American hospitals along with other health care industry segments, became the beneficiaries of relatively generous federal policies from 1950 to 1980. Hospitals, in addition to providing routine patient care, have been able to build and expand, increase their range of services, conduct biomedical research, purchase expensive technology, and conduct extensive education programs. Furthermore, hospitals have been compensated on a cost-of-care basis for care of the elderly (Medicare) and low-income persons (Medicaid).[12] Hospitals have charged what they wanted, and the federal government was unsuccessful in controlling costs. Along with other health care sectors, hospitals have been responsible for escalating costs to the extent that health care expenditures now constitute more than 10 percent of the Gross National Product.

Nowhere in the inner-city health care delivery system has the fundamental change in federal reimbursement been more pronounced than in the nonprofit teaching hospital. By long tradition, urban teaching hospitals have cared for low-income patients in volume, and this volume has made these hospitals ideal for the clinical education of physicians, nurses, and others. The low-income patient, the elderly patient, and the teaching programs have essentially relied on the same source of support: government subsidies in the form of Medicaid and Medicare on a cost-of-care basis. The 1980s have brought increased health care costs, a severe recession with particularly high unemployment among blacks, and an estimated 10 to 25 million uninsured persons, lower eligibility standards for Medicaid, and fixed-cost Medicare reimbursements to these hospitals.

Personnel in urban teaching hospitals feel strongly about their traditional role in providing often superior care for low-income persons and in having provided much of the equal access to care that was so lacking previously. Here, medical care is considered a right, and dismay is being expressed over the potential diminishment of quality care and inabiilty to hold the line on access due to the problems of reimbursement. Because it has become more difficult to shift the costs of care to other third-party payers (e.g., Blue Cross) and remain out of debt, some urban teaching hospitals will be forced to close, and all are having to reexamine their policies. Many have already restricted care: many will do so unofficially. Other hospitals have rarely shared in the burden of medical care for medically indigent patients to the extent that this sharing is meaningful to society. If patients without resources seek care at one of these hospitals, they are subjected to a "wallet biopsy" and are usually rejected for care. If care is extended, it is usually done by private arrangement on some ill-defined "deserving poor" basis. Increasingly, all hospitals are targeting their marketing toward the "upscale" patient—that is, the middle-class or upwardly mobile person with comprehensive, dependable health insurance.

Urban teaching hospitals have long been social policy instruments, a second line of defense against the unfortunate tendency of low-income persons to be more seriously ill than more affluent persons. These hospitals now are faced with an increasing volume of care with less funding, and most do not know how they are going to respond. Moreover, the hospitals have generally provided more costly care because a more extensive range of expensive medical services is required by their communities (full trauma care, for example) as well as ancillary services such as social services and substance-abuse programs. It is more expensive to provide care to low-income persons because their medical problems are more severe and complicated, and socioeconomic problems are more difficult to solve.[13] The chief concern being voiced is that all these conditions may encourage teaching hospitals to do too little for optimal patient care or to select and provide for less resource-consuming medical problems.

Some strategies for dealing with these problems successfully are developing on a localized basis. Many of these new strategies may improve delivery, but these will be useful only to persons in select localities as there is no longer a national standard of equal access to care.[14] The resulting difficulties created for urban teaching hospitals will be discussed in the financing section later in this chapter.

Public Health Clinics

The premises underlying the provision of public health clinics are based on concepts of the "common good," assuring a healthy, productive community, and protecting those persons least able to afford private ambulatory (or outpatient) care.

The clinical role of public health at the local level has been limited to activities involved in preventing the spread of disease and protecting identified at-risk groups through the provision of specialized programs. Beyond certain common areas, there often is great variation in different cities regarding how the role of public health is interpreted. Historically, these variations are dependent on how states and cities choose to interpret their public health responsibility, funding levels, local epidemiology and demographics, and degree of cooperation or resistance emanating from the private practice sector.

There has been and continues to be tension and ambivalence between public health and private medical practice over the amount and kind of medical care provided in public health clinics. The decision-making process is such that states and cities have left as much as possible to private practice and voluntary efforts, and federal policy generally has been to allow states and local government to determine the clinical activities of public health.[15] Because public health cannot compensate physicians in as enticing a manner as private practice, few physicians have chosen the field as a practice specialty. This situation may change with the present overproduction of physicians.

What has evolved is an often uneasy overlap and balance between public health's role in preventing disease and protecting the public, and the physician's role in diagnosing and treating the ill on an individualized basis. Most contemporary public health clinics conduct similar clinical activities that also are dependent on federal as well as state and local funding. Maternal and child health, family planning, disease control, and health education are the most common. Many public health clinics are also involved in nutrition counseling, care for the elderly and homeless (an increasing local and national problem), mental health, refugee care, adolescent pregnancy, and environmental protection. In many cities (especially where there is an absence of private practitioners and hospital-provided outpatient care) there is a well-developed system of primary medical care to indigent populations at ambulatory clinics. Nonetheless, public health has never had a mandate or the funding to provide medical care much outside the peripheries of community prevention and disease control. Therefore, increasing numbers of uninsured or otherwise medically indigent patients cannot be easily shifted (some would say dumped) to this sector. Furthermore, even if more outpatient care were shifted to public health and local funding increased, the crisis over inpatient care remains—and this crisis has not at all been within public health's domain in recent years.

Although the need may always exceed the provision, it would appear from the current situation that blacks residing in certain cities with large black populations will continue to receive care and attention in public health clinics. At what level this will occur is questionable, for federal funding for public health and related areas took cuts in the billions of dollars beginning in 1982.[16] These cuts affected maternal-child health, crippled children's service, community health centers, community mental health centers, family planning, child nutrition, and immunizations. The repackaging of categorical federal grants into block grants reduced funding by 25 percent prior to being turned over to the states. Food stamp eligibility, Supplemental Security Income (SSI), Medicaid, and Aid to Families with Dependent Children (AFDC) all experienced federal curtailment or federal-to-state cost shifts. The WIC program (nutrition supplements for Women, Infants, and Children) experienced cuts in the millions of dollars. All of these programs are candidates for yet more budget cutting as the Reagan administration continues into its second term.

However dire this outlook may seem for black inner-city residents, public health commitment at least remains more constant than that of the hospitals because serving the "common good" was always its purpose. Here, it is a question of more or less and not whether to provide care. Baltimore's public health department has operated since 1793 and has long experienced cooperation with major city health care institutions. Atlanta provides the standard public health services, as well as an impressive array of mental health programs for problems other cities choose not to acknowledge. Detroit, amidst a grim background of high unemployment, does yeoman work and asks, is health care a right or a privilege in this country? Memphis suggests that rational planning, practicality, and common goals among institutions can improve delivery systems for patient benefit, cost-effectiveness, and community welfare. Again, how blacks fare will depend on the community and state in which residence is held.[17]

Prepaid Health Care Organizations

The 1980s saw the advent of the prepaid mode of health care financing. The impact of this mode in delivery of health to minority populations is not well documented to date. However, it is universally accepted that this system is very attractive to blue-collar workers. Prepaid plans and their multiple penetrations have also ventured into the Medicare market and in some areas have experimented with Medicaid. The name "Health Maintenance Organization" was initially used as a promotional term in advocating prepaid health plans as an alternative to increased governmental regulation of health care systems. Prepaid plans are characterized by the following:

1. They include a defined population of enrolled members.
2. Payments on premiums are paid in advance for a specific period of time.
3. Only physician subscribers to the program are authorized to render services.
4. Enrollees to the plan subscribe to the plan on a voluntary basis.

Prepaid plans thrive economically primarily when the patient practices sound health maintenance principles. The patient is encouraged to have periodic examinations with the objective of detecting or preventing the occurrence of catastrophic illness and its concomitant economic problems.

When one considers the utilization pattern of poor ethnic minorities, it is quite apparent that their health care attitude fosters episodic care that is crisis-oriented and not preventive- or maintenance-oriented. It is no wonder, then, that prepaid plans consider minorities groups at risk, or, in the vernacular, high utilizers. The result is that as these plans become more popular, both the physician provider and the minority population he or she serves is at risk of being alienated from the mainstream. Prepaid plans are aggressively seeking out the elderly to include as their participants but, in contrast, few have to date actively sought out the Medicaid programs.

FINANCING

Quality health care that is accessible and equitable is expensive. Financing it for all segments of the population is a continuing problem. For those with low incomes and the elderly, financing is now a central dilemma. A piecemeal approach has been taken to assure Americans the means to purchase timely health services without having to sacrifice inordinately large percentages of income. The piecemeal approach consisting of private and public financing has not worked with any consistency or credibility over an extended period of time. Decisions are now being made almost purely on the basis of financial resources and market-place competition, and not on the basis of need. For low-income urban blacks as well as for others, this decision-making period represents an extremely treacherous situation.

We have come to rely on three methods of paying for health care: direct and indirect governmental expenditures, and private insurance. None of these is an endless source of payment, and it is regrettable that all parties did not achieve successful cost controls earlier. Medicaid and Medicare represent direct government expenditures. Indirect expenditures consist of uncollected tax revenues. These occur by not taxing employer-paid health insurance as income, and by allowing tax deductions for health care expenditures (currently those in excess of 5% of gross adusted income). Direct expenditures favor the poor and the elderly, whereas indirect expenditures favor middle- and upper-income groups. Neither form of government expenditure favors those under 65 years of age whose employers do not provide health insurance, those who cannot afford to purchase insurance independently, or those whose incomes are too high to qualify for Medicaid. (It does not take much income to be excluded from Medicaid—$576 monthly income for a two-member family in New York State, one of the more generous states.[18]) Persons not covered by some form of public or private insurance are the most at risk. When federal curtailments in health-related programs are added to those for health care, low-income black populations are at extreme risk. (Table 11.1 lists federal entitlements, and health-related and health programs.)

According to the federal government, the 50 states have approximately $18 billion in unallocated surplus income to take over all previous federal expenditures. The governors of the states feel that figure is misleading, so it must not be assumed that state (or local) governments will eagerly pick up the bill the federal government is shifting to the states. Some states are wealthier than others. Some compare economically to less-developed countries. There are some states that might be willing to pay if able, and yet others with a long tradition of little responsibility for citizen well-being. Local governments have been shielded from all but selected costs for many years and likely have no concrete idea of how much the federal cost shift will affect them.[19]

Private insurers and employers who cover American employees are also acting to control and reduce health care expenditures which are deemed too large and unpredictable a percentage of business costs. Approximately $100 billion a year is spent privately to cover employees and their families (or about 60% of the American population, according to the Census Bureau). Prospective and retrospective scrutiny of health care expenditures by employers and private insurers is now commonplace: expenditures are questioned and negotiated. Employee cost-sharing and rising deductibles are increasing rapidly. The private sector has decided that continual increases in medical costs (6% in 1984), hospital shifting of bad debts to private insurers, and inappropriate utilization by employees can no longer be tolerated.

It is worthwhile here to explain in more detail some of the intricacies, costs, and statistics associated with financing as these all affect minority populations. The details will more fully explain the human and health delivery problems discussed earlier in the chapter, and will provide the reader with additional insight for understanding public policy decisions.

Health Care Costs as Percentage of Household Income

Medical care costs are definitely inflationary. Although the charge for each item of care may seem reasonable, the composition of costs for any illness may increase rapidly and take a percentage of household income that is difficult to manage. The percentage of household income an illness costs varies significantly among different economic groups. Current and typical costs for a common medical problem requiring an uncomplicated outpatient surgical procedure to resolve the condition total $1,179 (see Table 11.2 for composition of costs). The cost is fixed regardless of insurance, income level, or ability to pay. Several different gross incomes, each with a typical insurance arrangement, are also described in Table 11.2. The percentage of household income required to

Table 11.1
Federally Funded Entitlements, Health and Health-Related Programs

Entitlements	Health	Health-Related
Food Stamps**	Medicare	Food Stamps**
Guaranteed Student Loans**	Medicaid**	Supplemental Security Income
Military Retirement Pay	Black Lung Disability Payments	(SSI)**
Medicare	Block Grants	Aid to Families with Dependent
Medicaid**	Maternal/Child Health**	Children (AFDC)**
Black Lung Disability Payments	Community Health Centers**	Women's Infant & Children
Supplemental Security Income (SSI)**	Centers for Disease Control	(WIC--nutrition)**
Aid to Families with Dependent Children	Public Health Service	Crippled Children's Services**
(AFDC)**	National Institutes of Health	Family Planning**
Veterans' Pensions	Community Mental Health Centers **	Child Nutrition
Social Security	Immunizations**	(School Lunches)**
	Guaranteed Student Loans	Head Start**
	(Health Professions)**	Block Grants
	Early and Periodic Screening,	
	Diagnosis and Treatment	
	(EPSDT--for children)**	

* Entitlements programs are administered so that anyone who is eligible may receive the benefit no matter what the cost to the program or how many people are eligible; some entitlements are means-tested.

** Means-tested (or needs-based)

Table 11.2
Medical Cost Composition/Percent of Household Income

Pap Test	$ 10.00	Preventive, diagnostic
Office Visit, M.D.	35.00	Diagnostic
Outpatient Surgical Suite	468.00	Operating suite and recovery room; includes nursing care; total time 4 hours, no meals
Anesthesiologist, M.D.	127.00	Treatment
Surgical Fee, M.D.	350.00	Treatment
Laboratory	125.00	Pre- and post-operative tests and interpretation
Prescription Drugs	29.00	Treatment
Office Visit, M.D.	35.00	Follow-up to diagnosis and treatment
Total Cost	$1,179.00	

A. $6,914 income (minimum wage, slightly over Medicaid eligibility for two-person family in New York state) -- no insurance. Percent of gross income to pay costs: 17%.

B. $10,000 income (above poverty line for family of four) -- comprehensive insurance paid equally by employee and employer at annual cost to employee of $600 each year; 80% coverage after annual $250 deductible paid. Percent of gross income to pay costs: 10%.

C. $20,000 income -- comprehensive insurance paid by employer; 80% coverage after annual $500 deductible paid. Percent of gross income to pay costs: 3%.

D. $35,000 income -- comprehensive insurance paid by employer; 80% coverage after $150 annual deductible paid. Percent of gross income to pay costs: 1%.

E. $50,000 income -- comprehensive insurance paid by employer; no deductible and full coverage. Percent of gross income to pay costs: 0%.

pay $1,179 in medical expenses increases as income and insurance coverage decrease. Similarly, the percentage of income needed to cover the costs decreases as income and insurance coverage increase. The variance among percentages of income to pay an identical expense is significant—in our example 17 percent.

As deductibles increase along with the employee share of insurance costs, and costs of care rise, it requires an increasingly greater percentage of household income to cover the costs. When Medicaid income eligibility is lowered and the number of those living in poverty increases, the number of uninsured persons at risk increases. For those without some kind of insurance, it can be financially devastating to experience even a relatively inexpensive but unanticipated, short-term illness. For persons needing to pay 17 percent or more of annual income out-of-pocket, the year-end tax deduction for expenses over 5 percent of income is hardly a comfort. What happens in these circumstances is that medical care is often foregone because the cost is unbearable. The illness may worsen and become more complicated, ultimately be more difficult to treat, or require extensive hospitalization. Treatment may be sought, but perhaps the bill will not be paid. Unpaid bills produce the bad debt which health care providers are required to write off every year. In the case of public hospitals, bad debt can grow, forcing reduced care or even closing the hospital.

Medicaid and Medicare

Medicaid and Medicare were enacted in 1965 to provide health service payments for the poor and the elderly. A retrospective, cost-based reimbursement system rapidly led to a skewed system of payment that favored more expensive inpatient and institutional care over preventive, outpatient, and office-based care. Certainly, Medicaid and Medicare worked for the purposes intended, particularly for the elderly; unfortunately, these programs worked so well that they became the largest nonmilitary federal expenditures. Federal cost controls were not effective.

Medicaid costs far less than Medicare because of restricted, means-tested eligibility. However, because of its arrangements with the states and linkages to AFDC and SSI, it is a far more complicated program than Medicare. Until 1981 the federal government provided between 50 and 83 percent reimbursement to the states by authorizing funds for each state's medical assistance program for indigent care. Funding to the states was based on state per capita income: poorer states were given more than richer states. Some cities financed their own Medicaid programs without state or federal assistance. In 1977 the federal government paid $9.3 billion and the states paid $7.3 billion for Medicaid.[20]

A main objective of Medicaid was to allow the poor to buy into mainstream medicine by choosing and maintaining a relationship with a health care provider. However, unlike Medicare, services were restricted to absolute essentials.

The low-income people who qualified for Medicaid coverage varied, as each state had the discretion to set income eligibility levels and to allocate eligibility emphasis among three indigent groups: (1) the elderly; (2) the seriously mentally retarded, blind, and disabled; and (3) children from single-parent families and their parents under certain conditions of unemployment and lack of insurance. All other persons and families were omitted, and continue to be omitted from eligibility, regardless of indigency. Because the states made different choices, it is estimated that, at its peak, Medicaid covered one-third to one-half of the country's poor. Another 5 percent were eventually covered by community health centers. Minorities received less than 20 percent of Medicaid's support services. The group receiving the most assistance (37 percent) have been the elderly retired who were either poor or became poor. (Poverty was not a difficult achievement for the elderly in the inflationary 1960s and 1970s.) Nursing homes received 72 percent of these expenditures owing to Medicare's restrictions for long-term nursing home care. The next largest Medicaid recipient group (30 percent) were those with severe permanent disabilities (mentally retarded, blind, and disabled). Expenditures covered medical care and nursing home services. The third category, poor children and unemployed/uninsured single parents, received 28 percent of Medicaid; more than half of this was for children.

By 1979, 2.1 million people were covered. This coverage coincided with a drop in death rates for major diseases and increased life expectancy. There is little doubt that availability and accessibility of medical care at a timely point in illness made a difference. Among the more stunning gains of the period was a 45 percent drop in black infant deaths. These gains also overlapped with a decrease in poverty levels until high inflation and high unemployment began to slow and, in some cases, reverse the trend of population gains in health.[21] Medicaid costs rose as the cost of health care rose and as more eligible people were covered.

After 1981, when the states began to bear a more equal share of the costs, the states received federal permission to limit a recipient's choice of provider as a trade-off for state cost-sharing. States can now determine eligible providers (who may well not be the recipient's choice or the provider who has maintained a relationship with the recipient), as well as control eligibility, and require nominal cost-sharing by recipients in the form of enrollment fees, premiums, deductibles, and copayment. It is difficult to compare the states' pre-1981 Medicaid policies because little comprehensive information is available. However, in 1981, 40 states reduced their Medicaid spending by cutting benefits, lowering payments to providers, and reducing the number of persons eligible by lowering income eligibility levels—all during a recessionary period that produced the largest number of unemployed persons since the Great Depression.

In 1983, 22.1 million persons received Medicaid; the federal government paid $19.5 billion and the states paid $17 bilion. It may appear on the surface that eligibility expanded since more people benefited in 1983 than in 1979; however, unemployment greatly increased, as did the number of persons living in poverty. It is not known how many persons who may have qualified in the 1970s for Medicaid were disqualified in the early 1980s, or how many of these persons were minorities.

The federal government has established minimal Medicaid requirements for the states to follow. States must cover all persons who receive direct AFDC or SSI support as well as the categorically needy (aged, blind, disabled, plus eligible children). One way the federal government assisted the states was by cutting the number of SSI recipients. SSI provides a small monthly allotment to the aged, blind, retarded, and disabled on a means-tested basis. Its cost to the federal government was $8 billion in 1984.[22] Federal requirements also mandate certain medical services the states are to allow recipients, and these services must be sufficient to achieve their purposes. It is left to the states to define "sufficient," and this loophole has resulted in such measures as limiting the number of hospital days and outpatient visits. Beyond these federal requirements are many intricate state regulations that further define eligibility and establish cost controls. As federal policy intended, states now have enormous power to manage Medicaid and indigent care as they choose. All indications are that Medicaid is now the fastest growing expenditure of the states, and the federal government is attempting to restrict its total annual contribution to the states. Capitation may force the states again to reduce the number of Medicaid recipients and the amount of expenditures in order to control costs.

What exists now are 50 different Medicaid programs with the following features:[23]

1. 25 states require recipient copayment.
2. 23 states have enrolled some recipients in prepaid health plans at flat fee premiums.
3. 14 states negotiate medical care and hospital services in advance rather than reimburse for costs; 6 reimburse hospitals a flat fee.
4. 44 states conduct pre-admission screening before allowing Medicaid to cover nursing home care; 2 require contributions from relatives of recipients.
5. 35 states encourage home care and community-based services as alternatives to nursing home care.

6. 11 states have commissions that set mandatory reimbursement rates.

7. 28 states have converted Medicaid from fee-for-service to some form of primary care case management, provider-risk contracting, or capitation.

Because of Medicaid's continuing linkage to AFDC, it is important to view AFDC as well. It is a state-administered, means-tested entitlement funded jointly by state and federal governments. At present, maximum benefits in the form of direct cash subsidy for a family of four range from $120 per month to $600 per month. The average national monthly case load is 19.9 million persons. As an indication of Medicaid eligibility cuts in the early 1980s, 500,000 families were dropped from AFDC and another 300,000 had benefits reduced an average of $175 per month.

Medicare is a federal trust fund for health services to those over 65 years of age; it is administered by the Department of Health and Human Resources but is operated as part of federal revenues and deficits. Until recently, Medicare reimbursed hospitals on a cost-based system and physicians on a fixed cost fee-for-service basis. Medicare has been and continues to be a major fiscal, political, and medical issue. As noted earlier, it costs the federal government more than any other domestic nonmilitary expenditure. It covers a great many voters who were promised its security, and it is an important income producer for hospitals and physicians. We all pay for it via a payroll tax, our parents and grandparents benefit from it, and the medical cost of illness in old age can be so staggering we know we need such a program. When the median income for an elderly person is $6,974, we are even more certain of its need. Current Medicare cost-control reforms may only delay Medicare's projected insolvency a few years. Actuarial estimates project insolvency between 1995 and 2000, with accumulating deficits thereafter. In 1984 Medicare cost the federal government approximately $64 billion to insure approximately 29 million persons over 65 years of age.[24]

Medicare's impact on blacks is no different from that on whites except in two respects. First, black life expectancy is shorter than that for whites and so proportionately fewer blacks will utilize Medicare for as long a time as whites will, yet they still pay for it. Women benefit more than men. Second, Medicare has been a critical source of income for urban teaching hospitals which, as explained earlier, have been major health care providers for low-income, inner-city blacks. The latter situation may prove to be the more important long-term problem for low-income inner-city blacks but in a less apparent manner.

The hospitalization portion of Medicare has been changed from a cost-based system of reimbursement to a fixed-cost reimbursement popularly known as DRGs (Diagnostic Related Groups). Now, instead of a hospital billing Medicare for the actual cost of patient care, the hospital is paid a fixed-cost based on diagnosis at the time of admission with a small differential allowance for teaching hospitals that is meant to offset the increased patient care costs resulting from clinical education. Prospective payment is aimed at making hospitals more efficient by treating illness faster with fewer hospital days: theoretically, hospitals gain income for efficiency and lose income for inefficiency (i.e., using more hospital days than the fixed cost covers). What this does is transform patients into production-line commodities to be turned over and out as quickly as possible. This transformation is vastly upsetting to health care professionals who want to provide patients with whatever is needed for whatever length of time is required to resolve an illness. The sick human body simply does not respond like an automobile in a repair shop!

There is great concern that hospitals may implicitly develop a system of admissions only for illnesses and conditions that lend themselves to low resource use and treatment, fewer hospital days, and more profit, and therefore screen out and reject high-resource-use-and-treatment illnesses and conditions. A second concern is that hospitals may continue to accept Medicare patients as usual but compromise optimal patient care by doing less. It will be difficult for patients to ascertain what "less" is composed of because many aspects of care are not apparent to the patient. One might be aware of fewer nurses but unaware that a diagnostic test has been eliminated because cost, rather than need, has been the deciding factor. A third concern is that DRGs are not going to compensate hospitals or physicians adequately for chronic illness or for certain difficult diseases. Relatives and spouses will find themselves faced with extremely difficult financial choices in attempting to provide long-term care for the chronically ill. Because the United States has growing numbers of elderly persons, it can be safely projected that there will be more elderly persons with more difficult and chronic diseases. These concerns establish another area of vulnerability for elderly black patients (see Chapter 10). As stated earlier, low-income blacks tend to experience very few single, uncomplicated illnesses and more chronic, multiple illnesses of a complex nature.

Medicare also has a cost to the elderly. If one has not worked enough quarters to qualify automatically, one can purchase Medicare hospitalization coverage for a mere $174 per month! For those who do qualify, the costs are:

1. Part A—Hospitalization: no premium; $400 annual deductible
2. Part B—Physician: monthly premium $15.50 or $186 per year; $75 annual deductible.

Using the median income of $6,974 for an elderly person, the percentage of income required to purchase Medicare is 2 percent. When Medicare is used and all annual deductibles are paid, it requires 9 percent of this income to meet the cost of illness.

Physician behavior with respect to Medicare is problematic. Physician fees have been prospective for some time, and many physicians feel they are less than adequate to cover costs. Medicare has frozen direct physician payment at a fixed amount and requires physicians either to accept the fixed fee as full payment for all cases or forego direct Medicare payments entirely, the same situation the hospitals are facing with DRGs. Only 30 percent of the nation's physicians have agreed to become direct recipients of Medicare payments.[25] This does not prevent non-Medicare physicians from billing elderly patients for usual and customary fees directly and having the patient collect a portion from Medicare.

What lies ahead for Medicare is difficult to ascertain specifically. It does seem clear that changes will consist of some mix of increasing beneficiary premiums, reducing or eliminating the DRG teaching hospital allowance, and freezing or producing payment levels to all providers. How and if Medicare can survive and be financed in the future is the larger policy question.

CONCLUSION

This chapter conveys gravity and concern but little optimism about the short-term conditions of stable, accessible, affordable health care provision for urban low-income black populations. However, it would be extremely unfair to discount the roles that social intelligence, political will, economic compassion, and pragmatism play in the United States, and how these characteristics tend to translate into innovation and action.

Our beliefs, values, and behaviors as a culture may not always mesh at private and public levels but have continuously evolved solutions to problems. It may be more hopeful to view the entire array of recent changes in health care as an opportunity and a challenge. More emphasis can be placed on prevention and ambulatory care, and restraint can be developed with inpatient care to reduce expenditures without sacrificing quality health care. Better service coordination is long overdue, as is a clear perspective on high-technology medicine. The health care sector must be able to provide more thoughtful care arrangements using fewer resources in as least harmful a manner as possible. The private sector of health must take on a meaningful share of the medically indigent health care problem; profit cannot be the sole criterion for service provision. The public sector in its turn must be able to assure at some level of government that the more vulnerable members of our society will not be expended in an effort to reduce the national debt.

NOTES

1. Socioeconomic effects on child and teenage mortality in the United States have been a neglected research topic. For a preliminary study, refer to Robert D. Mare, "Socioeconomic Effects on Child Mortality in the United States," *American Journal of Public Health* 72, no. 6 (June 1982): 539-547.

2. This study took place at the UCLA Center for the Health Sciences under the UCLA Robert Wood Johnson Foundation Clinical Scholars Program. See Nichole Lurie, Nancy Ward, Martin Shapiro, and Robert Brook, Special Report, "Termination from Medi-Cal—Does It Affect Health?" *New England Journal of Medicine* 311, no. 7 (August 16, 1984): 480-484.

3. For a summation of federal health policy for the poor since the Johnson administration, see John K. Iglehart, Health Policy Report, "Federal Policies and the Poor," *New England Journal of Medicine* 307, no. 13 (September 23, 1982): 836-840.

4. Income distribution as well as other aspects of health care delivery are discussed in this public health textbook chapter. See John J. Hanlon and George E. Pickett, "Medical Care Delivery," *Public Health: Administration and Practice*, 8th ed. (St. Louis: Mosby, 1984), pp. 579-603.

5. "Improving Longevity May Have Side Effects," Week in Review Section, *New York Times*, February 17, 1985, p. E-3.

6. The value and accomplishments of Medicaid are discussed in detail. See David E. Rogers, Robert J. Blendon, and Thomas W. Moloney, "Who Needs Medicaid?" *New England Journal of Medicine* 307, no. 1 (July 1, 1982): 13-18.

7. Lewis C. Robbins and Ronald Blankenbaker, "Prospective Medicine and the Health Hazard Appraisal," in Robert B. Taylor, ed., *Health Promotion: Principles and Clinical Applications* (Norwalk, Conn.: Appleton-Century-Crofts, 1982), pp. 88, 94-96.

8. The president of the Carnegie Corporation delivered this paper to the annual meeting of the Association of American Medical Colleges in 1982. See Alan Pifer, "The Social Determinants of Political Change," *Journal of Medical Education* 58, no. 1 (January 1983): 1-7.

9. S. N. Sherman, X. Tonesk, and J. B. Erdmann, "Datagram—1981-82 Enrollment in U.S. Medical Schools," *Journal of Medical Education* 57, no. 6 (June 1982): 495-498.

10. David Satcher and Ludlow B. Creary, "Family Practice in the Inner City," in Robert E. Rakel, *Textbook of Family Medicine*, 3rd ed. (Philadelphia: U. B. Saunders, 1984), pp. 226-237.

11. Emily Friedman, "Access to Care: Serving the Poor and Elderly in Tough Times," *Hospitals* 56, no. 23 (December 1, 1982): 85-90.

12. C. Thomas Smith, "Health Care Delivery System Changes: A Special Challenge for Teaching Hospitals," *Journal of Medical Education* 60, no. 1 (January 1985): 1-8.

13. Robert M. Heyssel, "Competition and the Marketplace for Health Care—It Won't be Problem Free," *Hospitals* 55, no. 22 (November 1981): 107-114.

14. Maurice A. Schwartz, "Health Care for the Poor: Changing the Rules," Editorial, *Hospital Practice* 17, no. 11 (November 1982): 15-17, 21.

15. This scholarly, readable book on the social history of American medicine has received much acclaim and several prestigious prizes. See Paul Starr, *The Social Transformation of American Medicine* (New York: Basic Books, 1982): pp. 180-197.

16. Iglehart, "Federal Policies and the Poor," pp. 836-840.

17. Public health directors and private physicians in several U.S. cities with large black populations discuss a range of issues, problems, and programs affecting health in their cities and the country as a whole. See "Medicine and Health Care in Urban America—Part One: Perspectives," *Urban Health* 13, no. 5 (June 1984): 22-41.

18. Andrew Stein, "Medicare's Broken Promises," *New York Times Magazine*, February 17, 1985, sec. 6, pp. 44, 82-85.

19. For detailed observations and commentary on state Medicaid decision-making processes, see the series of Health Policy Reports by John K. Iglehart, "Medicaid Turns to Prepaid Managed Care," *New England Journal of Medicine* 308, no. 16 (April 21, 1983): 976-980.

20. Daniel M. Wilner, Rosabelle P. Walker, and Edward J. O'Neill, "Financing Medical Care and Assuring Quality," in Daniel Wilner, ed., *Introduction to Public Health*, 7th ed. (New York: Macmillan, 1978), pp. 149-151.

21. Rogers, Blendon, and Moloney, "Who Needs Medicaid?" pp. 13-18.

22. The Urban Institute in Washington, D.C., has accumulated and analyzed current federal policies with respect to impact on cities. See John L. Palmer and Isabel V. Sawhill, eds., "Appendix C," *The Reagan Record: An Assessment of America's Changing Domestic Priorities; An Urban Institute Study* (Cambridge, Mass.: Ballinger, 1984), pp. 368-372.

23. For details of the states' Medicaid programs, see *Analysis of State Medicaid Program Characteristics* (La Jolla, Calif.: La Jolla Management Corporation, 1983).

24. See Palmer and Sawhill, "Appendix C," *The Reagan Record*, pp. 368-372.

25. "Reagan Again Proposes Medicare, Medicaid Cuts," *American Medical News*, February 15, 1985, pp. 1, 80-81.

12. Competitive Health Care: Assessing an Alternative Solution for Health Care Problems

Mylon Winn

The reduction of public services in favor of privatization is receiving increased attention in President Reagan's administration. Advocates of competition are portraying this change as the mechanism for providing equal access to health care for all Americans.[1] Public funds are being diverted from public health programs, and private enterprise is being promoted as a suitable substitute.[2] Dropping the present fee for service and initiating a competitive health care system would reduce government funding and policymaking in the health area.

Historically, access to health care in the black community has been poor,[3] although some scholars have noted that during the 1970s black access improved.[4] But these improvements were not enough to prevent J. N. Gayles from labeling the care in the black community as "health brutality." Gayles' label is based on his contention that blacks "suffer from higher mortality rates, higher incidence of major diseases, and lower availability and utilization of medical services."[5] Poor access has produced inequalities in health care between black and white Americans in the form of disparities in infant mortality rates. Among adults there are disparities in deaths caused by heart disease, diabetes mellitus, cerebrovascular disease, pneumonia, and malignant neoplasms.[6] For these reasons black scholars have concluded that black health care is inadequate.[7]

Proponents of a free market health care system agree that present health care is inadequate. Where blacks are concerned, they argue, health care will improve if black consumers are given the option of selecting health services from competing providers. The promise of improved health care has encountered skepticism from scholars who argue that government does not have the resources needed to support low-income people in a competitive environment.

For blacks, two concerns make adequate health care more than just a consumer decision about which health care provider offers the most efficient and cost-effective service. The first concern is whether making health care competitive will mean that low-income blacks will be unable to afford health care services. Without adequate government funding to pay health care fees, low-income blacks will not be able to purchase health care services. In addition, government funding is important in the training of health care professionals, the building of clinics, and the organization of services for the poor. Thus, health care for blacks is not simply a matter of reducing costs and providing consumers with a choice; it must ensure that health care will be available to low-income blacks.

A second concern is the impact that reducing government involvement in health care will have on blacks. Providing health care services to low-income blacks is a responsibility that is normally assumed by the government and not the private sector. Government's responsibility includes providing for the well-being of all Americans, whereas a business is primarily concerned with the consumers of its product. If the proponents of competitive health care are able to reduce government involvement in health care, there will be no institution that blacks can hold accountable if or when they are unable to get health care.

This chapter discusses the impact of a competitive health care system on black Americans. It is divided into four sections. The first section examines the argument that health care is provided best through competition and discusses the rationale for a competitive health care system; the second discusses government support of a competitive health care system; the third, general concerns about such a system and specific criticisms of the competitive health care system.

HEALTH CARE AND THE MARKET

Proponents of market health care argue that a competitive health care system is the best means of allocating health services because the availability of health services, like other commodities, is determined by consumer preferences.[8] Advocates have proposed two market approaches for providing competitive health care services. The first approach allows an individual to use personal income to purchase health care from the provider offering the best service at the least cost. When there are multiple providers, the market prioritizes the choices available to consumers through competition. Prioritizing is possible because the market identifies the provider offering the best service at a cost attractive to consumers. The second approach encourages consumers to join health maintenance organizations (HMOs) or some other form of prepaid group practice. Advocates argue that HMOs can provide health care more economically by offering comprehensive services to consumers who pay a fixed annual fee. HMOs have an interest in keeping the cost (per enrollee) of their services at a lower level than the annual fee; otherwise, operating costs are not economical. Once an HMO enters into a contract with a subscriber, there is no immediate way to recuperate excessive costs. Thus, HMOs have an incentive to offer effective health care because they share, with their subscribers, the economic risk of "ill-health."[9]

Proponents of competitive health care do not ignore low-income people; they actually support a moderate redistribution of income to assure that low-income people can purchase minimum health care. Open enrollment in insurance plans and minimum quality of health care would be established and required to assure that low-income people would not receive substandard care. Low-income people would use vouchers to purchase health care from the provider of their choice. Money to fund vouchers would be generated by tying them to the "mean health expenditure" of the general public. Thus, competition would make the best health care services available to all Americans, regardless of their income.

Advocates of competition reject government regulation of health care. Walter McClure argues that government regulation is a source of inefficiency in the delivery of health care, and that there are no incentives for health care providers to develop services that benefit the public when they are regulated.[10] David Mechanic contends that regulation shifts power from health care providers to "financial and administrative personnel whose responsibility it is to ensure compliance" with regulations. To focus on compliance and not on providing services does not create an incentive to providers that benefits the public.[11] McClure's solution is to reduce government's regulatory responsibilities. He argues that reduced regulation by government would free the market to determine the demand for health services and that it would create incentives for providers to offer efficient and economical health care services.[12]

In sum, these advocates propose less government and more reliance on competition to deliver health care to consumers. Their proposal depends on reducing government participation in health care policy-making. Efforts to decrease government involvement in health policy have been considered during the Carter and Reagan administrations.

GOVERNMENT SUPPORT OF
COMPETITIVE HEALTH CARE

One recent proposal considered by the Carter administration was Alain Enthoven's "competitive strategy."[13] The Enthoven proposal called for the following:

1. Multiple Choice
   Each consumer would be offered the opportunity to enroll each year for the coming year in any qualified plan for health care financing and delivery operating in their area.
2. Fixed Dollar Subsidy
   Each consumer would receive a fixed sum toward the purchase of a health plan membership, and the amount would be independent of the plan chosen.
3. Use of the Same Rules for all Competitors
   The same rules would apply to all qualified health plans. These rules would govern premium-setting practices, minimum-benefit packages, catastrophic-expense protection, and so on. Such a system would prevent preferred-risk selection, excessive costs for high-risk persons, and deceptive or inadequate coverage.
4. Organization of physicians
   Physicians would be in competing economic units. The market would include "limited-provider," "preferred-provider," or "closed-panel" plans, in which a health-care-financing plan would be associated with a limited set of physicians. The premium charged by each plan would then reflect the ability of its associated physicians to control costs.[14]

The Carter administration was divided in its support of Enthoven's proposal. The economists supported the proposal, whereas the noneconomists (health, education, and welfare personnel) opposed it. The noneconomists were concerned about how the poor would be affected by Enthoven's proposal. The noneconomists prevailed, and the Carter administration chose to support a regulatory approach.[15]

Ronald Reagan's administration has rejected the regulatory approach favored by the Carter administration. Reagan has chosen to promote a competitive system rather than to regulate health care. One effort to develop a competitive health care policy was made during former Secretary Richard Schweiker's tenure in the Department of Health and Human Services. The administration planned to develop a competitive health care bill to be unveiled in 1982.

The major effort in the Reagan administration to develop a competitive health care legislative package was proposed by the Office of Management and Budget (OMB) under the leadership of former Director David Stockman. Stockman's efforts with the administration started in 1980 when he outlined his views on the need for a competitive health system at the Health Opportunities for People Everywhere Conference. He stated that health care is an "economic good that should be purchased by people who understand the financial consequences of their decision."[16] He pointed out that health care is considered a "spiritual or social or collective good," and thus the ability of the market to regulate economic goods is ignored. Hence, competition is ruled out; the result is that the cost of health care is increasing, providers and consumers are unhappy, and the health care system is out of control.

Stockman outlined five premises which he believed would solve the problems of health care:

1. Consumer franchising. This premise calls for giving consumers a choice that involves the opportunity to select less expensive health plans that would benefit consumers.
2. Redistributing income. This premise involves redistributing "fixed monetary subsidies" that can be "controlled," publicly debated, and are "changeable."
3. Financial risk for health care providers purchasing new technology. This premise is meant to eliminate protection from failure for private sector hospitals that invest funds in expansion projects and cannot make enough money to recoup their investment. Stockman believes the market can introduce discipline to hospitals provided they are not protected from bankruptcy.
4. Structured competition between providers.
5. Marketing of retailed health care. Self-organizing markets would be created for providers.[17]

These premises were included in the House bill that Representative Richard A. Gephardt (D., Miss.) and Stockman submitted to the 96th Congress, which is still pending.

In sum, Gephardt and Stockman proposed a bill that strongly encourages competition to reduce health care costs, improve the quality of health care services, and create a risk for inefficient health care providers. The emphasis in their bill is on reducing the government's role as a regulator and policymaker of health care while decreasing competition among health care providers. Consequently, government's responsibility in a competitive health care system would be minimal.

CRITICAL ISSUES IN COMPETITIVE HEALTH CARE

In 1983 the President's Commission for the Study of Ethical Problems in Medicine and Biomedical and Behavioral Research issued a report that examined the ethical implication of differences in the availability of health services. Members examined equity of access, competitive health care, and equity as an adequate level of health care to determine which means would be the best to provide health services.[18] The commission rejected two of the three alternatives—equity of access to health care and a competitive health care system—on the basis of health care and the financial cost to society for providing services. Competitive health care was rejected specifically because it would be inaccessible to low-income people who lack the financial resources to purchase health services. In addition, some people would not get adequate health care if the distribution of service was left to the market.[19] Equity as an adequate level of health care mandates that "everyone should be able to secure an adequate level of care."[20] The commission endorsed this alternative because it believed that equity as an adequate level of health care would assure the availability of health care to all citizens without creating a financial strain on government. The commission's conclusion that all Americans should have access to health care reflects its sensitivity to the social responsibility of government to ensure that health care is available to all Americans.

The goal of providing adequate health care to all Americans depends on whether consumers are prepared to make informed decisions about the choices available to them when they purchase health care. A second consideration is whether a competitive health care strategy will include provisions to ensure that poor people will receive health care. Critics are doubtful that consumers in general and poor people in particular will fare well in a competitive health care system.

Daniel Wilker argues that consumers are not always educated about the complexities of health services and therefore will make uninformed judgments.[21] Amy Gutman points out that a moderate redistribution of guaranteed income will not cover the cost of a major illness.[22] Eli Ginzberg states that (1) competitive health care system will not meet the needs for the total population in the United States, and (2) there are no assurances that the resources needed to support the poor for essential care will continue to be available.[23]

Andrew Dunham et al. point out that the demand side of health care involves using receipts in lieu of currency (vouchers) to "allow members of group health plans and recipients of Medicare and Medicaid to select between alternative insurance packages."[24] Furthermore, they contend that whether or not the poor receive adequate health services depends on the value of their vouchers. They conclude that if actual medical costs for services exceed the value of vouchers, adequate health services will remain limited or unavailable to poor people.[25]

Dunham et al. express concerns about linking the value of vouchers to the "mean health expenditure" of the general public. They state that the "average cost of equitably serving the poor is considerably greater than current average expenditures; it is also considerably greater than current average expenditures on Medicaid." Thus, Dunham et al.

conclude that linking vouchers to current benefit expenditures would be inadequate to cover the costs of serving the poor.[26]

The concerns that Wilker, Gutman, and Ginsburg express have led Lawrence D. Brown to conclude that the argument for competitive health care is based on conjecture. Brown argues that the analysis by advocates justifying competitive health care suffers from "confusion over the differences among fact, hypothesis, and evidence."[27] He says their analysis fails to provide examples that the proponents of competitive health care can point to as proof of their claims.

Among the critics, Victor W. Sidel's indictment of a competitive health care system is probably the most stinging. Sidel contends that the rich will benefit from a competitive health care system by paying less in taxes to subsidize health care for the poor. The others who will benefit will be "providers who skim the cream off the medical market and leave the real problems to a diminished . . . public sector."[28]

Critics argue that adequate funds for vouchers will be unavailable, which means that government support will be unavailable to ensure that poor people can purchase adequate health care services.[29] Thus, health care in a competitive system where government activities are reduced will not improve the access low-income people have to health care services; rather, it will reduce their access.

In sum, it cannot be assumed that competition will improve the quality of health care services in America for poor people. What is apparent is that if a competitive health care system is adopted the consumers will bear the direct cost.[30] The major costs will be assessed against poor people. They will have less access to health care, and government will provide inadequate financial support to ensure access to health care for poor people.

IMPLICATIONS FOR BLACK AMERICANS

Impact on Health Conditions

Proponents of competitive health care argue that if black consumers have the option of selecting health services from competing providers, they will have access to better health care. The central problem, however, is whether competitive care will reduce their access to health care services they already have.[31]

John Holliman identifies three barriers that affect access of blacks to health care. First, he points to a survey of black welfare recipients who indicated "doctors were prejudiced against them." Second, blacks may be reluctant to get early treatment for illnesses because the care is provided by nonblack medical personnel. Third, access to medical care is reduced because many doctors refuse to provide services in poor communities.[32] Such barriers translate into acute illnesses, excessive medical costs, and higher mortality rates among black Americans; an inequality in the delivery of health care; and a disparity in death rates and life expectancy between black and white Americans (see Chapter 2).

Alphonso Pinkney contends that blacks have higher mortality rates and shorter life expectancy than whites because of racism.[33] Racial barriers to health care is not an issue for advocates of competitive health care. Their emphasis on market demands means that health care priorities would be responsive to health care needs of individuals and not blacks as a special group. However, concentrating on individuals ignores the fact that blacks experience shorter life spans, a higher rate of chronic and debilitating illnesses, and lower protection against infectious diseases (see Chapters 2 and 3). For these advocates, racial discrimination is not a consideration in the poor health that blacks experience; the real problem is the absence of a competitive health care system.

A competitive health care system would limit the access of low-income blacks to health care services because of their inability to pay. Inadequate voucher funding would still leave blacks with insufficient funds to purchase health care. As a result, their access to health care would be reduced. Thus, blacks would make fewer visits to their doctors, and their illnesses would be in advanced stages when they finally received medical attention. The mortality rate among blacks would increase, and their life expectancy would decrease. A competitive health care system would, therefore, place a disproportionate burden on those blacks with inadequate financial resources and benefit only those few blacks with enough financial resources to purchase suitable health care services.

Impact of Less Government

Reducing government involvement in health policy would ensure that economic interests prevailed, and in that event the result could well be increased numbers of low-income blacks receiving no health care because of inability to pay and increased death rates and frequency of illness among them. Hence, the government would not easily fulfill society's ethical obligation that adequate health care be provided for all Americans.

Reducing government involvement in health policymaking means that acceptable health care standards would be determined by the market. It cannot be assumed that the market would (1) establish a level of health care that would ensure treatment for all blacks, (2) emphasize access to health care for blacks, (3) focus on the quality of services that blacks receive, and (4) concentrate on eliminating the disparities (death rates, frequency of illness, and longevity) that exist between blacks and whites.

Brown points out that the proponents of competitive health care have not been able to furnish any examples proving the viability of competitive health care.[34] In the absence of such assurances, it is not in best interest of blacks to support reduced government involvement in health care policymaking.

To respond to the health care needs of blacks, competitive health care would have to (1) decrease the higher (than whites) incidence of serious illnesses, (2) reduce the extended hospitalization that accompanies poor health, (3) increase the number of black health care professionals in leadership positions, (4) encourage more blacks to enroll in medical schools to become doctors, and (5) recruit more blacks to allied health care fields.

Rice and Jones argue that black consumers must be involved in health care planning if their severe health care needs are to be reduced.[35] Black consumers would introduce issues and perspectives that would have to be considered by policymakers in any plan to improve black health care. Christian Bay points out that the kind of participation Rice and Jones advocate provides a sense of "equal say in shaping the rules under which one lives."[36] In this case an "equal say" means not relying on a market that favors the economic goals of providers.

Advocates of competitive health care maintain that the health care needs of consumers will be satisfied by those providers who offer the best services in the market. The market currently offers blacks inadequate services, however. Thus, from the blacks' point of view they do not offer an adequate health care alternative.

SUMMARY AND CONCLUSION

The Reagan administration has been an active advocate of competitive health care, proposing that a competitive health care system would (1) reduce the cost of health care, (2) eliminate unnecessary expenditures, and (3) give consumers an opportunity to purchase health care from competing providers. Proponents also advocate a moderate income redistribution to assist low-income people to cover the cost of health care.

Critics of a competitive system counter that (1) government funding of vouchers will be inadequate; (2) health care costs will not be reduced; (3) access of low-income people to health care will be reduced; and (4) health care is a collective good, not a commodity.

It would seem that competitive health care would indeed reduce government support of health care, which, in turn, would have an adverse impact on the large number of blacks who depend on the government for assistance. Therefore, a competitive system would have an adverse effect on the access blacks have to health care and would also reinforce the current disparity between black and white Americans in mortality rates and life expectancy.

Without government financial support and the accompanying assurance of health care, health care will be available only to those people who can pay the fees charged by providers. Hence, health care will become a privilege and not a right. If government's role in ensuring the availability of health care declines, blacks must rely on the "good will" of the private health sector in a competitive system to fill the void created by that decline. Consequently, those consumers who are able to purchase health care from providers who offer the best and least expensive services will benefit from competition. Low-income blacks will not benefit as long as the primary task of competitive health care is to promote economic rather than social goals.

NOTES

1. Woodrow Jones, Jr., and Mitchell F. Rice, "Black Health Care in an Era of Retrenchment Politics," in Jones and Rice, eds., *Contemporary Public Policy Perspectives and Black Americans* (Westport, Conn.: Greenwood Press, 1984); and Victor W. Sidel, "Health Care: Privatization, Privileges, Pollution and Profit," in Alan Gartner, Colin Greer, and Frank Riesman, eds., *What Reagan Is Doing to Us* (New York: Harper and Row, 1982), pp. 24-53.

2. Alain C. Enthoven, "The Competition Strategy," *New England Journal of Medicine* 304, no. 2 (November 6, 1980): 109-112; Robert M. Sade, "Medical Care as a Right," *New England Journal of Medicine* 285, no. 5 (December 2, 1971): 1288-1292; and Alain C. Enthoven, "Consumer-Choice Health Plan," *New England Journal of Medicine* 298, no. 2 (November 6, 1980): 650-658, 709-720.

3. Mitchell F. Rice and Woodrow Jones, Jr., "Black Health Inequities and the American Health Care System," *Health Policy and Education* 3 (October 1982): 195-214; John D. Reid, Everett S. Lee, Davor Jedlicka, and Yongsock Shin, "Trend in Black Health," *Phylon* 38, no. 3 (Fall 1977): 105-116; and Steffie Woolhandler, David U. Himmelstein, Michael Bader, Martha Harnly, and Alice A. Jones, "Medical Care and Mortality: Racial Differences in Preventable Deaths," *International Journal of Health Services* 15, no. 1 (1985): 1-23.

4. Paul Starr, "Medical Care and the Pursuit of Equality," in *Securing Access to Health Care: The Ethical Implications of Differences in the Availability of Health Services*, President's Commission for the Study of Ethical Problems in Medicine and Biomedical and Behavioral Research 2 (March 1983): 3-22; and Lu Ann Aday and Ronald M. Anderson, "Equity of Access to Medical Care: A Conceptual and Empirical Overview," in *Securing Access to Health Care*, pp. 19-54; and Karen Davis, Marsha Gold, and Diane Makuc, "Access to Health Care for the Poor: Does the Gap Remain?" *Annual Review of Public Health* 2 (1981): 159-182.

5. Joseph N. Gayles, "Health Brutality and the Black Life Cycle," *Black Scholar* (May 1972): 2-9.

6. U.S. Department of Health and Human Services, *Health and Prevention Profile* (Washington, D.C.: GPO, 1983).

7. Mitchell F. Rice, "Black Health Care,'Another Look at an Old Problem," *Texas Public Health Association Journal* 33 (Fall 1981): 17-20; and George P. Tolbert, "Meeting the Health Needs of Minorities and the Poor," *Phylon* 38, no. 3 (Fall 1977): 225-235.

8. Enthoven, "The Competition Strategy," pp. 109-112; Sade, "Medical Care as a Right," pp. 1288-1292; Paul M. Ellwood, Jr., M.D., et al., "Health Maintenance Strategy," *Medical Care* 9, no. 3 (May-June 1971): 291-298; and Walter McClure, "Structure and Incentive Problems in Economic Regulation of Medical Care," *Milbank Memorial Fund Quarterly/Health and Society* 59, no. 2 (1981): 107-143.

9. Ellwood, "Health Maintenance Strategy," pp. 291-298.

10. McClure, "Structure and Incentive Problems in Economic Regulation of Medical Care," pp. 107-143.

11. David Mechanic, "Some Dilemmas in Health Care Policy," *Milbank Memorial Fund Quarterly/Health and Society* 59, no. 1 (1981): 1-15.

12. McClure, "Structure and Incentive Problems in Economic Regulation of Medical Care," pp. 141-142.

13. John K. Iglehart, "Drawing the Line for the Debate on Competition," *New England Journal of Medicine* 305, no. 5 (July 30, 1981): 291-296.

14. Enthoven, "Consumer-Choice Health Plan," pp. 650-658, 709-720.

15. Eli Ginzberg, "Competition and Cost Containment," *New England Journal of Medicine* 303, no. 5 (30 July 1981): 1112-1116.

16. Iglehart, "Drawing the Line for the Debate on Competition," p. 293.

17. Ibid.

18. *Securing Access to Health Care*, p. 4.

19. Ibid., pp. 26-29.

20. Ibid., p. 20.

21. Daniel Wilker, "Philosophical Perspectives on Access to Health Care: An Introduction," in *Securing Access to Health Care*, pp. 109-147.

22. Amy Gutman, "Principles of Equal Access," in *Securing Access to Health Care*, pp. 55-69.

23. Ginzberg, "Competition and Cost Containment," pp. 1114-115.

24. Andrew Dunham, James A. Morone, and William White, "Restoring Medical Markets: Implications for the Poor," *Journal of Health Politics, Policy and Law* 7, no. 2 (Summer 1982): 488-501.

25. Ibid., p. 491.

26. Ibid., p. 490.

27. Ibid.

28. Lawrence D. Brown, "Competition and Health Cost Containment: Cautions and Conjectures," *Milbank Memorial Fund Quarterly/Health and Society* 59, no. 1 (1981): 145-189.

29. Sidel, "Health Care," p. 47.

30. Daniel W. Sigelman, "Palm-Reading the Invisible Hand: A Critical Examination of Pro-Competitive Reform Proposals," *Journal of Health Politics, Policy and Law* 6, no. 4 (Winter 1982): 587-620.

31. Ronald C. Lippincott and James W. Begun, "Competition in the Health Sector: A Historical Perspective," *Journal of Health Politics, Policy and Law* 7, no. 4 (Summer 1982): 460-487; and Mark E. Rushefsky, "A Critique of Market Reforms in Health Care: The 'Consumer-Choice Health Plan' " *Journal of Health Politics, Policy and Law* 5, no. 4 (Winter 1981): 720-741.

32. John L. S. Holliman, Jr., "Access to Health Care," in *Securing Access to Health Care*, pp. 79-106.

33. Alphonso Pinkney, *The Myth of Black Progress* (Cambridge, Mass.: Cambridge University Press, 1984), p. 73.

34. Brown, "Competition and Health Cost Containment," pp. 145-189.

35. Rice and Jones, "Black Health Inequities and the American Health Care System," pp. 211-212.

36. Christian Bay, "Needs, Wants, and Political Legitimacy," *Canadian Journal of Political Science* 1, no. 3 (September 1968): 241-260.

Selected Bibliography

Adam, C. T. "A Descriptive Definition of Primary Prevention." *Journal of Primary Prevention* 2, no. 2 (Winter 1981): 67-80.

Allen, V. L., ed. *Psychological Factors in Poverty*. New York: Academic Press, 1970.

Babor, T. F., and Steven Berglas. "Toward a Systems-Ecological Approach to the Prevention of Adolescent Alcohol Abuse." *Journal of Prevention* 2, no. 1 (Fall 1981): 25-39.

Berkley, George. *On Being Black and Healthy*. Englewood Cliffs, N.J.: Prentice-Hall, 1982.

Bloom, B. L. "Prevention/Promotion with Minorities." *Journal of Primary Prevention* 3 (Summer 1983): 224-234.

Blum, Henrik L. *Planning for Health*. New York: Human Sciences Press, 1974.

Bourne, P. G., and R. Fox, eds. *Alcoholism: Progress in Research and Treatment*. New York: Academic Press, 1973.

Brigham, John, and D. W. Brown, eds. *Policy Implementation*. Beverly Hills, Calif.: Sage, 1981.

Brill, Norman Q., and Hugh Storrow. "Social Class and Psychiatric Treatment." *Archives of General Psychiatry* 3 (October 1960): 340-344.

Brown, Lawrence D. "Competition and Health Cost Containment: Cautions and Conjectures." *Milbank Memorial Fund Quarterly/Health and Society* 59, no. 1 (1981): 145-189.

Cahalan, D., and R. Room. *Problem Drinking Among American Men.* New Brunswick, N.J.: Rutgers Center on Alcohol Studies, 1974.

Davis, Karen, and Cathy Schoen. *Health and the War on Poverty: A Ten Year Appraisal.* Washington, D.C.: Brookings Institution, 1978.

Dunham, Andrew, James A. Morone, and William White. "Restoring Medical Markets: Implications for the Poor." *Journal of Health Politics, Policy and Law* 7, no. 2 (Summer 1982): 488-501.

Gary, Lawrence E. "A Mental Health Research Agenda for the Black Community." *Journal of Afro-American Issues* 4 (1976): 50-60.

Gary, Lawrence E., ed. *Mental Health: A Challenge to the Black Community.* Philadelphia: Dorrance, 1979.

Harper, F. D. *Alcohol Abuse and Black America.* Alexandria, Va.: Douglas, 1976.

Harper, F. D., and M. P. Dawkins. "Alcohol and Blacks: Survey of the Periodical Literature." *British Journal of Addiction* 71 (1976): 327-334.

Harwood, Alan, ed. *Ethnicity and Medical Care.* Cambridge, Mass.: Harvard University Press, 1981.

Institute of Medicine. *Infant Death: An Analysis of Maternal Risk and Health Care.* Washington, D.C.: National Academy Press, 1973.

Jackson, Jacquelyne J. "Death Rates of Aged Blacks and Whites, United States, 1964-1978." *The Black Scholar* 13 (January-February 1982): 21-35.

Jackson, Jacquelyne J. *Minority Aging.* Belmont, Calif.: Wadsworth, 1980.

Joe, G. W., B. K. Singh, D. Finklea, R. Hudiberg, and S. B. Sells. "Community Factors, Racial Composition of Treatment Programs and Outcomes." *National Institute on Drug Abuse Services Research Report.* Rockville, Md.: National Institute on Drug Abuse, 1977.

Johnson, Bruce D. The National Institute on Drug Abuse Research Issues 21. *Drugs and Minorities.* Washington, D.C.: GPO, December 1977.

Klein, D. C., and S. E. Goldston. DHEW Publications No. (ADM) 77-447. Rockville, Md.: National Institute of Mental Health, 1977.

Linn, Margaret, Kathleen Hunter, and Bernard Linn. "Self-Assessed Health, Impairment and Disability in Anglo, Black, and Cuban Elderly." *Medical Care* 18, no. 3 (March 1980): 282-288.

Lowi, Theodore J. *The End of Liberalism.* New York: W. W. Norton, 1969.

Manton, Kenneth. "Differential Life Expectancy: Possible Explanations During the Later Aging." In Ron Manuel, ed. *Minority Aging: Sociological and Social Psychological Issues.* Westport, Conn.: Greenwood Press, 1982.

Markides, Kyriakos S. "Mortality Among Minority Populations: A Review of Recent Patterns and Trends." *Public Health Reports* 98 (May-June 1983): 254-255.

Mechanic, David. "Some Dilemmas in Health Care Policy." *Milbank Memorial Fund Quarterly/Health and Society* 59, no. 1 (1981): 1-15.

Melvin, H. Rudolph, and Nancy Santangelo. *Health Status of Minorities and Low-Income Groups.* DHEW Publication No. (HRA) 79-627. Washington, D.C.: GPO, 1979.

Naylor, Allen C., and Ntinos Myrianthopolous. "The Relationship of Ethnic and Selected Social Factors to Human Birth Weight." *Annal of Human Genetics* 31 (1967): 71-83.

Noble, Ernest P., ed. "Alcohol Use and Abuse Among Black Americans." In *Third Special Report to the U.S. Congress on Alcohol and Health from the Secretary of Health, Education, and Welfare*. Rockville, Md.: National Institute on Alcohol Abuse and Alcoholism, June 1976.

Nobles, W. "Black People in White Insanity: An Issue for Black Community Mental Health." *Journal of Afro-American Issues* 4 (Winter 1976): 21-27.

Reitzes, D. C. *Negroes and Medicine*. Cambridge, Mass.: Harvard University Press, 1958.

Rocheleau, B. "Black Physicians and Ambulatory Care." *Public Health Reports* 93 (1978): 278-282.

Rushefsky, Mark E. "A Critique of Market Reforms in Health Care: The 'Consumer-Choice Health Plan.' " *Journal of Health Politics, Policy and Law* 5, no. 4 (Winter 1981): 720-741.

Seham, M. *Blacks and American Medical Care*. Minneapolis: University of Minnesota Press, 1973.

Starr, Paul. *The Social Transformation of American Medicine*. New York: Basic Books, 1982.

Sullivan, L. "The Education of Black Health Professionals." *Phylon* 38 (1978): 225-235.

Taylor, Robert B., ed. *Health Promotion: Principles and Clinical Applications*. Norwalk, Conn.: Appleton-Century-Crofts, 1982.

Thompson, Frank J. *Health Policy and the Bureaucracy*. Cambridge, Mass.: MIT Press, 1981.

Thompson, Theodis. "Selected Characteristics of Black Physicians in the United States." *Journal of the American Medical Association* 229 (1974): 1758-1761.

Turner, Samuel M., and Russell T. Jones, eds. *Behavior Modification in Black Populations: Psychosocial Issues and Empirical Findings*. New York: Plenum Press, 1982.

Viamontes, J. A., and B. J. Powell. "Demographic Characteristics of Black and White Male Alcoholics." *International Journal of the Addictions* 9 (1974): 489-494.

Williams, Blanche. *Characteristics of the Black Elderly, 1980*. Washington, D.C.: U.S. Department of Health and Human Services, 1980.

Windle, C. "Correlates of Community Mental Health Centers' Underservice to Non-Whites." *Journal of Community Psychology* 8 (1980): 140-146.

Index

Contributors

PATRICK R. CLIFFORD is an Assistant Professor of Health Education at the University of Texas at Austin. He holds a Ph.D. in Community Health Science with a specialty in Behavioral Science from the University of Texas Health Science Center at Houston, School of Public Health.

NANCY R. COPE is a Doctoral Candidate in Counseling Psychology at Pennsylvania State University.

MARIANNE FOLEY was Education Coordinator for the Central Texas Medical Foundation in Austin, Texas, from 1979 to 1985. Ms. Foley holds a Master's Degree in Health Sciences Education from Case-Western Reserve University, Cleveland, Ohio, and a Master's Degree in Public Health from the University of Texas School of Public Health, San Antonio. She has served as consultant to the Minority Health Affairs Committee of the American Academy of Family Physicians and is a member of the American Public Health Association.

MALCOLM L. GOGGIN is an Assistant Professor of Political Science at the University of Houston. He holds a Ph.D. in Political Science from

Stanford University. His research interests include child health, implementation theory, and the politics of health care.

HOWARD R. HALL is an Assistant Professor of Psychology at Pennsylvania State University, University Park. He holds a Ph.D. in Experimental Psychology from Princeton University and a Psy.D. from Rutgers University, Graduate School of Applied and Professional Psychology.

DOROTHY C. HOWZE is an Assistant Professor of Maternal and Child Health at the School of Public Health at the University of North Carolina, Chapel Hill. She is also on the faculty of Bush Institute of Family and Child Policy. She holds a Doctorate of Public Health from Harvard University, School of Public Health.

GLEN R. JOHNSON has been Director of the Family Practice Residency of the Central Texas Medical Foundation at Brackenridge Hospital, Austin, Texas, since 1977. He received his M.D. from Howard University, Washington, D.C., completing a residency in Family Practice at Howard University Affiliated Hospital in 1975. He became a Diplomate of the American Board of Family Practice in 1975 and was made a Fellow of the American Academy of Family Physicians one year later. Dr. Johnson has served on the American Academy of Family Physicians Minority Health Affairs Committee and is currently the American Academy of Family Physicians Representative to the Joint Review Committee in programs for accrediting Physicians' Assistants. He is a Clinical Assistant Professor in the Department of Family Medicine at the University of Texas Health Science Center at Houston.

WOODROW JONES, JR., is a Professor of Political Science and Adjunct Professor in the School of Public Health at San Diego State University. He is co-author of *Indochinese Refugees in America* (Duke University Press, 1985) and co-editor of *Contemporary Public Policy Perspectives and Black Americans* (Greenwood Press, 1984). He holds a Ph.D. in Political Science from the University of Oregon and an M.P.H. from the University of Texas. He has written extensively on utilization behaviors, health behaviors, and the delivery of health services.

K. ROBERT KEISER is an Associate Professor of Political Science at San Diego State University. He holds a Ph.D. from the University of North Carolina. He has been published in the areas of congressional politics and behaviors.

VERNA M. KEITH is an Assistant Professor of Sociology at Texas A & M University. She received her Ph.D. in Sociology from the University of Kentucky. Her specialties include the elderly, demography, and public health.

ANTONIO A. RENÉ is a Faculty Associate at the University of Texas Health Science Center in Houston. He holds a Ph.D. in Community Health Science with a specialty in Epidemiology from the University of Texas Health Science Center at Houston, School of Public Health.

MITCHELL F. RICE is Associate Professor of Public Administration and Political Science at Louisiana State University, Baton Rouge. He is co-editor with Woodrow Jones, Jr., of *Contemporary Public Policy Perspectives and Black Americans* (Greenwood Press, 1984). He has written extensively on such topics as Equal Employment Opportunity and Affirmative Action, Black Health Care, and Urban Service Delivery Systems. He holds a Ph.D. in Government from Claremont Graduate School, Claremont, California.

MYLON WINN is an Assistant Professor and Director of the Ph.D. program in Public Administration at the University of Alabama. He holds a Ph.D. in Political Science from the University of Washington, Seattle.